The Long 1950s

Also by Andrew Duncan:

Poetry
In a German Hotel
Cut Memories and False Commands
Sound Surface
Alien Skies
*Pauper Estate**
*Switching and Main Exchange**
Anxiety before Entering a Room. New and selected poems
Surveillance and Compliance
Skeleton Looking at Chinese Pictures
The Imaginary in Geometry
*Savage Survivals (amid modern suavity)**

Criticism
The Poetry Scene in the Nineties (internet only)
Centre and Periphery in Modern British Poetry
The Failure of Conservatism in Modern British Poetry
Origins of the Underground
*The Council of Heresy**
Fulfilling the Silent Rules (forthcoming)

As editor:
Don't Stop Me Talking (with Tim Allen)
Angel Exhaust (magazine: 1992–98 and 2005–   )
Joseph Macleod: *Cyclic Serial Zeniths from the Flux*

*Shearsman titles

The Long 1950s

Morality and fantasy
as stakes in the poetic game

Andrew Duncan

Shearsman Books

Published in the United Kingdom in 2012 by
Shearsman Books Ltd
50 Westons Hill Drive
Emersons Green
Bristol
BS16 7DF

Shearsman Books Ltd Registered Office
30–31 St. James Place, Mangotsfield, Bristol BS16 9JB
(this address not for correspondence)

ISBN 978-1-84861-137-5
First Edition

Acknowledgements
Some of the essays appeared in earlier versions as follows:
'Spectral investments' was published in the *CCCP Review*;
part of the essay on Jeremy Reed appeared as a review in *Poetry Review*;
part of the essay on Pauline Stainer appeared in *Poetry Review*;
'The singer-songwriter genre' was published in *Hi Zero*.

For permission to quote from Jeremy Reed's *Black Russian: Out-takes from
the Airmen's Club* (Hove: Waterloo Press, 2011), our thanks go to
Jeremy Reed and to Waterloo Press.

CONTENTS

Introduction

The present work deals with a complex of issues, but started with the double twist, that two '50s poets, Christopher Logue and Geoffrey Hill, have dominated the artistic scene over the last ten to fifteen years (or, say 1996 to 2010) and that the death of the main '50s style has liberated the official English poetry, with the decease of certain inhibitions which were glued together and brewed up to weapons grade quality back in the 1950s.

Going back to the 1950s was also a way of recovering innocence, a time of more placid belief in poetry and in the value of education. This has always been symbolised for me by the association of marine watercolourists, whose exhibitions were held next to the Institute of Contemporary Arts and which I used to pass on the way to some modern-style event. I loved the idea that people were still painting perfectly precise pictures of ships. I wanted to write about *affirmative culture*. This is my venture into these intact worlds of the non-modern, although after some experiments I have stuck with poets of exceptional quality; there is a further step, beckoning, of looking at the vast lands of amateur poetry, offering potent difficulties of address.

Amateur calculations led me, a few weeks ago, to the suspicion that as many as 7,000 poets published volumes during the period of my interest, *viz.* 1960–97. Clearly the watchword for my endeavours as historian was incompleteness. This led me to wonder if I could start from the other side and cover the unknown poets in some way, leaving out the well-known ones.

A large number of people were writing poetry without any affinity with the academic base of EngLit and its professional orthodoxy. We can call the amateurs substream, or *s-stream*, and so pose the question: is the history of the mainstream the history of the substream? That is, if we write about a few dozen prominent poets, are we also writing down the history of the whole crowd of people writing poems? I think the answer is that there are many more styles in the substream, which is simply incapable of self-censorship, and the m-stream is bound to High Street commerce and so to fashion, so that it jettisons styles quickly and imitates cleverly. We all wonder if public poets are actually better than amateur poets, or if they get picked up by calculating editors because they are photogenic, because they have the right biography, because they are compliant enough to write what editors tell them, etc.

We are recovering the history of whole areas usually ignored by connoisseurs of poetry. The prerequisites for me taking part in it were partly the expiry of previous passions, all too intense. *Indifference* is the prelude to a wider understanding. Partly, too, the discovery of extents of poetry unknown to me. The present work is a draft history of the mainstream, although only of a few strands in a vast complex of texts.

Part of the Sixties intellectual Left sensibility was a wish to scrap the author as individual. One of the more successful paths towards this was to study genre—a system which went much deeper than individual experience and which structured the creativity of individuals, showing shifts in time which were not conscious and which could be seen as symbolic machines—impersonal programs running in the literary realm. Apparently, anyway. So the study of genre was the object of a classic essay by Hans Robert Jauss and offers us a way of dealing with poetry as a mass event. (The project is *also* to write a book without mentioning the left-modernist Underground.)

The second watchword was typification—a mass of several thousand poems would yield only some which can be attached to a genre without too much classification compromise. The genres I offer do not cover the whole ground, and they relate to real poems only as types, schemas. They have the advantage of clarity in a terrain darkened by an excess of information. I reserve the right to talk about brilliant individuals who have used genres—a literary critic is unwilling to get away from those.

The attempt to find changes in stable conventions is difficult. Securing shared space requires the attempt to create a shared vocabulary which captures the meaningful units of modern poetry and makes discussion possible even if we disagree after our discussion. Jauss deals with many genres, at one point listing "the *exemplum*, the *fabliau*, the legend, the miracle, the *lai*, the *vida*, the *nova*, love-casuistry, oriental narrative literature, Apuleius and Milanese love-stories, local Florentine histories and anecdotes" (as sources of Boccaccio), an astonishing wealth of conventions. The stability of magnetically charged clusters, as deposits and sites of recursion, may be more necessary to oral cultures than to literate ones. Everyone agrees that the genre system has collapsed in the 20th Century—along with the class system and other organised conventions. There is a lack of names for the kinds of modern poem, and it is possible that their variety is much greater than in the 14th century. Both poets and readers set a high price on originality. So maybe genre is a set of limits and failures—lines where energy runs out rather than the features of success. The limits around the poem can be seen as simply inhibitions, and certainly we are glad when they are moved. It doesn't seem that marketing poems is like marketing Westerns. I dragged on Genre as something that was not property, but there is still the possibility that dominant individuals who occupy these temporary identities can leave them changed—that the way the game is played might therefore be different in 1980 from what it was in 1960.

I discuss domestic anecdote, the Pop poem, the academic poem, the communalist poem, the Oxford Line, the late Christian poem, the poem of star culture and high glamour. Other genres like the avant-garde, the myth poem, the New Age poem, have been covered in other works of mine. I use the terms m-stream (for mainstream) and u-stream (for the Underground) to speed things up. (M-stream possibly comes from the phrase "central current" in the introduction to the 1963 anthology *New Lines 2*.) There is also substream (the sub-literary) and the J-stream (Jungian poetry). For more exact definitions of these terms the whole of my work is relevant.

The advent of postmodernism came through what Lyotard defined as the collapse of the *grands récits*, the grand narratives. The arrival of *petits récits* is accompanied by the spread of indifference to moral considerations in art. However, within poetry the migration towards *petits récits* was very closely linked to a focus on the concrete situation and on the individual, and the purpose of this was, massively, to make moral relations clearer and to avoid the vagueness of splendid theological language. Human freedom and choice take place on the small scale. This puzzling fact conceals the possibility that the new small scale will bring the return of moral considerations to the centre of poetry.

Anxieties and Lures

Spectral investments and revisionist muzzle-flash
Anthology of 20th Century British and Irish poetry,
ed. Keith Tuma (New York: Oxford University Press, 2001)
941pp.; 137 poets)

The new book shows a fairly thorough wipe of both Yeats' (1936) and Larkin's (1973) view of the landscape. No-one would claim objectivity for either of these previous Oxford anthologies or for Enright's *Oxford Book of Contemporary Verse* (1945–80). Both those recent anthologists were Movement poets, and it is widely said in print nowadays that the Movement was a gang of not very talented people who were expert in publicity and politics and brutal in their attitude to outsiders. The popularity of such accounts does not quite amount to proof that recent anthologists—Sean O'Brien, Jo Shapcott, Neil Astley, Robert Crawford with Simon Armitage—are less prone to selectivity, self-interest, and corruption. My colleague Richard Price has said that "anthologies are [...] always personal"—somewhat underrating the defensive/connective work of pleasing patrons, hitting the market, and avoiding criticism.

Clearly such a broad-spectrum anthology does not have the reach or comprehensiveness of more specific works like *Conductors, Floating Capital,* or *A Various Art.* The course steered here is halfway between *The Democratic Voice* and *Conductors of Chaos.* Because I have checklists lying around as part of a private project, I was able to count that 51 poets I consider significant are in the anthology and 104 are not. But really, what does this mean? I could not say I was happy with Tuma's choice, but no true quantity is here to be measured. My list is full of poets who wrote very little I like (e.g. Ruth Pitter), or who, like Betjeman, are important but wrote not one poem I enjoy. In general, counting a few column inches in an anthology makes you quarrelsome, and makes pleasure impossible, whereas worrying about a few syllables, or one syllable, makes pleasure possible (if not inevitable). Small-scale space works in this odd way. I am not certain this book is too short. I am sure it would be revolutionary if it were to reach the bookshelves of all municipal libraries, secondary schools, High Street shops, etc., because it is a momentous break with the official propaganda of Movement critics, Bloodaxe Books, *Poetry Please, PN Review,* Peter Forbes,

Michael Horovitz, etc. But it threatens too many investments of those who would give it publicity. I feel that the view here offered of poets emerging in the last 20 years [*written 2001*] is quite implausible, and already seems to have collapsed. This is a difficult area. Sean O'Brien (agreeing with me, so far) did a spectacularly nasty review (in *Poetry Review*) because Tuma hadn't included his favoured raft of larkinesque northerners (or followed his anthology, *The Firebox*; or secured a short stock of Sean poems). O'Brien is easily upset, because he would like to be intelligent, Auden, and left-wing, and is by daylight blunt-nosed and conservative. How many other people think that British poetry has *declined* since 1960, and the high-point is represented by Larkin? Far better to ignore the vagaries of choice and look at the whole hundred, the polycyclic centurial curve.

At the outset, we would expect good language to follow from basic rules of benignity and attentiveness. If you want to enjoy such a verbal kind of experience, you need to cultivate the virtues of a listener. The act of feeling bored can be interpreted as aggression—a rejection of someone's demand for your neurological resources. Fortunately, no one seems to insist on the virtue of reading Cecil Day Lewis—it's OK to feel bored and to avoid what induces boredom. Just as a critic who is bored too easily is called supercilious and arrogant, so also a poet who masters the primary function of seizing attention may lack virtue; we only wish for screaming and banging on dustbin lids if there is a secondary load, of complex information, to occupy our attention once it has been seized. Conversely, we may feel that the poet who acquires the socially admired, Anglican virtues of self-effacing presentation, careful control of urges and desires, loses touch with the primary artistic drive, and produces poetry which is civilised but tedious. The social office of poet tends, thus, to be awarded to someone who cannot write good poems (Robert Bridges and Andrew Motion being candidates here).

Also at the outset, we may think that good poetry is a by-product of exciting social scenes with crackling emotional exchanges. Hence a line which is moving on—not "formal progress" but the nervous instability of human energies. Topics become "significant" because of the group attention which charges them up, eyes tracking the light of flying objects.

Since language is a secondary medium, it can accommodate any kind of experience; the poems here are not linked primarily to each other, and we need to think about what the poem is about in order to make headway with it. To go beyond the personal, poetry likes to use shared symbolic sites—supra-local, sublime, but also *familiar*. These sites, composed of stored associational chains, retain what is dumped at them. The 1880s saw a rise in interest in "national myth", and a player on the field of such myth was the government—still by proxy, since it was the mass media (appealing to the newly literate mass audience) which were pouring out a wave of imperialism. Kipling had a vision of the national cause which saw multiple dangers for England's little ship and called for constant shifts of course. The newspapers brought "national" issues into local communities and made it easy to identify friends of the nation and their ideological duties. A cigarette card series of the 1890s, *Picturesque Peoples of the Empire*, sums up the new data flow: aimed at a mass audience, attractive and highly coloured, brilliantly stylised (and desperately fragile as soon you look more closely), imperialist, recruiting the exotic in the cause of commerce, solidly based in real information. Poets who tried to argue about politics were inevitably drawn into doing "sociological sketches"—Auden's 30s poems can usefully be compared to these cigarette cards.

Just before the (chronological) outset of the century, was the startling arrival of Kipling, Housman, and Hardy, preoccupied with poor people as protagonists, with practical subjects and urgent material need, with low life and plain language. Even before Kipling, "sordid" and urban poetry was being written by W.E. Henley (the original for Long John Silver, allegedly), a Tory imperialist, preoccupied with heroism—and quoted by Tim McVeigh *in extremis*. The Noughts saw the emergence of poets like Sturge Moore, Wilfred Gibson, Walter de la Mare, John Masefield, Anna Wickham, Charlotte Mew. There was a split between the "peasant" strand and a Parnassian, elaborate version of poetry, dreamily open to all phases of European culture. Sturge Moore and William Watson were writing such poetry. Irving's production of *Faust* (originally 1885) gave a concrete image of the ego being shown all times and all countries. This wonderful access also brought awareness of the decay built into all institutions. This privileged spatial figure, often referred to with words such as *pageant*, *panorama*, or *cavalcade*, was also realised as universal exhibitions; in compact form as the Albert Memorial, with its checklist of subject races and climates; and, possibly, in the new gallery shops, with all their glass.

The view "from above" seems to open onto what Victor Turner describes as a liminal space, lifted above the ego and social oppositions. The disconnection of touch stimuli or near-by objects produces a boundless feeling. The more you abolish the egocentric perspective, the more blurred and flat the view seems. Where identification produces a spectral investment (locked on a bandwidth), the liminal integrates the whole spectrum. The liminal viewpoint relates to a personal standpoint as an object relates to a plane. Most of the poets I have examined wish for the liminal at some stage—at great risk of reaching the banal sublime. Great poetry shows a power of movement between the visible and the invisible. The gap or *diastema* between the temporal and the sublime is a moving line, and indications are that it was destabilised around 1900. The Nonconformists refused to accept the gap and wanted to bring about the Kingdom; they were vehemently emotional (which is why the literary world equates "emotional" with "low") and often excluded from public life ("particular"). The focus on social reform, the Welfare State, argued about quantitatively through statistics, threatened to efface the diastema going the other way, and abolish the transcendental (except as the minutes of the Poor Law Commission). Because the becoming-human of Christ is the classic moment where temporal and transcendental meet, it is significant that a new theology of the incarnation and atonement developed at this time, wrapped up in a new explanation of the relationship between scientific, sensory knowledge and the Revelation. It is associated with the word *kenosis* ("emptying"), and the name of Charles Gore—who is also given credit for moving the Anglican Church from the Tory party to Labour.

There is a special relationship between poetry, songs, and advertisements. All are lyrical, hedonistic, irrational, enthusiastic, and individualist. All have given up the "objective" function of language, their information is oriented towards sympathy and so to a (virtual) "personal" relationship—a shared fantasy. The expression of personal choice is most often seen in purchase decisions. Because the culture around it is based on possessive individualism, it is conventional for poetry to pursue individual expression, for example through a personal style. Since there is (apparently) a cultural imperative whereby art expresses possibilities denied during workaday experience, and transcends individual self-aggrandizement, poetry is also pushed towards the egoless and collective as the place where the Sublime is found. This has meant an intimate and vexed relationship between poetry and the collective imagery, which is highly stylised and coded, recognisable to all, and controlled by "central issue agencies". Making statements about the "spiritual" and the "communal" without signing a deal with the Established Church and the political parties has not proved easy.

The song side of poetry can be divided into relationships with hymns and with popular song. The problems of the latter would shed light on the parallel problems of lyric poets: we have virtually lost English song culture of before 1960. We can, provisionally, consider a poem in terms of its *offsets* from the universal and "banal" topoi of the common song patterns: selfless, generalised, and moralising in the case of hymns, individualised, hedonistic, and insouciant in the case of pop songs. When nervous tension fails, the poem simply *flops* back onto these worn models.

The 1910s saw the emergence of poets like Edith Sitwell, Gordon Bottomley, Lascelles Abercrombie, T.S. Eliot, D.H. Lawrence, Siegfried Sassoon, Harold Monro, Isaac Rosenberg, Wilfred Owen, Edward Thomas, Walter James Turner, Richard Aldington. The Georgians have had their revisionist moment (in Robert Ross's classic *The Georgian Revolt*). According to the historian Robert Ensor, the arrival after the 1870s of a new group of secondary schools not teaching Classics produced a new wave of literate pupils with no attachment to Latin & Greek models and was the basis for the return of English speech rhythms. It seems that accentual meter came first, and was followed by free verse. One of the striking features of the 20th century is the disappearance of drama and narrative as the most popular genres of poetry. The reduction to the individual as site, and to states of mind as subject, goes right across the literary spectrum. The Georgians simplified the poem as part of an attempt to become ordinary—part of a political urge towards socialism, a social urge towards blurring "educated" status. The "stellar perspective", its power/knowledge, is replaced by a walking perspective—vulnerable yet exploratory. This was the first kenosis of the new century, the first abandonment of knowledge in order to make present experience more vivid. Free verse was linked with this belief in walking, and with the abolition of a certain, Classical, sublime.

The War saw the entry of the government into the propaganda business, or alternatively the entry of hundreds of literati into government service. If Kipling and Newbolt wrote for young male readers, it was because there was a mass war coming along, and this *pedagogic process with lethal outcome* had to culminate before its outcome. Newbolt was effectively made head of propaganda policy, as chief of a committee. The functional link between government and the newspapers was forged, with Northcliffe and Beaverbrook taking up government posts.

Because speech has much to do with the signalling of status, poets are very concerned about class as a subject. However, reading poetry does not necessarily have to do with the reception of status. (There is a distinction between class politics and status politics.) Class awareness has a lot to do with housing patterns, and so its rules are specific to communities, not existing anywhere at national level. Of course "single class streets", or estates, cause polarisation, which damages cultural discourse. Detailed tracing of shifts in class relations during the century helps to pass the time, but does not amount to an explanation of the poem as a complex of information. What is palpable about "class" is strain and anxiety before speaking, before writing the poem. Imagined rejection is captioned as "you hate me because I'm middle class", or "you don't think my awareness is significant (because I'm not educated)". Poetic anxiety takes a million forms; it is the *doppelgänger* of insight.

The decisive event of the 1920s was the reaction against invested social authority, which had burnt up its reserves in promoting super-patriotism. A sense of confident irresponsibility produced wonderfully light and experimental poetry. This reaction was divisive and spread around the country at uneven rates. Graves records that everyone he knew in the Army in France thought, in 1918, that there would be a revolution when they came home. The old system was rotten, there was no saving it. The new electoral act of 1918 multiplied the number of voters by four—a dangerous experiment with democracy which was followed by 20 years of Conservative dominance. However, in poetry (a fairly small and autonomous area), Newbolt and the whole genre of naval-patriotic-historical poems came to seem ridiculous. A split between advanced and conventional taste now emerged; it is hard to decide whether this was the "Victorian—anti-Victorian" split based on revolt, or the "university taste—old middle-class taste" split.

In the 1920s, poets like Sacheverell Sitwell, Hugh MacDiarmid, Robert Graves, Edgell Rickword, and Edwin Muir emerged into the light of day. Sydney Bolt's *Poetry of the 1920s* is a successful capture of the decade and of its exoticism. The period 1926–28 saw a remarkable number of the century's best-selling poetry books. *Collected Poems* by John Masefield, *The Testament of Beauty*, by Robert Bridges, *The Land*, by Vita Sackville-West. The lack of resemblance between these suggests that there is no abiding "structure" of the market, but rather a series of excitations, unrelated to each other, which are self-reinforcing but also pass a cusp after which their size makes them unsustainable. The duration and rhythm of such excitations are of great interest. We can guess at a preference for long forms—short poems are less likely to induce the shopper to part with money. The reader wants to be immersed—and does not wish to experience distantiation. Heaven knows what proportion of turnover attaches to the "modern style"—very low, I imagine. The Empire Exhibition of 1925 (with a "programme", a "concept", by Kipling) was no doubt closer to the "actually existing middle class" than 'The Waste Land'. The twenties style was "fashionable but unpopular", and was forgotten in the new, depressed, decade.

English Literature degree courses were now being set up. The Practical Criticism method conveyed a taste for the Metaphysicals, and for paradox. When I look at European poetry, one of the basic contrasts with English poetry is the lack of paradoxes. These can be equated with sarcasm, as a feature of English speech. The package of the New Criticism was complicated and permissive. Because of its institutional investment, it represents one of the few points of continuity in taste. As a package, it is also part of the typical differences between educated and uneducated poets—visible in the small-scale texture of poems. The Anglican taste for 17th century language was highly compatible with the Metaphysical taste—but obviously not all New Critics are Anglicans. Prac Crit is a key classroom practice, but now has to compete with others, such as the "imaginative" creative writing approach associated with Holbrook. The ideology as packaged and distributed was a lot cruder than the "central" original; for example, the new critics clearly stated that myth was the highest form of poetry, but in the classroom "trained critics" came out firmly against myth, and poets who liked myth were identified as "loose" and "unacceptable".

The sublime panorama manner derives from the Temptation of Christ via *Faust*. The doctrine of suffering man is probably what led to the loss of the narrative quality which Kipling or Masefield excelled at. The human in jeopardy is now allowed to stay there—an existential plight containing the poem. The egocentric quality of modern poetry is probably related to the christological partiality of Anglican theologians. The displacing of the boundary between the spiritual and the temporal naturally affected the pacing of the book of poems. A sociological concern with stable (statistically large) structures (with fluctuations cancelled out) cancels out the movement of narrative—which resided in fluctuations. The urge to be "typical" is the universality of the Redeemer's mission at one remove. So we have the reduction into banality and finitude but without the element of excitement and reversals of fortune. We can speak of the structure-revealing or *struidical* tenor of the poem—shedding "local" detail to be solemnly, generally, valid. Myth without narrative. The kenosis of *subjectivity* was for poetry much as the loss of the congregation was for the Anglican church.

Newbolt was writing two volumes of the official naval history of the war. He was thus handed virtually the *Palladia regni*—the supreme envy objects. He had the real possession of what *The Orators* plays with the fantasy possession of. Newbolt's national epic had obvious links to the Right (at least, to spending on dreadnoughts rather than social welfare), although social knowledge was seen as a Left agenda; just as documentary film is seen as Left but was founded by Stephen Tallents at the Empire Marketing Board—an imperialist propaganda shop. Myth or documentary?

The Navy ran on Persian oil, the Empire's blood circulated through the canal at Suez. The expansion of Italy in the Mediterranean, her aggressively anti-British propaganda to the Arabs, and the deep-seated problems of co-operating (or suborning?) Dominion governments at a time of shocks for the world trade system, permitted Stephen Tallents to revive the propaganda structures mothballed after the Great War. His pamphlet, *The Projection of England* (1932), with a snappy cover design by the modernist graphic designer McKnight Kauffer, set out the basic iconographic programme for promoting Britain. Reconstruction using certain anomalies in the published accounts (and this certainly isn't in the official records) would "out" him as the chief of ideology for His Majesty's Government. This would include, for example, managing cultural exports to the Empire and vetting BBC scripts for concordance with Foreign Office views. The willingness of British poets to dissent from the *theatre of patriotism* has always been rather faltering and easily fatigued. The permeation of the public realm by images of the idealised Britain developed in government commissions swept away or buoyed up poets, who wanted to use basically the same imagery and could not detain the inculcated chains of association from their sequence. He projected England, and so it was discovered. *I thought it was a mirage but it was a collective representation.*

It's curious that one of the people most drawn to modernism was Stephen Tallents. He makes it quite clear how much more impressive he found Modernist entries at international exhibitions than English entries and their vein of historicism, rurality, and domestic comfort. He made Soviet films the explicit model for the new British documentary movement, set up under his tutelage.

The Thirties saw the emergence of poets like Joseph Macleod, Hugh Sykes Davies, W.H. Auden, William Empson, Charles Madge, George Barker, John Betjeman, David Jones, Ruth Pitter, Dylan Thomas, Ronald Bottrall, Idris Davies. As modern warfare relied increasingly on the morale and education of the civilian population, the envy-formation came to be "knowing how the country really is". This was an unsuitable object of contention—because you can write great poetry without it and because the character of a good witness requires you to surrender subjectivity. The struggle for expertise remained a major distraction. The shift from "fact" to "critique of acts of knowledge", signalled by Macleod's *Script from Norway*, where the diegesis is quite literally about how to fit the shots together, moved the action to epistemology — quite palpably with Prynne, Crozier, and Denise Riley. In Auden and MacNeice (partly also with Macleod), we find endless scene-setting for a drama of ideas which never starts. Finally, with *White Stones*, we get the drama of ideas.

After forty years? Backpacking through the deserted wastes of numerous anthologies forced me to posit a "mid century malaise", a cultural sterility reaching from 1930 to 1960. The "modernist salvation thesis" can perhaps be re-cast as a fantasy reaction to this weariness rather than as a real poetological programme or a proper thesis about history. Auden's *Poems*, of 1930, can be picked as the start of this malaise. Mottram's belief that there was a Poetry Revival starting in 1960 clashes with the belief of American nationalists that the malaise has lasted until the present day. It is very difficult for me to get interested by the most favoured products of the mid-century; recently I re-read Kenneth Allott's *Contemporary Verse* and felt bewildered and uninvolved—as I had done in 1973, first reading it. I don't think we need to explain it too much, since the poetic creativity of the period since 1960 is more urgent. However, reading biographical material of the period suggests material problems of the intellectual stratum (bringing pessimism and exhaustion), combined with an uncertainty about their role, and about the credibility of the educated classes in general. The welfare state made ease and leisure more available to the marginal educated—the dominated fraction of the dominant class, as Bourdieu calls them.

Yeats' 1936 *Oxford Book of Modern Verse 1892–1935* is an authoritative statement of a school which has no books written about it, but which for all that is still active. This is a curious and personal anthology. Catchphrases like Symboliste, Theosophist, mythical, New Age, spiritual, Jungian, occult, archetypal, set the scene. It may be helpful to think of it as a semantic opposite of the "objective" new university taste based on the New Criticism, and of the "Russian Ballets" or "modernist" taste. Newbolt's *New Paths on Helicon* is a broader-bottomed anthology, good for roughly 1900–1930.

Joseph Macleod wrote an interesting analysis of the change of mood around 1930 (in the *Festival Review*). He abandoned the style he had used for *The Ecliptic* and *Foray of Centaurs*, and began writing something more politicised and closer to the language of the people. Reading what he wrote about the style of the 1920s, a period he had just lived through, writing major poetry, casts deep doubt on the concept of "modernism" distributed to university students today. The idea that developments since 1960 follow a curve parallel to events of the 1920s, that the course of future poetry is already contained in the events of the past, that the preconditions for artistic success today are prefigured in aesthetic frameworks discovered in the 1920s—all this is deeply implausible. I would suggest, instead, that a wave of critics avoided the task of facing past poetry within its own horizons, by setting up a test of prestige, which they had all learned, and judging the poetry, inflexibly, by that test. The whole area of shifts of taste can thus be avoided. The ambiguity of the past disappears. Doubt disappears. Recognising the in-style lets you be recognised as in by the in-group. Clearly, most poetry of the last century is not worth revisiting. The decision which poets should be revisited cannot be resolved by applying the "modernist" ideology. It is simply a way of cutting down the info load and not "throwing yourself" back into a past intellectual horizon.

The problem with utilising modernist techniques in poetry is still that they have been so thoroughly assimilated by advertising that they make the audience flash into the mental state demanded by advertising.

The 1920s were a "good" period, but the arrival of the Depression made the '20s attitude (*ballets russes*, exoticism, neo-classicism, all those glittering toys) seem out of date, and commitment was the burning issue. Recent writers on the Thirties (Dai Smith, Valentine Cunningham) have pointed out that lack of commitment was a class quality—the privilege of the privileged. The most typical response to the crisis was to vote Baldwin, someone who stood for no response except serenity. The rise of Fascism made world-view an urgent matter for discussion. The camera now began decisively to challenge or reinforce social memory; the wish for precision came out as documentary. Charles Madge founded Mass Observation, which had a strong surrealist influence, and (rather later), wrote documentary poems.

Macleod's least favourite person, Stephen Tallents, tied the "image of England" firmly to consumption, leisure, sport, affluence—so also to individualism and to leisure practices developed by the land-owning families. The growth of leisure and a "consumer society" has been a long process of stratified diffusion of upper-class codes to the masses. The British pavilion at the 1937 Paris Exhibition showcased this vision of leisure, traditional quality, and individualism. Cultural successes have typically been mediators of gentry culture to everyone else; Betjeman being a classic figure. A '40s magazine like *Horizon* described the favoured days (the *très riches heures*) of Oxford aesthetes and is the model for the colour supplements which arrived, classless but affluent, in the 1960s. The aesthetes rejected work to evolve better play and inevitably became the godfathers of the leisure culture. The new status game affected language, in which status is central, and made it possible to define poetry as an individualist practice in which style was a form of self-differentiation. By becoming privatised, in subject matter and style, the poem fulfilled Tallents' strategic conception. Britain as a product, Britain as a range of products.

The images with which politicians, advertisers, and poets depict the desirable state are essentially similar. This similarity perhaps encourages struggles for legitimacy; it means that the rival claimants to social wisdom compete on a shared pitch, with the disagreement encoded in slight modifications of the central imagery. Poets (preachers, etc....) cannot invent new primary scenes, but generally wish to combine the sublime with the personal; the switches where personal, local experience, and invariant, symbolic experience are tied together or "interleaved" are few in type, and each type is used by many different poets. They are "common carriers".

Changes in the opinions of Christian writers (and orators) are still central to an educated public still dominated by Anglicanism. The history of these changes in Anglican opinion has not been written— but if we see poetry following a curve, we can ask what drew the curve. Because Socialism lacks a morality (as also the Church lacks a theory of politics), and because poetry deals with personal relations, Christianity remained the source of models for poetry. A recent preoccupation with Christology and the difficult concept of kenosis probably influenced the way English poets wrote about suffering in the trenches. It is hardly coincidental that a new dogma which emphasized the suffering and fear of Christ on the Cross, His immersion in human muscles and senses, arrived together with a public preoccupation with the health of the working classes. In the 1930s, rejection of modern war, and so of the modern state, led to personalist positions, and was probably influential on poets in their wish for "a personal stance", on politics but also on how to write. It is likely that the shifts in the way poets understand their "millimetre of distinctiveness" as a legitimation for speaking, modulating from Personalism to political protest to existentialist quest to intellectual thesis to "lifestyle statement", are the arena where the soul of British poetry has been exposed; where the grand stakes are lying around free; where the battle is lost and won.

Magazines and the radio demanded a new light entertainment poetry to stock their shelves with—a new product brilliantly supplied by figures like Betjeman, with borrowings from popular song channelled through nurseries like the Oxford revue. Auden began by imitating Brecht and went on to imitate Betjeman. Time and print are not kind to chorus-boys. Looking at the BBC just reminded the historically minded of a whole chain of relationships in which the patron dominated the artist. The convention is that in the 20th century the artist supplies the ideological programme—whereas in the 17th century it was the patron, or a "civil servant" working for the patron, and the artist drew the figures. A cherished illusion? Figures like Newbolt, Tallents, Melvin Lasky, made the terms of employment clear, at various times, and by controlling usage made the associational paths repetitive—to internalise the message was to internalise the code. To fail to internalise it was to be a lout—someone who couldn't hear the music.

It would be interesting to analyse styles, for once, in blocks beginning in 1905, 1965, etc., instead of "zero to nine". Emergence is not a simple concept, and some of these cases would need some further research. What exactly constitutes emergence? And what about demergence, an event rather more common than we would like? (And could it be transitive, e.g. "Andrew Motion demerged them all one especially bad Friday night.") The problem with a list like the one proposed here in segments is that readers immediately start to barrack you about the poets you haven't mentioned. Aiee! A much-loved myth is that of the neglected writer, stubbornly individual, who after symbolic years in the wilderness achieves recognition. The problem with this curve is that it doesn't make the reader the central thing in the reading experience. The myth of neglect thoroughly confuses the history of innovation—most neglected writers are perfectly conventional. It seems to help in selling books. There is a special lien between the reader and a writer they can buy shares in—a kind of debenture. The theory, rightly or wrongly, is that such a heroic Legend dramatises the reader's path from dependency, to originality, to struggle, and to—becoming the Marquis of Carabosse, I suppose. The governing of the spectrum auction by rules like:

> if you own it, I don't
> if I own it, you don't

—produces something like a suburban tract of houses and gardens, each partitioned off from the others. The handling of the wilderness of the imaginary reproduces the everyday if the poet applies a suburban logic and treats other poets as competitors. The fragmentation of the market is the *realisation* of a social structure.

The organisation of an anthology by the authors of the poems invites us to organise a competition between them. Or, we may enjoy judging the relative success of poets. Starting to write a poem is never a more certain undertaking than setting out on a journey carried by Railtrack. Perhaps we do not wish to see the poems as lumps of property, as indices of performance and personal prowess, etc., but prefer an exit into a space where ego boundaries are weakened, and transcended.

Could we imagine the separate poems as a population of realisations showing the geography of a pre-existing space? We begin with uncertainty and end with morphology. We can alternatively see the period as containing a series of brilliant possibilities, which poets compete to capture—and which have nothing to do with individuals. Individualism is artistically productive—in swiftness to vary formal constants, curiosity abut "inherited assumptions", fearless debouching into unoccupied and boundless space, the fantasy of frequent replacement of the centre by a periphery. But also, I see the urge for self-aggrandizement squeezing the poetry out of the poem.

In the 1940s, we have the emergence of poets like JF Hendry, Roy Fuller, Glyn Jones, Lynette Roberts, Sorley MacLean, W.S. Graham, T.S. Law, Kathleen Raine, Roland Mathias, George Campbell Hay, Douglas Young, Sydney Goodsir Smith, F.T. Prince, Alan Ross. My colleague James Keery is undertaking a large-scale revision of traditional interpretations of this decade, of which his recent edition of the poems of Burns Singer is just the start. He is contemplating a revisionist anthology—which, no doubt, should be followed by parallel interventions for each decade since, overturning the verdicts made by partial literary journalists at the time (and apathetically followed by conformist academics). What stands out from the list above is the pre-eminence of Scotland and Wales at this time. In wartime, the closeness of death brought out the priestly function to assure the living that grief would pass. Poets were the eschatological guards carrying out the *apocalypse*, the unveiling, as death unveiled itself. As civilisation vanished, poets evoked immortality and eternal values. Revelation "falls, like lightning, vertically from above" (Barth); is the "downrush from the superconscious" (Charles Gore). The polar ice appeared in the poetry of Graham and Hendry as a liminal substance, frozen, changeless, but carrying life. Rexroth's 1948 *New British Poets* is the classic anthology.

In the 1950s, we have the emergence of poets like George Mackay Brown, Edwin Morgan, Iain Crichton Smith, Christopher Logue, Geoffrey Hill, Philip Larkin, Charles Tomlinson, Ted Hughes. This was a miserable decade, and it was traumatic that the culture managers it threw up controlled so much of the (tiny) poetry industry for the next 25 years. Reinfection by interpenetrative elites.

The decline of Christianity in Britain is the single unambiguous fact of the last 40 years. The Anglican Church was undergoing a defensive crisis in the '50s (although it seemed like a revival to some people), and so the efforts of the clergy to find relevance for their message to an urban, proletarian, and increasingly secular society were firm and radical—if sometimes called desperate. The loss of significance of the established clergy prefigures the loss of the literati, including the poets, and posterity will see these processes as parts of the same thing. It is not quite clear to me, for lack of time-stamped evidence, whether poetry got into simple language, live performance in clubs, "relevance", "protest", the youth market, because the Church had already done that, or whether they led (in any way). The shift from Apocalypse to Movement was a shift within concerned Christianity, and the move on to Pop poetry and the "reading" was also a shift within the Christian communion. So many of the poets of the '60s write from a virtual youth club, and cannot be understood in any other context.

James is researching the underground survival of the New Romantics (the origin of the Underground?); for me it was just a miserable decade where the Conservatives won three General Elections. The Cold War saw most European countries debating the virtues of Russian and American models for art. With the Welfare State, the Left was stepping into the shoes of the Church, as source of security and of collective ideals, ready to undergo a parallel decline at 20 or 30 years' delay. The (poetic) failure of the Left in the 1950s is either the key to the whole decade, or a result of some other failure, still obscure. Books by Macleod and Christopher Logue are tantalising and anticipatory. For committed leftists, the surrender of artistic judgment to Party officials, who themselves lacked artistic judgment, led to portentous and wooden poetry. The sense of middle-class guilt was too disabling. So it was that Left poetry had to wait for the arrival of a generation of educated working-class students who were turned on by the idealisation of the proletariat. The exodus from the Communist Party in the wake of destalinisation and the Russian intervention in Budapest may also have cleared the air.

While the Left was shedding its addiction to Nonconformist hymn and sermon figures, the Anglican Church was positively copying Nonconformism. Endless triumphant repetition had associated sincerity with poverty of means, artistic splendour with faintness of heart; the rise of the working class meant the triumph of Nonconformism, by weight of numbers. One result was the abolition of high art, but with the mundane conquering all, instead of the sacred flooding the mundane. This pressure to fail struck a bizarre alliance with the spread of light entertainment, demanding trivial poems. This is the heritage of Forbes and Astley—the Empty Quarter. But the same situation, the same readers, could sustain a completely opposite result.

The advance out of a wartime/emergency economy, and a shift from heavy industry to light, drew on a consumer society, with the image-makers paid to direct consumption rather than make propaganda for the government. Individualist consumption scenarios called for individualist poetry. Along with the white goods came the genre of domestic anecdote. As higher education spread and spread, the expanding academic cadre of EngLit had a remarkable degree of homogeneity, which in many ways went all round the universities of the capitalist world. This consensus had staying power rather than creative energy. It was the citadel of defence for a certain approach to the poem which we can describe as disenchantment. Poets from within that citadel had as watchwords empiricism, toughness, the rejection of rhetoric, the criticism of ideology. Of course there were other stylistic preferences in the poetry world, but the disenchanted faction had remarkable impetus and retained power over opinion and central magazines at least until the 1980s. A very high proportion of poets published, all through, wrote from inside that consensus, to be read by others inside it. This stylistic register presented itself as freedom and modernity to those inside it and as a massive array of inhibitions to anyone else. If you read 100 cultural or social histories of Britain, they will all say that the Swinging Sixties changed everything. However, the decline of poetry in the culture market is equally clear. One way of writing the modern history is to say that the lyrics of pop songs replaced poetry and that the line of musicless poetry was a province by-passed by modernity—thinly populated by pastoral clans of conservatives and malcontents. The disenchanted were more disapproving of Youth Culture (as embodied in students) more than anything else, and they simply had to stand fast in their positions, as "bourgeois guardians", in order to survive until 1979 and the triumph of neo-conservatism. That is, key figures born around 1920–1930 fulfilled the usual length of a writer's career rather than being crated up and delivered to the scrapyard by around 1966. One theme of this work is necessarily how the long 1950s came to an end.

At this point we break off from Tuma's anthology, because the problem of which poets to select has become too urgent. It is easy to depict the period since 1960 in the terms classically stated by Eric Mottram, that is as the collapse of everything organic to the old social system and the old middle class, and the emergence as dominant artistic formation of a wave of innovative poets who had constitutively absorbed "the lessons of modern art", and in particular of a package of American poets flourishing in the 1950s. Tuma's selection supports this, to a great extent. This tenet, which might seem to be just a personal matter of taste, goes beyond that because it identifies a conflict within the poetry world. Now that decades have rolled by, there has emerged a depolarisation project, where we try to grow out of the mutual hostility of the factions which lined up against each other in the '70s. The present work is trying to discover the truth about the mainstream, as a step towards mutual understanding and respect.

There's this dance going round like an awful disease. The "British Poetry Revival" developed such kinetic energy as to achieve an effect of shock and awe. This covered the full spectrum of cultural endeavour and drew everything from architecture to anthropology in its train. All this had a certain effect of dazzle which may have reduced clarity of mind even while injecting a million milligrams of Theory. Too high to look down? *If I stop running I'll fall out of the sky*, as The Creation sang in yesteryear. Catalogue work allowed me to make a count of "Underground" poets publishing up to 1990: 2,000 names. This was a whole world. Of these perhaps 100 were artistically significant. If there were 2,000 poets publishing in the Underground, it is futile to go into the new cultural process under a banner saying that they were all good. Surely there are excellent reasons for admitting that the slack, messy, inattentive Underground boys were inattentive, messy, and slack. This is the truth and will found a society of poetry in which we can talk to each other. The disputes were originally about theories of poetry. If there are so many bad poems, the theories responsible for them must be wrong, and there is no point going to war for them. Perhaps there are better theories, which regrettably most poets have failed to understand. The theories we abandon on the way to the truth probably weren't going to be very good paths to follow into a joyful future. Being delusions moves them out of the frame for shining paths. The lie seems to be inclusive but all the falsity it entails means that the shared thing crumbles at every step. So it's better to tell the truth.

A community has been defined as a group of people who share a version of the past (or, share a past preserved in narratives). In order to build a larger poetic community, we go through a process of filtering which builds an ever larger stock of truth. To investigate the Underground poets was a mammoth critical undertaking which filled my horizon for a great portion of my life. However, reaching that horizon revealed another landscape, new extents of cultural and linguistic space. This raises a number of questions.

Q1 What did the Sixties and Seventies achieve, if not to make us all so hip it hurt? Could the reversals of traditional perspective be repeated and still work? could this happen twice? What is the Underground now *for*?

Q2 Has historicism played out its hand? is modernism still striking out into the unknown, 100 years after the first Modernist wave in Europe and fifty years after the start of the "British Poetry Revival"? What style does the time recommend, or does the Time have an organ which shapes style? Has the obsolete ceased to be obsolete?

Q3 Has the refusal to innovate worked as classicism, that is something which is timeless rather than tedious and used up?

Q4 In the 1950s, an established poetic style was identified with the middle class in power. Has the mainstream or the middle class evolved since? Is there a new middle class? What changes have occurred within the mainstream?

Q5 Has the BPR evolved since 1977 or become a genre? has innovation continued to be innovation or become a range of recognisable and beloved moves?

Q6 Far from the tier of cynical/urban literati, is there a world of poets, provincial, innocent, untouched by fashion? are they productive?

Q7 Is there an "innovation wave B" following the maximum polarisation of the 1970s, which has been accepted by the mainstream without sinking back into the conventional? We could call this the "suave postmodernist" vein.

Q8 Is there a modernity, in terms of what gets through emotionally to a modern audience, which is quite different from the self-reflective "in" sound of the Underground?

Q9 Did the box of beautiful things really get burnt?

I do not feel able to answer all these questions. I went through a project of trawling bookshops and the Net for mainstream poetry books, but a count of the total makes it clear that I only caught a drop in the ocean. It is a dubious basis for generalisation. I am not trying to take the Underground out of the Museum of Culture and dispose of it in some car-boot sale of finished experiments. Instead I am trying to reach another part of the spectrum and collect new experiences. The "truth and reconciliation" process must involve truth, and the way to this is research.

A necessary idea is that, as you shop and consume in the poetry world over decades, there is a shift from intense reaction to a classificatory recognition of surface features, which degenerates into a classificatory inertia. That is, as a dumb teenager you try lots of things and work out what you dislike from inside it, experiencing it, but a few years later you are just recognising surface features to "recall" what you are going to like. You don't repeat the bad experiences but you tend to converge on what you already own (and what is called your "identity"). If this (unproven) idea is true, you stand to benefit from depolarisation, there is a dividend from it. Maybe a genre is really a repetition neurosis. Of course a critic who simply charges in and tells a well-informed market of readers "your taste is wrong! your knowledge is wrong! your deeply held preferences and precious learning are just mistakes I am going to liberate you from! just wait!" is advancing into idiocy territory.

The existence of genres derives from this "classificatory nostalgia", the wish to return to the pleasurable experience. So can the wish be a wrong decision? Or is it the voice both of self-knowledge and of connoisseurship? Is there a profession of managers whose function is to *annul my wishes*?

It is possible to disbelieve in the existence of the mainstream and the Underground and the geometry which opposes them to each other. However, the opposition is a fundamental feature of the social space in which poetry happens. There is an exact line between the two realms even if an individual poet can write on both sides of the line. This fuzziness is the nature of human behaviour, and the overlaps never amount to an erasure of the opposition. Equally, the opposition is at the level of the Gestalt and cannot be reduced to a single feature which we could quantify and count off with bureaucratic accuracy. Several other classificatory oppositions have something to offer, but this one is soaked in the energy and ideals of several generations.

People channelling Wilfred Owen or W.H. Auden are likely to show up in any store of amateur poetry. An obvious trait here is retardedness—time seems to have stopped for these people. Self-insertion occurs into a literary situation which already exists. It may be that the eminent can be visualised as the apex of a large column of literary sensibility in which hundreds of other people participate. In fact, we can conceptualise genre as being the abstraction from the concrete activity of dynamic individuals, frozen and yet diluted by the passage of time. The way in which people write poems comes out of the shared past—new poems embody a shared past. The task here is to refurbish the past by finding out which poets achieved excellence.

The problem of self-insertion

I wondered about the total count of poets active in the period I write about, viz. 1960 to 1997.

One way of getting at this is to use sample points which are, or possibly are, counts of the complete numbers of books published in a particular year. Three are: *1995*, 1944; *1960*, 131; *1976–7*, 906. If we make some major assumptions and take the value for each year as the average of those two points (so 1960–76 and 1977–1995), we can build a model for the total number of books in the period. (This involves taking 1944 as the value for 1996 and 1997.)

This model yields a figure of 40,139 books for the period. If we assume an average of five books per poet (ASSUMPTION), in a 40-year span, this gives us 8000 poets.

I found the catalogue of the Association of Little Presses for 1990. It was organised by writer, so I could count 1,571 individual writers listed there. The ALP is roughly the Underground, although some mainstream poets may sneak in. I then looked at some ALP lists for the 1970s, although the way they are organised makes them hard to use, and did some more counts. If we assume a thousand "alternative poets" in the '70s, cut down a few as possibly not British, possibly writers of prose, etc., then we get to 2,000 for the whole period 1970–1990. This is a numbingly large figure, and I am certainly not proposing that everyone in that set is worth resurrecting, but it does suggest how important the Underground realm was. You have this tradition of eccentricity in Britain, and the idea of being personal, original and nonconformist appealed to large numbers of people.

The assumptions in the model above are pretty huge. Anyone is welcome to provide better figures at any time. As you can imagine, collecting and cleaning up the data is pretty tedious.

If the count is really 8000 then the count of 140 poets discussed in my work as individuals is amazingly selective. As I described in the introduction, the present work aims to talk about the wider community of poets writing, not by dealing with such numerous works one by one, but by identifying artistic conventions or moods which they had available to them.

The crux of writing history is that people are convertible. That is, that you can assume that the differences between a poet on scene in 1960 and one on scene in 2000 are so few that they can be isolated and articulated. This is an act of equivocation, saying that y=x, which one would have to carry out on a grand scale in order to start saying "this is how the scene changed".

I had an hour of enthusiasm for mapping historical change and during it built two spreadsheets of about 450 names to sum up the scene in 1975 and 2005. I had the concept that you could map one onto the other and the transforms involved would be a descriptor for the historical change over a generation. Unfortunately, brief yet serious consideration of the raw data, schematic as it was, showed that the processing involved was quite intractable and beyond the means of even a team of scholars.

Having failed in front of those intimidating (200x200) matrices, we can imagine a path out in which we simplify the setup to a smaller set of entities, two or three dozen, which are capacious because they are stylistic areas. If we could succeed in fitting the poets into these clusters, without violating the rules of pattern matching, we could map entire clusters between times without an excessive load. That is, we could compare avant-garde poets of 1955 with avant-garde poets of 1975 and avant-garde poets of 2005, and we would have a data object with few enough features for us to work with it. (Actually there were no avant-garde poets in 1955.) These shapes would have the dual quality that a poet at the start of their career could learn them and use them to generate poems, and that they survive and evolve over time.

The problem then is to identify what the clusters are. Most of the work is in analysing the *candidates* and weeding them out. Within this volume I discuss domestic anecdote, the Pop poem, the academic poem, the communalist poem, the Oxford Line, the late Christian poem, the poem of star culture and high glamour. I use the terms m-stream (for mainstream) and u-stream (for the Underground) to speed things up. There is also substream (the sub-literary) and the J-stream (Jungian poetry). This choice is one I made, although all the terms are already floating around in shared space. Other genres like the avant-garde, the myth poem, the New Age poem, have been covered in other works of mine.

If we tried to take on all the poets listed here, our consciousness would submerge, drowned by hundreds of conversations running simultaneously. This is failure. If we schematise, leaving out the mass of details flourishing in each poet, we may reach coherence—but we have lost most of the information. How could this not be failure? If we average out over a few thousand points we can produce something completely grey, a sort of sludge. In fact, any attempt to average out over several poets, or many poets, will tend to produce this grey amorphous effect. The price of moving to the plane of genre is incompleteness. If you look at a mass of poems from any moment in time, most of them cannot be assigned to a genre. It could be that only 1% of the poems in any large sample can be so assigned. In fact, less skilled poets may be more amorphous because they simply have less control over their material—there is no overriding purpose and so no stylistic identity. However, the stylistic clusters identified are also ideals: they represent aspirations, and it is valid to see poets as driven by idealistic dream states in which they yearn for artistic goals. These goals sometimes belong to a time and to a whole swathe of poets. In fact, if we look at the most gifted poets we are also seeing to some extent the ideals which other poets saw. It can be argued that poetry which is cut off from these dream states cannot truly succeed.

Perhaps if we suppress individual traits in order to develop groups which have a history longer and more flexible than individuals, allowing a story to develop across time, we can follow changes. It may be that these styles had histories, external and internal; times of invention, flourishing, falling out of fashion, decay. They contained symbolic assets and these assets could fluctuate in value or be captured by other groups.

If everything starts, everything stops. The currents of poetry which are no longer around must have come to a halt sometime. I was constructing a time-line diagram of recent British poetry for an American magazine. This was fun but was abandoned in the end. It was easy to show things starting—these were events. But most of the area of the diagram was featureless and boring because it was just things going on—they just flowed on for decades. The typical thing was for a major poet to find a groove and to go on creating inside it for thirty or forty years. This did not make for a diagram that caught the eye. So I became interested in things stopping. Everything runs out, everything consumes vital energies which in the end are burnt up, but it was too difficult defining the moment when something ran out. Perhaps the crash and exhaustion of great creative rushes provide the key moments of poetic history—buried by denial, muffled by endless attempts to reproduce the effect when it's too late, but definitive. In this work I have tried to write the life and death of genres—admittedly with blurred results.

Identifying these crises is another source of controversy. I could probably find 100 essays which say "free verse has shot its bolt", but it doesn't seem to be true.

The proposal is that if you fit all (or, say 200) poets of 1960 into a matrix of cells, and take that matrix and fit all (or, 200) poets of 2010 into it, you could compare the poets within each cell and come out with a notion of how things have changed in 50 years. Everyone would deny resembling other poets but at the level of capturing fabulous linguistic objects from the past they are all for it. They want to be compared to the great, and comparison is already categorisation. Identifying such clusters might expose a landscape whose parts are moving slowly but inexorably in relation to each other, of which some are perishing and some fabulously and greedily growing. The markets or fan bases evolved at the same time, allowing for a vivid competition for dominance, with some groups irresistibly accumulating power and attracting new members. This could resemble the manoeuvring of rival groups at a court, displaying in order to acquire prestige, intriguing to acquire influence, spreading rumours to weaken other factions. This is an economy of pleasure, although for some people it goes well beyond a game. The game can be lost, with rafts of poets breaking away and sinking. The phenomena of cliques and mobbing have as a corollary the act of withdrawal, where entire groups move out rather than tolerate a false linguistic environment. This was taking place on a large scale in the mid Sixties and the split of that time has notoriously not been closed up even now.

To recapitulate. The approach through genres is a way of opening the perspective out to the whole range of poets, including the conventional and the amateur. Its efficiency is low but we can fill a book with it and completeness is wholly unattainable. The choice and definition of genres are to a great extent arbitrary, and I have preferred to deal with the genres which have an identifiable composition and a history.

Blind panics and glittering fevers

Amateurs don't get to write Theory but we can get at their decision processes indirectly via a reconstruction. The way I have chosen is to list explanations of why modern poetry has gone wrong. These are germane because most amateur poetry has gone wrong, somewhere. I assembled a collection of panic stories. The statements are all genuine but the composition, regrettably, is my own. They also reveal intense aversions, bursts of energy which fuel people's journey into conviction and counter-error. With every poem comes a justification. These judgements are also social in part, the product of public debate and of accumulating critical commentary. They are the stones which anxiety forms. All of them represent attacks on official and prized poetry. They also suggest how the amateur world is split—they object to different things. The line of division between professional and amateur is discontinuous and follows a perverse route. So, modern poetry has gone wrong because of:

- rejection of the avant-garde; fear of ideas.
- the myth of the avant-garde; historicism and the myth of progress in the arts; the worship of technique and the territorialisation of technique.
- the domination of the poetic realm by the traditional upper middle class with their investment in conservatism and their peculiar way of pressing meaning out of language.
- the abandonment of traditional culture and the heaving of flat and vengeful masses from beneath, dumbing down in the slime of rip-off degradation.
- Christian inhibition and diffidence, meekness, greying every texture, flattening every drama, soothing away every conflict, evacuating problem areas, ignoring the issue of power.

- the exploitation of the appeal of a certain voice with its tint of ease and privilege, and the quiet rejection of any poetic content in case it disturbs the self-assured flow of this voice and the heedless narcissistic investment in it by those who possess it or those who merely envy it.

- the reliance on intuition in the fear of ideas; the fact that intuition turns out to mean imitating the artistic procedures of those of a generation earlier, or two generations; the fact that the voice of intuition can direct you to the place where bad poetry happens and even dictate bad poems, entire and word perfect, to you; the lack of technical training in poetry; the inability to theorise because the faculty has never been developed by formal training or discussion with peers; reliance on infantile strata of the mind to produce artistic schemes because the later and more intelligent strata are stunted and ineffective.

- the decline of rhetoric as the means appropriate to poetry and the only dimension in which it can achieve greatness; the discrediting of any means by which language can work on the imagination; the assumption that flatness is the sign of authenticity in language; the traditional Nonconformist dread of fine language, Italian art, exalted music, Mediterranean culture, anything grand or beautiful.

- loss of the high oral: poetry formerly relied on skills of delivery developed and massively enjoyed in high oral genres such as courtroom rhetoric, the sermon, and the stage; the overwhelming deterioration of quality of the sermon and the language of plays has drawn in its wake a deterioration of poetry; a fatal lack of labour agitators; the disappearance of politicians who can make great speeches.

- the elimination by the Church of England of its own High Oral tradition in favour of dumbing down in an attempt to appeal to urban youth who are perceived as essentially non-Christian; the development by the Church of an anxious, socially committed, oral register of banality adopted by numerous poets of conscience.

- the spread to vast numbers of people of a belief that poetry is where you can be completely unconstrained, so that you just write down anything you feel like and it is like conversation without the constraint of having to interest other people; the reduction of poetry to a kind of domestic snapshot without any technical ambition or originality; the equation of unqualified self-talk with authenticity. the equation of literary devices with inauthenticity.

- as set out in Thurley's classic *The Ironic Harvest*, the betting of poets on a position of ironic detachment as superior to writing directly about emotions or about positions they actually believe in; the dominance—within the group of people who dominate poetry—of scholarly analysis, which makes people anxious about expressing emotions; sneaking feelings that anyone writing about emotions is inferior; an ironic style of acting; the slightness which makes full-blooded acting seem exaggerated; a professional ethos which knows that if you can't argue on both sides you can't work for the side which offers you the highest fee.

- the audience's love of the past and their indifference to living poets

- the belief that there is a way of writing which is inherently moral and that this can be detached from acting in a moral way; the reduction of morality to a competition which can be won; the allocation of morality chiefly to a few people in an intellectual elite, as if it were like a grasp of theoretical physics.

- the Pathology of the Impresarios; the grip on the business and marketing side of the scene of a few cultural managers with pathological weaknesses and a lust for vengeance on the talented; the tragic limits of otherwise great figures who led people into strange predicaments even when enabling them to write important poetry; hundreds of different and totally inexplicable personal deviations and manias of dozens of impresarios; mass investment and employment in malformed cultural projects; the design of the public image of poetry and of shared enthusiasms or movements by impresarios tripped into delusional states by glittering fevers.

- a narrow intake of talent; unidentifiable feelings in much of the population that poetry is not for them; a door on the second floor.

- the vagaries of the Oxford Model which has remained dominant for the entire century and which had greater successes in the past.

- the lack of any technical training in any institution, so that many poets write in an ineffectual and naïve way, and others have to snatch time for self-teaching away from other commitments, including demands to write essays and other useless forms of approved activity; the amateurism of poets when compared with musicians, actors etc.

- domination of business values, the loss of leisure, reduction in the number of "younger sons" who are interested in culture rather than in practical and money-earning activity; the sudden rise of academic life which has taken "useless intellectuals", employed them, and reduced their lives to the productivity model.

- the disappearance of arts patronage except by the government; government patronage run by people who hate modern poetry and in their complete misunderstanding of artistic values promote other values according to an iron whim.

- the self-identification of the new dominant class with a register of language, between naked power, degraded systems theory, and sheer vacuity, which is incompatible with poetry.

- the rise of feminism making the sphere of intimacy, the preferred topic of poetry, unavailable because the signal is drowned out by waves of dispute and contention and made subject to rules of fashion, display and competition.

- the oppression of women, causing them to write voluminously and badly about themselves in order to prove their importance.

- the ritualised nature of English social life.

- the absence of ritual as the organic site for intense poetry full of social symbolism.

- dumbing down; the elimination of information from poetry; the elimination of critical thought from poetry; the elimination of emotion, as this creates conflict; aiming poetry at bored 15-year-olds with literacy problems.

- the factional struggles within the residual "poetry world" as dominant figures lead followers into pathology, and as elementary style choices became hopelessly politicised, territorialised, and subject to dispute and rage; the success of your rivals becomes an offence to you and audience reactions cease to be based on a generous artistic appreciation.

- the use of artistic choice sanctimoniously to reveal character flaws in the poet/reader needing therapeutic intervention; the trickling down of Utopian projection into an authoritarian plan to repress phantasy (via amateur psychoanalysis); the medicalisation of any artistic imagination; the reduction of artistic knowledge to a social worker's dossier.

- the advent of poetry in performance, leading to uncontrollable narcissism and insecurity which drown poetry in formulaic repetition and super-obvious effects.

- the failure of the New Left.

- the advent of Identity Politics persuading people that everything they write should be an advertisement for themselves and that self-criticism is a form of disloyalty and internalised oppression, and that all poetry is equally good; this was possibly a kind of fungus growing in the burnt-out site where the New Left had failed.

- lack of shared ideological beliefs, loss of norms; the difficulty of inventing a vocabulary of symbols in which to say anything; the impossibility of writing without radical originality, which is a strain to acquire and takes years to work out technically.

- obscurity of language.

- the loss of a specialised language of poetry which demarcates poetry from everyday life and marks out a separate world with learnt psychological patterns of leisure, detachment, contemplation, high associational rate, pleasure; a psychotope.

- people don't love each other any more and so can't write love poetry, which is the main urge to write poetry.

- cynicism; the inability to believe in other people, to believe in talented people, to surrender, to believe in exalted language and exalted experiences.

- privatisation and the active rejection of shared values so that there is no vocabulary left for art; the corrosion of the sphere of the collective by possessive individualism, a revolutionary and unregulated creed which has seized Britain since the 17th century; the corrosion of art by individualism.

- the dominance of personality as a heretical departure from the great traditions of European art (according to C.S. Lewis, *The Personal Heresy*); poets should forget about their tedious personalities and write something more selfless and ideal.

- fake Third World poems going down in a dessert bowl of pastoral sentimentality and communalist kitsch; poetry as the travel poster with sun, fruits and beach pastoralism.

- exhaustion of folk culture; the wreckage of folk culture to an extent greater than in any other European country by urbanisation and commercialism; the disappearance of folk song as the basis for all "high" poetry over the last 3000 years.

- the loss of a peasant culture to act as a substrate for the imagery of poetry, not enough poems using the eternal imagery of ploughs, birds, weather, potato digging, etc.

- the dominance of a fantasy of rustic language and a wilfully fake pastoral; writing poems about potatoes.

- abandonment of artistic values in favour of obligatory commitment to doing things you don't want to do and staging poems in such a way as to demonstrate your moral superiority.

- because Standard English is worn out and politically compromised and only dialect is authentic, but as no one has ever written any interesting poems in dialect it is undeveloped and comic.

- the decline of myth.

- the imitation of Blake; the belief that imitation of a pre-modern if voluble psychopathology is the be-all and end all; developing a comprehensive envy of phony cult religiosity as an exit from the "Western box"; the wish to reject physics and cosmology and rewrite them in terms of Zoas, emanations, mundane shells, voodoo rays etc. before getting to the poetry.

- the worship of purely personal and irrational associational patterns which reach the terrain of myth formation only at the cost of infantilism and obscurity recovered only by a cult structure; faith in the unconscious when language is all to do with making conscious and clothing in external form.

- an addiction to realism and communalism as artistic ideals, preferring "naked experience" to any kind of high language and recording the typical, the massively over-familiar, the wretched, the comfortless in a triumphalist brandishing of intentions which prevent any kind of artistic success; the willingness to throw away the language and ideals of poetry in favour of a romance with sociology, starting in the late 19th century; a cult of the ordinary.

- the addiction to the values of Georgian poetry which was largely a surrender to realism and the cult of the ordinary; superficial updating of Georgian poetry to write senseless poems about virtuous urban workers instead of virtuous rural workers as in days of yore.

- apathetic reversion to the iambic pentameter and to worn out rhythmic patterns familiar in the 19th century.

- surrender to free verse and so to subjectivity and a rhythm that does not entrain the reader.

- the loss of shared measures to an extent which means that only radical originality of rhythmic organisation can have any success.

- the attachment of poetry to a national interest which was in geopolitical decline in mid century and was visibly in the process of losing most of the assets it originally possessed.

- succumbing to theory in a form which traps the poet in rigid ideas like a bean in a can—even if these theories are original and produce novel results.

- hysterical surrender to French philosophers whose work depends on impossibilism in politics and irrationalism in language.

- the cult structure of avant-garde groups where unique possibilities are abandoned for palpably false ideas and the monomaniac preoccupations of charismatic leaders; the millennialism of avant-garde salvation cults where self-criticism is unheard of; the occultist belief that babble, spatter, squawks, endless photocopying of scrumpled sheets of paper, represent destiny and infinity.

- hatred of the English, leading people to submerge in a ruinous swamp of rural infantilism as expression of their "ethnic identity"; folk revivals where Death came along for the ride.

- the domination of American poets.

- the hatred by American poets of English poetry.

- the domination by American poets who write awful poetry which when imitated turns out to produce awful poems in an English accent.

- different problems in each successive period of 5 years (or 4 years? or six months?) so that counter-tides of reaction roll in and lead to new failure.

I can't succeed with describing the mass of poetry because you can't make the rules of the hegemony conscious. We can offer flashes when a grey world is lit as an intense greyness. What seems like a translation from sludge into consciousness turns out sometimes to be the opposite. Poetry is supposed to express uniqueness, and poets may not like being "inserted" by me into a genre, however comforting and powerful. Aversion suits them better, as bourgeois individualists—it is a moment of high energy and also amounts to consciousness. It is the theory of untheoretical people.

There is another intention in collecting all these statements—to contextualise the claims I made (in *The Failure of Conservatism*, 2003) about the devastating effects of the rejection of modern innovations, above all in the 1960s and 1970s. However convincing that thesis, failure has a much more vast and impressive anatomy. It is not convincing that everyone could have been a good poet by taking on modernity—there are many examples of rather old-fashioned poets who wrote effectively. Also, of the poets who failed, it is not reasonable to think that it came about for this reason, and not hundreds of others. In fact, the problems of conservative poets, who ignored the innovations which were so attractive after 1960, are in no cogent way their lack of modernity. Their problems would still be pungent if there were no modern style poetry around. No more is it likely that all these puzzled and inept poets would have succeeded if they had taken on Pound and Olson without any reservations.

We have set up genres and uncovered tides of aversion. But as well as aversion poets also engage in self-insertion.

Fanfic

There is a genre of literature known as "slash" where people write freelance alterations to famous stories such as *Star Trek*. Within this genre, there is a line of naive self-projection defined as follows. MARY SUE (n.): 1. A variety of story, first identified in the fanfiction community, but quickly recognized as occurring elsewhere, in which normal story values are grossly subordinated to inadequately transformed personal wish-fulfilment fantasies, often involving heroic or romantic interactions with the cast of characters of some popular entertainment. 2. A distinctive type of character appearing in these stories who represents an idealized version of the author. 3. A cluster of tendencies and characteristics commonly found in Mary Sue-type stories. 4. A body of literary theory, originally generated by the fanfic community, which has since spread to other fields (e.g., professional SF publishing) because it's so darn useful. The act of committing Mary Sue-ism is sometimes referred to as "self-insertion."

The Mary-Sue Page

Her bearing will not easily be forgotten; the great red and cadmium cape thrown across her shoulders, her strange, hieratic countenance painted like a plaster mask, set off by a collar of diamonds and a blue wig surmounted with a sparkling crown. If, at the climax, the daughter of Minos and Pasiphae dies, Mlle. **Mary-Sue** does not cease to live because of this.

First **Mary-Sue** as Saturnian melancholic studies the sciences of number; then she gains prophetic insight into British imperial destiny; and finally vast universal religious visions are revealed to her.

I **Mary-Sue** wrote like Prynne and Crozier in the 1960s, and figured that if I went on doing it for long enough, no-one would realise that I hadn't invented the style. Preceding her friend Pauline Kael by more than a decade as a nonconformist thinker about movies, **Mary-Sue** got her start writing reviews for *The Iowa Republican* in the 1940s and proved as comfortable deconstructing gay Westerns as detecting ideological deviation in Latvian neo-realism. An acknowledged broker

43

in the cultural redemption of Mexican wrestling pictures, and a seminal influence on the early work of Kevin Nolan, **Mary-Sue** is *the* name to drop for instant Crit Snob credibility.

The episode with the ducks produced a sensation that was so profound that it seemed to take **Mary-Sue** into another mode of consciousness where the boundaries between the dead and the living were traversed.

Neither Washington nor Moscow but **Mary-Sue.**

The Long 1950s

Structure of the cultural field around 1960
Or, decoration and repression

"For various reasons I wasn't interested in writing poetry. What passed for poetry in the early Fifties seemed to me worthless, apart from some of Dylan Thomas. The Movement did not and does not seem to be worth the paper it is printed on: the poetics are boring, the subject-matter egotistical, smug and slightly repulsive. If that was what current poetry had to be like, I wasn't interested." (Eric Mottram, from a 1986 interview).

"Nothing could be so dead as the publication of poetry in this country, and my own efforts at Routledges are now at an end. … I am now met by an absolutely blank refusal to consider the publication of any poetry… The publication of poetry, of all but the most vulgar, has become a secret activity, carried out in catacombs. But one must live in the catacombs."
(Herbert Read, from a 1951 letter).

The 1950s were a child-centred decade and I was a child in the 1950s. I feel very positive about the era. In 1960, poets born in the 19th century were of course still publishing, and readers born in that century were still a segment of the reading and purchasing public. Actually, poets over 70 had the most prestige, and people over 60 had the most leisure to read. Why do I see it as foundational? Probably because I reached consciousness around 1964 and anything unconscious for me dates to the years before that. If we look at the pronouncements of Lord Dunsany (born 1878), (for example in *Poetry Review* for 1952), we realise that his attack on free verse, modernism, free association, and so on, was part of the dominant programme or feeling of the decade, that the roll-back to stanzaic regularity was key for poets. His consciousness had stopped before the Georgians.

A certain German book on '50s style says that the kidney-shaped table (*Nierentisch*) was the Gothic Arch of the 1950s. My mother had a set of three stacking tables like that, from Ercol. I can remember them arriving. For me the 1950s are something precise, like *that*, not a mixture of things. I have a clear notion of an ideal '50s poem, but no one in Britain was able to write it; Richard Wilbur and Jean Garrigue, in another country, brought it off. Garrigue writing about *eaux d'artifice* in 'A Water Walk by the Villa D'Este' sums it up, that combination of being musical, ornamental, flawless, and having a sense of the past. This book started when I bought, in a retro shop in Nottingham, a plate which has a transfer print of a kidney-shaped table as part of the design. The plate shows a range of things you might buy when setting up a household—this is the classic scene of the 1950s. Hitler destroys or damages 4 million houses, the '50s build new ones. You move into one and buy all the things which had been stopped to allow for war production. The plate shows you the corkscrew and salad serving cutlery which you have just bought.

The reading of the era was dominated by the accounts of the war which were coming out in hundreds. It takes a long time to recover from a world war. Very many of the generation which had fought the war had started families in the baby boom and were preoccupied with looking after the children and working to equip a home to have the family in. Focussing on children, who are so vulnerable, they were obsessed by security and predictability almost by default. Culture and politics had been put on the back burner—not necessarily for bad reasons. The 50s begin with thousands of gifted people involved in propaganda for the war effort and the war aims. The new era begins, so to speak, as the ruins of this supreme and intricate body of symbolism— something ornate, artificial, as strange as the faith which was expressed by a mediaeval cathedral; based on shared metaphors, or set scenes, which became incredible as soon as the collective need to believe in them vanished. The Ministry of Information (i.e. propaganda) closed down, and the writers and film-makers who had worked for it flooded out to find other work. The media also lost patriotic propaganda as a staple. Where did they go? Well, the mid-1950s saw the release of the economy for producing domestic goods—following 15 years of suppression of consumer demand. The recovery of consumption was delayed partly by the impoverishment of Britain's trade partners, partly by the need for capital reconstruction such as building ships to replace the ones sunk during the battle of the North Atlantic, partly by the Cold War and the atomic bomb programme. The pent-up consumer demand was a mighty river. Production shifted from heavy engineering to white goods. The experts at manipulating public opinion shifted from promoting democracy to promoting domesticity. The first big push was to build homes—symptomatically, the minister who made an outstanding success of this became Prime Minister, partly as a result. (The government was involved because basic commodities were still rationed and in short supply—he directed the raw materials.) The shift in scale took poetry with it—and so came the era of domestic anecdote, as described by Andrew Crozier. The coincidence of a narrow domestic range with the narrow focus of moralising poetry was an artistic disaster of historic magnitude.

We need a leitmotif for this vanished era, and I find this in Alex Seago's book on generational conflict at the Royal College of Art during the 1950s. It is called "burning the box of beautiful things" because of a legend that the teachers of graphic design had such a box, full of the beautiful and delicate things of England: a vocabulary of objects to dream about and to fill paintings or decorative designs. It was burnt because the students hated it and wanted to make images full of sex, violence, and speed. A typical feature of these students was the interest in cameras. Older commercial artists had been attached to the use of their hands, to the intimacy and patience involved in craft skills. Advertisements had been prepared with love, suggesting, also, intimacy and patience as the qualities which consumers would bring to the act of consumption. Even ads for women's underwear (a ware associated with sexual power) had usually been drawings—emphasizing style at the expense of fleshly impact. With the new wave, British advertising came to be dominated by the camera. From the perspective of a de-repressed era, the imagery of the 1950s seems to have been swept away like the Church of England—the people who loved the painting on barges, who made watercolours of wild flowers, who admired parish churches, were thrown off the building. Our leitmotif is decoration and repression. Something revisits to the auditory world of that time bring back with painful clarity is the coy voices of glamour actresses. Avoiding the bludgeon quality of sex as presented since the 1960s, they offered inauthenticity—either fake West End accents (combined with a cultivated and unreal cooing and twittering quality of delivery), or (like Alma Cogan) fake American accents. These voices are the sound equivalent of polka-dot tulip dresses and white elbow-gloves. The style of Auden, Fry, and Betjeman must also strike us as something whose lack of integrity is appealing, as a gesture towards shared fantasies which were too fragile to last into the 1960s. Louis MacNeice summed up Betjeman like this: "When is a pastiche not a pastiche? When is a satire apt to turn into an idyll and a giggle into a prayer? When does a jumble of bric-à-brac assume both significance and symmetry? When does an outmoded prosody ring once more true—and new?" (*Poetry London*, #15, p.24).

A good idea of what was in that box of beautiful things can be found in Barbara Jones' books, *Follies and Grottoes* and *The Unsophisticated Arts*, which came with her water-colours of popular arts, such as "wooden fascias to be found on the canopies of old Victorian railway stations, roundabouts, taxidermy, jelly moulds, waxworks, tattooing … and the curious rustic porches she discovered in the Victorian model village of Canford Magna." (Patrick Wright) Such recording was, after all, second-hand—the avoidance of new creation. Jones described the merry-go-round horses as "demountable baroque". If we consult Jones, we find the horses were given all-over coats of gold paint with "glazing afterwards with transparent colours in a limited range, such as carmine, yellow, viridian, and prussian blue." It suffices to pick up Lützeler's history of German art to find a sculpture by the Asam brothers of a completely gilt saint—genuine Munich baroque, then. How far is it from this to Billy Fury in a silver lamé suit—and the beginning of de-repression. When was that—1960, '61? Somehow popular art switched itself from naif watercolours to the teeming savagery of rock music.

The story we have to tell about the 1950s is one of cultural repression—a social network equipped to say no to the possibilities of the imagination and of language. If we look for the nubs of what was to emerge as modern culture, we find that in 1955 they were obscured by ridicule, and laughter is a telltale of the limits of the cultured world of the 1950s. Everything which was to create the new scene was seen as comic in the "high" 1950s—and in return my approach will not discuss the works of the era as books you might want to read. Instead, it takes advantage of the forgotten quality of this decade in order to evoke something strange, protected, nostalgic. Any version of events has to admit the counter-argument that the suburban 1950s bred the dynamic rebels who created a cultural revolution in the succeeding era: the Cold War establishment could not switch off the dialectic.

When we look back at those years, we see that there are no specialist markets and there are almost no little magazines. There was no avant-garde. There was no poetry of ideas. There was no modernism. The peripheral literary scene barely existed. There was a tunnel effect—whereby everything was either forced into a narrow range of verbal patterns or else was made invisible and "ridiculous". Attention has to be given, therefore, to the central bloc and to the inhibitions which prevented other tastes from defining themselves. Almost everything which happened in the 60s took the form of developing parallel markets, and was driven by groups who had been suppressed and disapproved-of in the 1950s.

The business arrangements of the period meant that there was a pull effect from publishers. Poets would approach them about the suitability of a book of verse, and if the publisher said yes the poems had to be written to fill out the book. As this implies, the absence of significant books at this time has a great deal to do with the commercial perceptions of publishers: they discouraged the poems from being written. To be sure, they were reflecting the responses of reviewers and the public, rather than imposing some haughty aesthetic fiat. I have been unable to uncover any stockpiles of unpublished work from the 1950s. Today, poets are far more inclined to write as they see fit, and so to stockpile unpublished work even in lean times. Today, there is much more leisure, and much more of a leisure aesthetic, whereby artists have to express their inner intuitions rather than aim at the market. There is much more tolerance for outsider figures; in the 1950s, people who were rejected by the cultural organs simply gave up writing poetry, drawing sinister conclusions about their own character and talent. The shift occurred directly through the arrival of vast numbers of little magazines in the 1960s, along with (a few years later) underground publishers, so that unpopular work could still come out. The point is, partly, that people didn't bother to do this in the 1950s—because they didn't find art mysterious and thought that failure was a straightforward, accurate, diagnosis. Further intellectual variations were seen as impractical and morbid.

Perhaps we can try to characterize the cultural managers. A life-cycle from bright Oxford undergraduate to BBC producer to sage to pontiff. How many jobs were there in poetry? Let's try to count. At the Arts Council, no-one. At the Third Programme, a few producers—six? At publishers, a dozen jobs but not full-time in poetry except for Eliot. Probably, poetry publishing was more to provide rewarding tasks for the editors than to make money for the publishers. At universities, quite a few specialists in English Literature, but none hired to lecture on modern poetry—unless in their spare time. As for postgraduate students in the field, it is hard to count them, but there certainly weren't very many. In magazines, no full-time jobs, but some paid work for reviewers at the richer ones (the *TLS*, the *Observer*). As magazine editors, only one full-time job (at *Poetry Review*), but a few spare-timers on magazines like *Nine*. As events organisers, arts administrators, etc, no one—this branch hadn't emerged yet. The unpaid committee of the Poetry Society. These people must have seen each other all the time. They formed the reception hall to poetry as a *group*—each one relied on the others, and was dependent on their good opinion. A small world which punished nonconformity but rewarded new commercial ideas. It must have been hard to envisage an opinion outside the professionals—experts in the finances and in the art of selling.

Two examples of poets who joined the BBC in the period are Terence Tiller and George MacBeth. Alfred Alvarez, a frequent contributor to BBC radio, is someone who actually made a living, without a job, out of literary work mainly related to poetry. Success must have meant impressing in conversation—the rest of the company coming away with the impression that you are desirable. You got the job by pleasing an informal audience—saying the right things, and, of course, not saying the wrong things and acquiring enemies. These talented young men were inclined to become so fixed on their talent object that they defined it as the one desirable thing. Although the milieu of metropolitan literati was liberal in many ways, it was also self-satisfied and inclined to blind spots in areas that were distinctive and unestablished.

An obvious feature of the period is the dominance of light verse. This verse is today largely unreadable. Was this a society without intellectuals? The '50s saw the triumph of Oxford—possibly also a fatal investment in Christian light verse at Oxford, which has failed to produce significant poets since. Poems were surrounded by an envelope of prohibitions which emptied every feeling of depth, every idea of complexity. Emotion and ideas suffered the same fate—they were excluded to preserve the lightness. These resemble the rules of broadcasting, which became far more important in the 50s—and was prominent in the thinking of bright university graduates. Betjeman writing guidebooks (to Oxfordshire and Shropshire) is a key register—someone putting over the cultural heritage in a smooth and accessible language. Wonderful presentation, prohibition of creativity. Books of beautiful things. The air of the time was fruity with Oxford voices being charming and affable, saying things which when we look at them appear perfectly banal. Poetry recovered by slowly losing its fear of intelligence. Obviously, it was the cultural managers who administered these prohibitions.

Historians generally treat the period in terms of the Movement, whom I want to look away from, and who are responsible for an almost universal belief that the 1950s were a deeply tedious era. John Press' book *Rule and Energy* is in effect a one-volume history of poetry in the 1950s. We can start, though, by a look at Kenneth Allott's *Penguin Anthology of Contemporary Verse* (originally 1950, new edition 1962, later editions issued with title change to *English Poetry 1918–60*). We are using the 1962 edition, which has about 150 pages worth of remarks on the poets, which are in effect close to a book about the '50s. The 1962 edition has a cover design (by Stephen Russ) of what look like woodcuts of snowflakes or dandelion heads, set in repeating groups of three against an ochre background—it derives from patterns shown to the Festival Pattern Group, a team working in the build-up to the Festival of Britain (1951). They produced a lot of scientific photographs, showing natural forms, to inspire artists and designers. The "snowflakes" come from X-ray crystallography, and the point of this theme was that Britain had two Nobel Prize winners in Physics, father and son, who were both X-ray crystallographers. This was in its way a display of national power. It is also an attempt to rush forward into the modern age. The result is a "geometrical-organic" set of forms which is recognizable as 1950s (and deeply evocative of the era) but not recognizable as British—designers from other nations used them too.

Depressingly thorough grubbing around in the papers does turn up the names of good poets writing in the 1950s; the names David Jones, Hugh MacDiarmid, Edith Sitwell, Robert Graves, Edwin Muir,

Glyn Jones, Joseph Macleod, George Barker, Norman MacCaig, F.T. Prince, Francis Berry, Terence Tiller, W.S. Graham, George Mackay Brown, Alan Ross, Eithne Wilkins, Roland Mathias, Edwin Morgan, Charles Tomlinson, Christopher Middleton, Christopher Logue, Roy Fisher, Geoffrey Hill, and Ted Hughes revive our interest, even if most of them were marginal, silent, or barely published at the time. When you look at the books actually published during the decade, the picture looks gloomy and you start to wonder about the problems. Much of the excitement of the '60s was because of slightly older poets breaking out, who had been prevented from emerging during the '50s. This was not a period in which publishers were striving to launch a new generation. If *New Lines* plays such a large role in available accounts of the decade, it may be because there were only two "new poet" anthologies of the time—the other being the feeble *Mavericks*. An alternative view of the state of poetry can be found in David Wright's Penguin *The Mid-Century. Poetry 1940–60* (1964), which presents the later work of the New Romantics of the '40s—a very interesting selection which was, however, disguised by its title, and in Thomas Blackburn's anthology *45–60. An Anthology of English Poetry 1945–60,* which comes from the same sector as Wright.

A hypothesis is that the "mid-century death" started in 1930. This was the moment when the Depression hit the English economy, and when Auden's first book was published. It was when Modernism ended—with the collapse of the milieu, the shared sensibility among a band of cultured people, which had made the 1920s style—Modernism—possible and credible. The successive years saw a world war, the post-war poverty following the more or less complete liquidation of the economy in winning the war, and the Cold War. The problems of the writer were the exhaustion and anxiety besetting the society he had to describe. The spiritual problems of the writer, and even the economic ones, were not new in 1930. One could so easily list hundreds of problems prevalent at any time. No one is so simple they haven't got complex problems. Clearly, the country was in much better shape by the 1950s. The reasons why the deathlike trance of poetry continued no longer have to do with poverty and insecurity.

Despite all the waffle about England being dominated by tradition, my perception of the 20th century is of poetic currents petering out rather quickly. Nothing ever reaches a second generation—we can equate this with the nuclear family, which has to be refounded in every generation. The French method of "movements" at least takes care of the succession problem; it is much more benign to younger writers arriving. It was quite a natural diagnosis of the mid-century death that what was needed was a return to modernism, indeed that this was the only legitimate 20th-century art, and that everything else was a deviation from the way, not to be approved of by people with the best taste. We have to ask what the state of the modernist lineage was, in the 1950s; because it certainly became very important after 1960. Nostalgia for the 1920s was probably felt by some people. It is strange how the 1920s writers were still there but unable to write. The canonization of the avant-garde follows on from the dominance of surveys of the whole 20th Century in which the measure of anyone's artistic success was frequently how far they had adopted avant-garde practice. These were written by academics, and Modernism came by, say, 1965, to define the university taste—something which would have amazed the art world of 1920. In the 1950s, whole university literature departments worship Eliot but no-one writes like him. To start with, Eliot had moved, poetically, towards conservatism; his artistic extremism had become identified with a Christian asceticism and unworldliness familiar from other millennia. His intelligence had brought him authority, and he identified with the institutions of society. Someone could write conservative Christian verse and still think they were plugged into the Eliot succession. There was Pound—still in a mental hospital at this time, round the bend and off the map. There were his followers— visible for example in magazines like *Nine*. This whole line had fallen on hard times. Pound appealed to people by his arrogance, and attracted followers with fantasies about their own superiority to the rest of the human race, and the superiority of their way of writing over all others. This selected for a group of people of Rightist and monarchist sympathies, ready to look on events since the French Revolution as a mistake. Worse, this arrogance made it very difficult for them to write anything at all; and they had little wish to test their qualities by writing—when they already thought they were God's gift. This little conspiracy was alienated rather than self-sustaining; carrying out a *Vathek*-like scenario of gloom, remoteness, and hypersensitivity. There is a volume, *Clear Lake Comes from Enjoyment*, by Denis Goacher and Peter Whigham, which represents Poundians and actually got published, in 1959. It is totally unimportant. Pound had acquired no significant new disciples since 1930. Another eccentric is Terence Heywood whose right as a modernist in the line of Aldington and Joseph Macleod must be conceded. This line drew to a close around 1930, and he published *Architectonic* in 1953 (according to Amazon—the copy I have is not dated). Titles like 'Principles of Temporal Aerodynamics' 'The Quince and the Kaffir-orange', 'Ultrasonics', 'Villanellified Rondeau for a Jet-Propelled Tom-Tom', 'Heavyside Layer', 'Medallion in Quicksilver' tell it like it is. Artistically these poems stand rather low. I noted the use of words *hyphae* and *mycorrhiza*, showing weird erudition about fungi. He was aware of the importance of nitrogen-fixing symbionts. But even if the reader gets the picture the poet has limited interest in the worlds of fungi and the poems are poorly motivated and disconnected. The pretension which dresses 'Architectonic' up as a single huge poem whereas the parts obviously don't relate to each other and were composed at different times seems to dissolve the poetry, leaving something mannered and exaggerated which never coheres. What is the link between fungi and architecture? Well, dry rot I suppose. You can't eat dry rot. Dry rot omelette is not called *omelette heywood*. Bunting published no poetry in Britain between 1951 and 1966; it is not certain that he wrote even one poem in the 1950s. If the Modernist, Poundian, method was so great, surely it would have enabled people to write poetry. What other test of a poetic can you set up? There was something critically wrong with this method. No one could possibly have expected the revival to come from this group, who in 1959 sounded like trilobites who had missed their exit line in the Cambrian Era—it was a million to one gamble made by eccentrics. Elsewhere, poetry—no doubt the finest of the decade—was being written by other modernists: MacDiarmid, David Jones, W.S. Graham. Looking back, this appears as a reproach to everyone else: the time spent arguing about Larkin or Betjeman was wasted. But these authors were too difficult for most of the poetry-reading public. Anyway, a total of three books is not much to fill a decade with; argument was bound to focus on other possibilities, because people who love reading new poetry need a constant supply of it. Of course, to believe that the supply can ever be constant is a great illusion. Edith Sitwell (1887–1963) is the English modernist who was cleverly removed from the record before the university canon of modernism was set up. Allott's anthology, which excludes her, is possibly a step in this operation. Her reputation collapsed during this decade; during which she published little new poetry and converted to Roman Catholicism. Sitwell published a pamphlet (*The Songs of Poor Men*) with Fore Publications, a front for the Communist Party (which had offices just opposite). Earlier, she had published biographies of two Queens. Between the Queen (and head of the Anglican Church), the Roman Catholics, and the Communist Party. This mixture seems bizarre to me—but presumably it seemed normal to her. Bracketing by male rationalist critics just never works for Sitwell. I think the story is that the academics, all male, just couldn't identify with her persona and characters. It was beyond them. She wasn't "difficult" in the way that Jones or Graham was; but the critics had forgotten about the Russian Ballet and couldn't enjoy her *Symboliste* fantasies. She had got religion (during the '40s) and moved on to moralising verse about the conscience of the world—things which should have appealed to the 1950s. But, there were no women priests at that time, she wasn't theologically conventional, and, again, they blanked her. The introduction to the 1950 edition of Allott (the 1962 edition omits this) tells us that he couldn't agree with the poet on which poems to include. Mina Loy was excluded without comment. It would be only fair to discuss the other modernists—it isn't as if everyone who had been young in 1925, or 1915, had died or got religion. But in fact I couldn't find any traces here. Tracing the other contributors to *Wheels* (edited by the Sitwells around 1917, and the classic showcase for English modernism—as well as a magnet for hostile criticism) is a depressing task. By 1950, they had pretty much left the business. Figures like Richard Aldington (one of the few to publish modernist work during the 1930s) or Herbert Read (an anarchist who became an arts administrator and accepted a knighthood) do not much trouble the 1950s.

Piling up historical evidence lures us towards the idea that the explanation lies in this evidence. Some caution is needed here. West Germany had very similar post-war experiences to Britain, and yet the 1950s were one of the great decades of German poetry. Proper historical modelling compares the society in question to similar societies, and asks why there were differences. It is unpopular with historians, because it almost always ends up with a blur—and entails large-scale loss of ideas which were beautiful in themselves, simply because they proved to be wrong. The concept of a blur as the design of history is attractive—large numbers of people are never going to form a shape with sharp edges. If it's not a blur, maybe you aren't looking closely enough. The possibility of talking about poetry historically comes from the mutual imitation of poets—the social imperatives which mean that, effectively, they are in a conversation with each other, and so are thinking about the same thing at the same time. What makes this convergence visible is looking at amateur poetry—poems being written by people who are not involved with the literary world, aren't involved in the conversations, and don't know what the fashions are. They provide a way of contextualising the "inner circle" poetry. Fashion consists of rules for what you have to talk about and what you must not talk about. Comparison with a context exposes both sets of rules. The observations we make about the rules from this comparison can be checked by looking at explicit statements which have survived in print. If we look at the remarks Allott makes in his ochre anthology, they imply imperatives (what to do and not to do) which we can correlate with the poems of the time.

The factor which made a theme of poetry full of brilliant possibilities was that there was a cloud of people interested in that subject and willing to be excited by someone talking about it. This image of an *excitable network* implies that, when the scene goes dead, there are neither poets charged up with hot ideas nor an audience charged up to listen to them—the whole scene is cold. So perhaps we could describe the 1950s as being like a fire which had gone out. This points us back— to the demise of the New Romantics, in the late 1940s, as the key moment which predisposed the failure of the next 10 years.

The '30s and '40s were also bad decades for poetry, and it is difficult to find political factors which could apply to the whole period of 1930–60—in the 1950s, there was no major war, no bombing, there was full employment, affluence, etc. So if poetry didn't recover, it was presumably disconnected from politics. Perhaps it was more like sport. What poets do connect to is other poets. If we sink to this simpler level of social events, away from UN resolutions, newspaper headlines, etc., we are likely to think of the (more or less) chance deaths of Dylan

Thomas (died at 39) and Sidney Keyes (killed in Tunisia, aged 20). If these two exceptionally gifted poets had survived, the 50s might have looked completely different. Imagine if Thomas had published three entire volumes of new poetry during the 1950s. Chance also meant that reliance on Eliot and Auden—the leading Anglican poets—was a deadening influence, as both had regressed into conservative modes. So looking at only four people already seems to have yielded major steps forward—if we expanded this to 400 people, we might have a very impressive causal analysis of the poetry that got written in the period. Trying to relate the state of poetry to the Korean War, the discovery of oil reserves in Arabia, and the rise of synthetic fabrics, as well, may be wasted effort.

Theorising about the adequacy of Anglicanism, Communism, individualism, etc., as bases for poetry may be beside the point. It might be more accurate to suggest that high-profile failures in any of these lines could put off young poets and make success seem remote. This excitable network theory suggests that there is no abiding value in ideas about poetics. When models come along and use an idea of poetics badly, it stops working—because they cover it with a local and temporary *redefinition*. When models come along and use a poetics brilliantly, the idea becomes hot and generates new works of brilliance. This gets us out of a hole. For, we want to explain how it is that "Christianity prevented '50s poetry from achieving itself" while simultaneously accepting that "Christianity allowed Geoffrey Hill to achieve himself during the 1950s", "Christianity inspired the majority of great English poets in history", and "some Christian poets excelled in the 1980s (or 1990s)". It is extremely difficult to look at 50s poetry without seeing Christianity as its biggest problem. But this was because the Christian writing accepted as norm-giving was uninspiring to poets. Something similar would apply to left-wing poetry. This has been around since Chartism in the 1840s (if not since Shelley), and probably at every point since then there have been people standing by and saying that it was worn out and obsolete. This belief makes it extremely difficult to explain why it keeps coming back with new great poets in every period. Allott hates praising people and gives very high praise to Roy Fuller: "neither of his post-war volumes really prepares us for the authority of the writing in *Brutus' Orchard* [published 1957], which seems to me one of the most important books of verse to be published since the war". Let me quote:

With yellow teeth the hunter tears and crunches
Whole boughs of the quince, then walks away,
His hind legs on a mannequin's straight line.
The clipped back (ample as a bed, unyielding
Save for a slight threat like an anchored ship)
Returns what always astonishes—the warmth
Of a new embrace.
('Monologue in Autumn')

The poem is about the Cold War, evoking in stanza five the other "half world", with its "furs, fuming breaths, ardours of moral striving" [...] "for which our own/ has manufactured all its cruel swords and faces/ Whose profits surround us here as love affairs". Robert Conquest, the other ideologist in tune with the most repressive aspects of the era, also praised *Brutus' Orchard*: "Even when young, Mr Fuller was setting his chisel to harder stone. He never fails to try to illuminate all the segments and fragments of experience before putting them back into synthesis. [...] he seems to me to be the one truly serious poet of his generation, as well as one of the finest." This is a little surprising given that Conquest was such an anti-Marxist (although, as a Sovietologist, he was presumably very well able to decode Fuller's symbolism). Thurley and Homberger, who are seldom wrong, say quite devastating things about the same poetry. Thurley says "For Fuller, it is impossible for the poet to be right in anything: his action and his inaction are alike culpable and dishonest. (…) The only course left open to the poet is a continuous unmasking of himself (…) What he can do is give constant expression to his sense of his own dishonesty. Bad faith (…) is really the theme and substance of Roy Fuller's poetry." Thurley comments on the mixture of light verse and conservatism that, "form, for Auden and Fuller, is both a genuflexion to the reading public, and a kind of interior decoration. It confesses their guilt at the same time as it apologizes for the insolence of breaking silence…" For Homberger, "But in the decade after the war Fuller wrote inconsequential, polished poems about finding a spider in a bathtub, a robin singing in a garden, walking alone through snow, a visit to a derelict church, and poems on reading Soviet novels, and on Gide's death. This was an "abdication from responsibility" of the kind of which Fuller himself had accused Lewis."

This level of disagreement is perturbing and my difficulty in fixing Fuller's exact merits has not gone away after re-reading his work. Upsettingly, I agree with both sides. Let me side-step by saying that this uncertainty is close to the heart of the era and so that if you read Fuller's books of 1949 to 1961 you are at the heart of the 1950s and their proper uncertainty. It is hard to answer questions like "did Fuller stop being a Marxist". The answer may be that he was still a Marxist but states of burningly clear Marxist optimism did not reach him every day. His radio set, so to speak, was playing up and reception wasn't so great. Or, "when did his talent burn out?" Fuller's decline may be connected to disillusion after the exposure of Stalin at the 20th Congress in 1956. The problem with this is that the last section of the *Collected Poems 1961*, at pages 213 to 243, is the best, so that he was reaching a creative peak around 1959 to 1961. Clearly the 1973 volume *Tiny Tears* is a failure, empty twiddling.

It is appropriate to argue about these questions because the act of putting those symbols together and trying to make a pattern of them is the fullerian thing, the complexity and recession are where his artistic powers lie. 'Autobiography of the Lungworm' describes a tiny parasite which for its life-cycle relies on being ingested by an earthworm and then, on the worm being eaten by a pig, it breaks out of the pig's intestine, and then develops and thrives inside the pig's lung. The detail is dry and precise, like an anatomical drawing. But why is he telling us this? The point is that we are in situations which we did nothing to bring about, in which our prosperity depends on slight variations, in which the decisive patterns are immeasurably beyond the reach of our senses and are not detected by our consciousness. This is the chiliastic serenity of Marxism, the realisation of the weakness of individual consciousness and of the inability of that inability to hold up the process of forward change. The poem gives us a glimpse of Theory as a way out of this carnal burial, the muffling cloak of sense data which hides the significant processes.

The master metaphors in *Brutus' Orchard* are evolution and the birth of freaks, holy isolates which contain the key to the next stage in the process of change. Evidently what these represent at the level of humanity is intellectuals. Five times he describes tumours or growths. The tumour is actually the intellectual, violating organic form and its inevitabilities. The blueprint for a new organism. He speaks of

> ... eras when the sensitive reported
> Doom through the deformation of a pot,
>> False quantities, and sounds
>> Too harsh for memory,
>
> Were secretly incubating even then
> Bravery out of freaks, ethics from hate,
>> And valid economies
>> Of starving theorists.
>>> (from 'Discrepancies')

Fuller describes the impedimenta of bourgeois consciousness in the way he does because the larger processes are still continuing and the jumble of mundane moments is almost an illusion—a screen, a jamming signal. He is upholding the radical nature of intelligence, like lightning from above. The human subject is torn between intellectual awareness of the long term goal, and of large-scale processes, and the connection to immediate sense-data, with the endless tangle of quotidian and predictable patterns.

'Discrepancies' continues with a key passage:

> In trying to be just our systems hunt:
> Too violent man's feed-back. Hector's shield
>> Lies under a massive floor
>> Of hideous ornaments.

This reflects the interest in science which makes the book echo the crystallography-derived imagery of the Festival Design Group. The lines refer to cybernetics, a branch which did not exist until the Second World War and its military research (Fuller worked in a technical branch at the Admiralty dealing with "air radio"). When a self-stabilising system is oscillating before finding a mode it can settle down into, this is called the "hunt" phase. The poem says that human social systems have stabilising feedback circuits but reproduce themselves discrepantly: the offspring is unlike the parents. The feedback cannot find a stable mode and so social systems are prone to collapse and the British system of 1957 in particular. The "just" bit is as in "adjust". Cultural expression reflects social process flows: this is why the collapse of taste in Bronze Age times shown by the "hideous ornament" in the stratum of deposits above Hector's shield (a symbol of archaic splendour, no doubt) is an example of something classical failing to reproduce itself, but also why recording the pulses of utterance of a poet of average sensibility is worthwhile, and why specially the things that fail to fit a pattern are worth writing down. Over the long time series, the oscillations entrain a complete new system. The same theme is stated again in 'Summer':

> All living matter's power
> To reproduce its form
> Includes occasional error:
> In air and water swarm,
> Gorgeous beyond their title,
> The creatures; and the mother
> Sends out into the battle
> Past her retreating force
> Fresh notions of brow and feather
> To perpetuate the race.

The *notion* may refer to recognition by another member of the same species: the mutant has to be recognizable to sexual partners in order to reproduce. Also the development of feathers for sexual competition is a proof of evolutionary theory. The brow bit must refer to the growth of the cerebral cortex in the genus Homo. In an age of nuclear atmospheric tests occasional error could be sterility as well as hopeful invention of form, and two other poems refer to the possible radioactive end of life.

I am offering more detail on Fuller's poetry because the standard work on him is so uncomprehending and goes to such lengths to pretend that his political beliefs were not expressed in his poems. Peter Levi says that Fuller lost his powers and then they came back. I haven't tracked this.

To "get" the 1950s you have to be receptive to people losing faith in Marxism and in Christianity and to the *possibility* of writing great poetry about the deconversion experience and about the emergence of a disenchanted but concrete world. The ruin of the sheltering building seems a strikingly *similar* passage for Christians and Marxists. This possibility is blurred by the inevitable co-acting effect that people in deconversion lost faith in *poetry* and that poetry became the object of doubt.

One of the conventions of the avant-garde is that it offers moments of doubt and subversion, with the key techniques offering as their special effect *the breaching of shared symbolism.* Maybe this breach *is* the long 1950s. Maybe the idea that the ruin of the building was the most precious moment, that doubt in poetry could be the subject of poetry, could only have arisen during the 1950s.

The best anthology of 50s poetry is Thomas Blackburn's *45–60. English Poetry 1945–60* which is closely related to John Press' book *Rule and Energy* and gives a strong emphasis to the irrational and exalted line which Press identifies (and places Blackburn in). That is, it highlights the continuing 1940s style, the thing which Conquest and Allott were trying to burn out and do away with. It looks as if the best poetry being written in the period was breaking rules which the critics of the time were rather particular about asserting, so that the official voice of the period was promoting something that was not happening and suppressing something that was.

The thesis put forward in Robert Fraser's biography of George Barker is about sexuality, randiness, logic, education. He suggests that GB is superior to rival poets because they were educated and he left school at 14; because he was highly sexed and they weren't. Fraser also suggests that Barker represents a breakthrough, and the future. The implication is that Objectivity is the product of years of servitude, and involves submission to male authority figures—it disables you for writing poetry, which requires vigorous subjectivity. Study and office work seem to have much the same effect—Barker said no to secondary education, and resisted having a job because he thought it would cripple his poetic gifts. This thesis looks good if we compare poets with rock singers, but unimpressive if we compare modern poets with poets from past centuries. It's interesting, it does explain why Barker is better than most of his contemporaries, but it only covers one set of relationships out of thousands—it has explanatory value only in a very confined area. Inhibition is certainly a problem—but the formula which says "academic=inhibited" is not convincing. There is sex life on campus. Also, it's hard to see Barker as the forerunner of a revolution, when the general pattern since 1950 is of poets becoming much more educated, graduate poets becoming the norm—and much more sexual frankness in poetry. I think the story is of theology falling out of poetry, society becoming much more educated, poets having great initial resistance to the penetration of ideas into the poem (felt to be a "primary" area, sacrosanct, filled with sensuous data), and gradually, enormously slowed down by these inhibitions, allowing ideas to fill the poem—and bring a new kind of poetry. Barker's later poetry, despite his reputation for lyric passion, has far more about theology and philosophy than it does about interpersonal relations. It fails, most of the time, because of his extreme lack of qualification for talking about ideas. All the same, his last 12 books are full of ideas—thus paralleling the movement of poetry in general. The story of modernity is not academicism stealing poetry away from naïve poet-shepherd types, but the endlessly prolonged inhibitions of poets about the tide of intellectuality which was going to prove the salvation of poetry.

What is difficult to recover in 1950s art is a sexuality which is wholly understated by 1960s standards—this is what we find in Christopher Fry's plays. This passage from *Venus Observed* (1950) describes the effect of an eclipse (the transit of the moon across the Sun) on a rural scene:

> Daylight, you see, is shamming twilight. (...)
> The crows, with much
> Misgiving, talk themselves into their trees. Even
> The usually phlegmatic owls
> Care a hoot or two. The bats from the barn
> Make one flickering flight, and return to hang
> Their heads. All of them tricked and fuddled
> By the passing of a small cadaverous planet.

The bit about the hoot refers to a piece of obsolete slang, "I couldn't care a hoot". The deception of the creatures by an effect of the light is a sly reference to the influence of sexual attraction (which so often seems to have been a trick of the light in retrospect) on human beings; the replacement of illusion by truth is the traditional denouement of classical European comedies of a pre-modern period, with which Fry tacitly aligns himself. I like this passage—I think it is a good example of Fry's charm, which hasn't dated. Allott refers to Fry's "twists and swirls and quirks of rhetoric" without sufficiently noticing that these embody an aesthetic, although a decorative one. Of course, it is pastiche, and the insistent replacement of sharp urgent sensations with delicate, deceptive, unaffecting ones means that the play can never get louder than a tinkle. The Duke has invited three ex-mistresses round so that he can decide which one of them to marry now that he is reaching the autumn of his life; one of his servants is an ex-burglar, one an ex-lion-tamer, one has a daughter who was imprisoned for active membership of the Society for the Desecration of Ancient and Modern Monumental Errors. This eccentricity reduces the inner life to something comic and arbitrary, while being combined with an insistence on being charming and sociable, as an exit from eccentricity. The domestic cosiness—everyone is either the Duke's servant or his ex-mistress, there are no strangers—is telling for the decade. The manner does embody a view of human ethics, to be summed up as "human emotions are dangerous and cause blindness" and "our duty in life is to be attentive to those close to us and overlook their faults". To be sure, this is a residual theology—it leaves all the dramatic statements to the priesthood. It covers a residual domain, within which the mundane individual (and not the Church, the government, etc.) can decide what happens—this dictates the *domestic* range of the poem. If other people don't act selfishly, you lead a better life—this is a genuinely Anglican approach to personal relations, and the message is one which everyone in the audience, in the St James Theatre in 1950, was able to pick up.

What shut down Fry's career was of course *Look Back in Anger*, a hit of 1956 at the Royal Court theatre in Sloane Square, whose daring and realism made his plays seem intolerably feline and fanciful. Logue saw this production and said "His [Osborne's] play broke the mental spell cast by our role in the Allied victory over the Axis powers. The acceptance of poverty, class obedience, unquestioning loyalty to the Crown and the Church, the power of bad, blind patriotism, things that had once bound us, had been changed, for ever." The qualities people saw in 1956 have mysteriously vanished from the text. Incidentally, the qualities he mentions were not present in the poetry of the 1950s—to which, nonetheless, Barker & Logue were thorny exceptions, as disreputable free spirits. They wrote from a *demi-monde*—geography is the key, in a literary world consisting apparently of endless, world-wide suburbs. In Soho, the nucleus of something new and altogether less worthy was coagulating whenever it didn't feel too hung over. The thing about Barker and Logue is that they are moving so fast, a thousand times faster than the staid academics who are sure they are right—hormones have such a powerful effect on the male brain, they speed it up. Logue called his second book *Devil, Maggot, and Son*—the three things which pursue a man, which are trying to catch him and tie him down; he is on the run the whole time, what he says is rapid and to the point. Sexuality transforms everything—and when they come to deal with ideas, it's so much more exciting, more involving, than with the moralists. Perhaps we can draw an equation, like this:

MORALISTS courtship behaviour
morality as a test of fitness for marriage

LYRICISTS courtship behaviour liberation, exaltation,
interest in sex, as tests of fitness to be lovers

Both of these devise poetry as something written by men and passing tests set by women—they are pre-feminist but already show the tendency of male culture to be dominated by women which was to influence the next 40 years so much. The strain in the moralist version is that they are trying too hard to be judges themselves—they want to set and judge the tests, and award the prizes, as well as undergoing them. Women are the adequate judges of male excellence—seizing this function is an offence against the basic standards of the species. Meanwhile, the function of actually behaving, describing human events in words, actually writing poetry—sinks into atrophy.

Reading either the Marxist critiques (praising folksong) or the conservative critiques (asking for poetry to be restored to the quality of song, whether hymns or love-lyrics) calls attention to the relationship of poetry to song. Printed poetry is constantly striving to get away from the archaeological connection to song structures—in an era of profound artistic failure of (printed) poetry, the advocates of song are bound to go on the offensive, and try to win back lost territory. So it is of interest to look at the state of English song during the period. To sum up:

Hymns	disastrous loss of nerve. Thorough reliance on the past. Deep resistance to anyone writing in a modern idiom.
Popular song	disastrous loss of nerve. Thorough dominance by American songwriters. Tendency to pastiche American, and African-American, idioms. Disastrously low level of achievement.
Folksong	disastrous loss of nerve. Very limited audience. Strong Communist Party presence. Heavy reliance on models from the past. Virtual inability of writers to compose new songs. Thorough reliance on American models.

Looking at this sorry state of affairs, we may have the glimmerings of a feeling that poetry *was* intimately linked to popular song, and that they were in the trough together (and revived together, in the '60s). It does not seem that nestling up to popular song was going to prove a radical stimulant for poetry in 1955. Maybe some of you can name even one song written in Britain during the 1950s. Poetry had to get close to popular songwriters who actually existed—it could hardly get close to songs that didn't exist. The management at the BBC were embarrassed at having to deliver light entertainment—and what they delivered, although extraordinarily popular, seems to have been of ruthlessly low standard. This was a really corrupt example of a connection between the educated class and mass culture. The generically low level of light entertainment in '50s Britain sheds a light on the light verse which dominated poetry. When people wanted to write songs like Brecht, deeply internalised habits meant that they had to go through the idiom of English vaudeville to get there.

Incidentally, when we look at poets hanging out in Soho, it is not completely coincidental that the best jazz musicians in the country were hanging out in the same few streets—Archer Street was where musicians hung around endlessly, waiting for chance calls to make up a band for a gig. When pop music got going, its headquarters was in Wardour Street—a few yards away.

Mass culture, the leisure consumption of the working classes, had been almost completely taken over by imported American goods. High art, despite having quite strong elements of European influence, was after all British—and being anti-American also meant being against the working classes (or against what they did, at least!). For some groups, there was a struggle between Russia and America, paralleling the Cold War—not too much should be made of this, as the pull of Russia was too weak. The Nonconformist sects were also a significant part of working-class culture, but their artistic achievements were of a very low order. The group which did combine artistic prowess with Englishness was the Anglican church. This needs to be borne in mind when we look at the constant decline of the Church throughout our period—it left "art" poetry high and dry.

The weakness of left-wing verse in this decade is very difficult to explain, although it is hardly unexpected after contemplating the weakness of Christian and modernist verse. I stumbled across the world of pageants while trying to locate the text of the 1937 Peace Pageant staged by the Women's Co-operative Guild (which my great-aunt was active in). Fore Publications, an imprint of the Communist Party, launched in 1951 a pamphlet series called Key Poets, priced at 1/-, which was very promising but was nipped in the bud, according to Andy Croft, by envious elements at CP headquarters who were alarmed at the prospect of middle-class culture being so popular. Croft has written a book on the Communist poet Randall Swingler—I really couldn't believe that anyone could write a whole book about Swingler, when his poetry is so uninteresting. But there we are. The basic story is a generation of Left literary intellectuals being forbidden from doing creative work by the commissars of the Left, and running aground. Then to be comprehensively ignored or despised by a rising generation of Leftist lit intellectuals. Key Poets are listed on the jackets as being George Barker, Edith Sitwell, Stanley Snaith, Jack Lindsay, Maurice Carpenter, Dorian Cooke, Randall Swingler, Jonathan Denwood, Jack Beeching, and Norman Cameron. Taking into consideration the low points, this series was utterly brilliant—the range from Cumbrian dialect poetry (Denwood) to Sitwell's neo-Symbolisme is awesome. "This book is one of a series of Poets that aims at breaking down the barriers between poet and audience…" Considering the total disappearance of most of these poets, shortly after the barriers, may explain why Communist poetry was so little heard-of in this period.

Swingler's attempts to write about Historic Destiny are very stagy, and his group had problems writing poems about history without links to the pageant mode obtruding. Marxist history, in its house organ *Past and Present*, was just getting out of the shadow of the holy texts. It was due to produce an astonishing harvest in the next two decades. George Thomson's *Marxism and Poetry* was the most convincing polemic of the whole century. Thomson (1903–87) was a Stalinist who converted to Maoism when the Soviet Union began to de-stalinize. This was published in 1945, rather outside our horizon (numerous re-editions, for example as *The Human Essence*, 1968) but still significant as a showcase for marxist ideas. It is wrong about more or less everything, but very exciting to read. It was possible to write great Marxist poetry in the 1950s (Hikmet, Neruda, Brecht, Arendt brought this off), but Thomson's pamphlet is all about disqualifying poets who can read and write (and explaining, kindly, that we don't recognize the superiority of oral poetry because our taste has been corrupted by books).

Marxist theory is captious because it is too complex for its defects to be rapidly visible, and consequently I cannot reduce the problem to a single paradox—there are hundreds of them! To pick, nonetheless, a single one: Thomson writes off all English poetry since the Renaissance for belonging to bourgeois individualism, and for not being folk poetry. Thus, Keats didn't really write lyric poetry—it doesn't count, because he was part of the bourgeois era and it wasn't collectively composed. We will return to the claims about bourgeois individualism. Without trying to rewrite the whole of British history, perhaps we can agree that Shakespeare, Milton, Keats, Wordsworth, aren't such a bad thing, and that writing poetry like theirs probably isn't such a total disgrace. The classification isn't incompatible with Arnold Hauser's—in his work, of the 1940s, which hasn't been refuted and so is probably as solid as literary history can get. The willingness of intelligent people to shoulder the burden of middle-class guilt, at the behest of talentless bullies, and destroy their own artistic gift, never ceases to amaze me. Hamish Henderson, probably the most significant new poet of the 1940s, became a folksong collector—harnessed to rules which physically destroyed the structures which make poetry poetry. In this sorry tale of Left cultural suicide, there are very important exceptions—*Script from Norway* by Joseph Macleod and *Songs* by Christopher Logue. Logue's songs of the 1950s were recently reissued on CD—just about the only English music from the 1950s anyone would think about listening to, except the documentary radio ballads (1958–63) by the equally left-wing Charles Parker and Ewan MacColl. The classic folk shop in London (a few years ago) was owned by Collet's, the Communist bookshop (it had a large Russian-language section which didn't stock anti-Communist authors). I find this embarrassing—I didn't identify with the Soviet Union, but it would be ridiculous to overlook the merits of folk music. MacColl was a Communist.

We have to mention *Dail Pren* (1956), by Waldo Williams— possibly, with the exception of *The Anathemata*, the most distinguished volume published during the decade. Williams was a Quaker, a pacifist, and a radical; his deliberate humility of means allows him to reach for the transcendent within the humble limits of verse. He didn't have any problems with the principles of Christianity being applied rigorously enough to destroy the State; and he didn't have commissars telling him how he was allowed to write. The title means *leaves of a tree*, and is taken from a letter of Keats which describes poetry as being as natural as leaves.

In 1953, Michael Tippett was commissioned to write a Coronation Ode for the new Queen—and got Christopher Fry to write the words for him. The whole episode is a little hard to believe if you recall that both men were (Christian) conscientious objectors during the war— Tippett went to jail, Fry worked in a battalion of the non-combatant Pioneer Corps. The moment is ludicrous—but artists have to do this kind of thing in order to get money. Ignorant and possibly rather unpleasant people tell them the terms in which they have to create, in order to get paid. The result is necessarily sweet, evasive, superficial. It develops minor virtues in order to distract us from the absence of all the major ones. It draws on styles from previous centuries in order to avoid the deep emotional commitments associated with the present day—and in order to give the audience something they understand. It doesn't give the mighty and exalted what they want—which is to own modernity and its prestige—and doesn't give the artist access to power and majesty either. Both sides end up frustrated. Pompous art for the king or aristocracy was the complement of folk art, representing the two halves of local culture as it had existed in, say, the 13th Century.

If we want to look at poetry which took place in public, as opposed to being read in private from a printed copy, we can look at the pageant. I can definitely say that you wouldn't want to read the texts of these pageants. (There are plenty of them in the British Library—they were printed as a way of raising extra revenue.) However, they are composed in verse. It is functional and not difficult for amateurs to memorise and deliver. There is a 1954 book on how to stage them by Pageant Master Anthony Parker. He refers to them cheerfully as Parker pageants, and supplies a photograph of his grandfather, Louis Napoleon Parker, in the middle of the cast of a pageant he had devised in Warwick in 1906. The grandfather wrote a volume of memoirs which gives us some carefully filtered insight into the history of the genre. The grandson remarks that the Warwickshire Coronation pageant of 1953 had three thousand participants. It also sold something like 30,000 tickets—a fairly low ratio, but not unfavourable compared to some later poetry readings by single poets. It is significant that Parker staged a pageant for Coventry (which is in Warwickshire) in 1950 and then a Coronation Pageant for all of Warwickshire (it travelled around) in 1953. Clearly the response to the 1950 one must have been very favourable—or the civic authorities wouldn't have splashed out the money for the 1953 one. This is nearly the only example of popular poetry to be found in the 1950s.

Although the tradition of civic pageants genuinely does go back into the mists of the Middle Ages, the British Library catalogues of printed texts show a clear concentration of them around 1905–30. The wave of 1951 (linked to the Festival of Britain) and 1953 (linked to the Coronation) seems to have been the end of a tradition—even if the participants saw the events as demonstrations of continuity and proofs of faith in the future. Because no town had a pageant frequently (except London), and most audiences had never seen a pageant before, the genre was able to evolve drastically without the audience realising or objecting. I find it plausible that there was a stylistic change around

1905, as A. Parker claims, in the direction of a model in which the text deals with local history and legend, there are as many participants as possible, and the stress is on carefully co-ordinated mass movement, with simple pleasures offered to the eye by historical costumes: "As an Interlude before the spectacular Finale, there is a short but effective ballet, 'The Peacocks of Warwick Castle', danced by 250 young girls. In their shimmering dresses under the changing floodlights, and with the gay and vivacious music, they present a delightful picture." There may be a link between this dating and the movement of the period called municipal socialism. There may also be a link with new myths of imperialism, invented to fill the syllabus of the new elementary schools where the whole mass of the population was now being taught to read and write; and because they had to fill the ranks of armies in imperial wars, and because some of them (male, and if they were lucky) had the vote and could overthrow governments. Defining the "English way of life" was significant if you were asking people to acquire an emotional commitment to it.

The pageants had focus, in the sense that there were lead characters, distinct from a mass of moving, costumed, walk-ons. These characters had speaking parts. (Tantalisingly, Parker speaks of separating the voices, having all the text delivered by speakers, through a public address system, who did not make themselves visible.) An excerpt from the text:

> Great Ethelfleda, vanquishing the Dane,
> Built Warwick's fortress, and brought Peace again.
>
> At Gosford Green, King Richard harshly sent
> Norfolk and Hereford to banishment.
>
> Vesey at Sutton, prevailed on Tudor grace
> To grant his folk a Charter and the Chase.

etc. These lines were sung by a Choir, part of the grand finale, where all the tableaux appear for the second time, simultaneously. Parker tells you how to write a pageant (in fact they appear usually to have been written by amateurs), and specifies a grand finale. These parts were very undemanding and un-individuated; most of the difference between amateur and professional theatre was that the latter had actors who could play strongly individuated parts, and suggest an unconventional inner life. Again, we find that this capacity differentiates between amateur and professional art. Virtually everything which made the 1960s interesting was the revolt of one or other strands against the bland collective presented by the Pageants, as repressing and boring them. The expansion of poetry is like the growth of rock and roll radio—confined, around 1960, to two hours on a Saturday morning, by the BBC (the only body licensed to make public radio broadcasts within the United Kingdom). The 1950s ended, we could say, whenever someone realised that the sweet, vacuous, comforting flow offered as leisure filler by the light entertainment industry was not all there was—that there were things that you could enjoy as well. It was boredom which discouraged people from revolt. All the revolts led to the privatisation of symbolic experience, and to the fragmentation of the market. That is, they developed the logic of a society based on status competition through consumer goods. This was true even when the individuals concerned had collectivist ideologies. Parker's version of history is peculiar and also inspired people to narrate their own versions of history in retaliation. It is hard to be precise, but it seems to correspond with narrative pictures of the 19th century. The entanglement between these and written accounts is complicated (didn't painters paint scenes which the audience *already* knew as stories?), but these paintings seem to be the prehistory of the tableaux on which Parker's pageants dwell. I can imagine that, for example, the Warwickshire audience could remember the illustrations in the history books which they had read at elementary school (possibly many years before), so that they didn't find the tableaux bewildering. Parker's stories had been reduced to visual, frontal, dramatic, unambiguous form many years before his birth. I can imagine that there is a connection between the processions which supplied such a striking (and time-consuming, and expensive) feature of Irving's productions at the Lyceum, over most of the late 19th century, and Louis Parker's colourful version of a civic pageant. I can imagine someone, in that crowd in the grounds of Kenilworth Castle (or elsewhere) gazing at the endlessly flowing crowds of performers in deep disbelief, and wanting a broader view of history to appear, one which showed social conflicts or the mechanisms of status and exchange. Such people filled a niche in the cast of the time—as spoilers, people unable to identify. They had the choice between enduring in boredom and withdrawing from where the people were—going somewhere silent and lonely, like a library. They were asked to feel a good deal of guilt for not cooperating. The possibility of taking this vice for a strength, and building a counter-pageant, getting together with other people like them, was not really on the horizon at that time. We might say that dissociated people were logically disqualified from taking a part in collective symbolism. Dissociation is one of the peculiar signs of high intelligence—this was a society which had a horror of intellectuals, and which didn't expect artists to have high intelligence. Complicated speeches would anyway have held up the programmed movement of masses of people, a kind of precision which the cast evidently enjoyed, and which is probably a feature of any really populist theatre. In the '50s, musicals were popular in East Germany as well as the USA. The Poet Laureate at this time was Masefield. I well recall the first time I heard his poetry read. It must have been 1966 or 1967, the poem was *Reynard the Fox*, and he was still in office. I didn't appreciate, then, that the theme of the poem was a society pursued and destroyed by the First World War (a "hunt"), or that this catastrophic social break had also brought an end to his vein of poetry. He had gone on writing, following a code of conduct which he observed scrupulously. In 1912, he had been seen as the "modern" poet, and as part of a new wave of democratisation—the introduction of disreputable characters, plain language, and physical action into poetry. His explorations—into verse speaking, verse drama, and liturgical drama—opened new possibilities for poetry, identifying genuine crisis lines around an art committed to solitude and silence. I believe the first modern religious drama was the one by Masefield presented in Canterbury Cathedral in 1928: *The Coming of Christ*. This was at the behest of the then Dean, George Bell. Bell showed Fry's first play, in 1935, in the garden of his bishoply palace in Chichester.

Masefield was not far from the world of pageants—that wish to put the whole of society onto a canvas, the mass action, the wish to break out into three-dimensional space. The evacuation of personality from his poems is depressingly complete. The shift away from narrative and into the expression of character (which must seem essentially static, and also solitary, monologic) happened over his head; although obsolete, his *Collected Poems* (1928) sold 200,000 copies. People *liked* narrative verse.

The Church was in a crisis. Admittedly, this is one of the preferred stances of priests. Being in turmoil suggests that you are intelligent, sensitive, compassionate, humble—possibly even holy. However, what they were contemplating was a once-only event: the eclipse of organised religion. Having survived into the age of management and statistics, they could find out just how few people attended church on Sunday, just how few of them were working-class or under 30, and how sparse they were in the cities. Demographics said that their future was bleak— and the claim to be the established church, the nation at prayer, was in question. The priests were not increasing in numbers, while the numbers of secular intellectuals like academics and broadcasters were growing daily. The response of the priests was very complex, as the behaviour of any organism in peril often is. They were shell-shocked at the massacre of the Jews, humiliated at the failure of the German churches (the rock of Protestantism) to resist Hitler, queasy about justifying atomic warfare in any circumstances whatsoever. Some of the responses to anxiety were impressive. The young priests of the time (recorded so vividly in Alec Vidler's collection, *Soundings*) ran towards life in the immediate present, with the draining of complex interiority. Language dominated by the present was the signal of this. The need for commitment was overriding, and urban social problems were the chosen field. The Church made big efforts to reach working-class youth, moving into different media after a recognition that the prose of Lancelot Andrewes, however rich in associations, was not going to reach these youths. The classic form was the youth club, but a radical simplification and modernisation of language as spoken by priests was another result. It is a big question, whether this took place before the simplification of poetry. The priests seem to have pioneered the sense of guilt about being (and sounding) middle-class. How far is it from the (amateur) drama in a church to the poetry reading? from singing Christian songs with a guitar to the poetry and jazz event, with protest poems? You throw out suffering in the abstract, you try to shift to contemporary issues which disaffected youth might respond to, you state things in plain emphatic terms—bingo, suddenly you've got the protest poem. You add a guitar (because the organ is trad and a drag, daddy-o), a chorus to join in, and, bingo, you've got a protest song. Out in the boondocks, the '50s saw stirrings which were due to become big-time in the '60s.

A line of religious drama had thus begun in 1928; Eliot wrote choruses for *The Rock* (1930), a pageant-play devised by E Martin Browne, who thereafter made his career in religious drama (most of it in verse). This recursion to mediaeval form was a late reflex of the arts and crafts movement, possibly even a reflex of Anglo-Catholicism, which emphasized the continuity of the Anglican church with the mediaeval traditions of the church. As a symbolic physical activity carried out in churches and defining their architectural space as something to be moved through, taking its sense from motion, it was probably related to the Liturgical Movement, an attempt to clarify and reform the movements around the Mass. The yearning for a spatial and collective aspect to symbolic utterance has not been without influence on poetry. *Murder in the Cathedral*, produced by Browne, was a hit in 1935—and transferred from Canterbury Cathedral (the building where Beckett had been terminated, *High Noon*-style, back in the 12th century) to the London theatre, in fact the one managed by Ashley Dukes. Here was the home of verse drama for the next ten years—not something Dukes sounds very excited about in his 1942 memoirs. Browne showed verse plays for two and a half years, just after the war, at Dukes' Mercury Theatre—which only had 136 seats. This was a tryout for authors and plays. The breakthrough, in a larger theatre, was Christopher Fry, in 1950. We must insist that the current was tied to Anglicanism— almost all the plays were of Christian theme; and Browne was ardently Christian. No new dramatists appeared in the 1950s. I find this bizarre, almost irritating, but this is what the dates say. The '50s saw productions of writers who had pioneered (with Dukes or Browne) in the 30s and '40s—Fry, Ann Ridler, Norman Nicholson, Ronald Duncan. What people in the early 1950s thought represented the poetry of the future was the plays of Christopher Fry. Conventionally, theatrical verse is rarely good poetry by the light of day. I think Fry is underrated at the present moment, but I can't really see people returning to read him.

James Lees-Milne's diaries, which belong essentially to the 1940s, describe the life of a son of the minor landed gentry whose job is to go round stately homes to examine their contents and discuss transferring their ownership to a public body, the National Trust. Since the funding for these transfers came from the government (in the form of waived inheritance tax revenues), this was a kind of socialism, of taking the symbolic wealth of the landowners into public ownership. Lees-Milne's ambivalent role, as someone springing from the gentry class who was nonetheless working for socialism, who identified with the old families but was nonetheless an expert (a traditional gentleman could never become an expert on anything), is symptomatic of the relationship between the new middle-class expert and the culture which was really the heritage of the families which had inherited it. The question is still with us: can one become an expert on this noble culture without absorbing the values of those who had owned it? His diaries, which exert a great fascination, are obnubilated by a mass of buildings and objects which are making a transition from being tokens of prestige and ownership to simply being works of art, to look at and appreciate. Visiting these stately homes became one of the favourite cultural diversions of the whole population, and wherever such houses existed; as these days out became an institution, the historical residue of hostility against those families and what they stood for vanished. Aristocratic culture (with its mainly Italian style of visual art) was unconsciously redefined as national culture. Lees-Milne's diaries are full of entries describing visits to the London salons (Cunard, Colefax), which were places where intelligent conversation about the arts was to be had. They exhibit an archaic system for changing public taste and launching artists on the public—a system definitely reaching its end in 1955. It was essentially similar to the mechanism of fashion in women's dress, where there were clearly defined centres which other places imitated, and where couturiers made their name in close alliance with aristocratic clients who displayed their wares and put them on the map. The system applied, of course, to restaurants, jewellers, and all kinds of luxury goods equipping the lifestyle of the fashionable. One has to admit that aristocratic patronage did a lot for European art over several thousand years—what we see in the '50s, though, is victories for the middle class, and for professionals invading the world of arts policy and leading public taste. I think the insecurity of these revolutionaries led them to overwork to compensate, since after all their qualification was technical knowledge. This tended to weaken the factor of pleasure in art expertise—and there is a specific strand of resistance that draws on this image of someone who has risen through passing exams, who knows too much and doesn't enjoy any of it. This is perhaps the impression which Allott's work, or Davie's, makes on us. But this was a transient moment in the history of culture. The image of people who didn't enjoy art is only intermittent—for every middle-class child crossly and unwillingly doing piano practice, there is another enchanted by the sounds they are making. All over the English-speaking world, I think, there was a moment of being exhausted and emotionally inhibited by the rigours of the New Criticism method, and then a reaction in which literary pleasure reconquered the field, and people became more confident about the fragility and subjectivity of their responses.

This late classical atmosphere is echoed in literature—Auden's libretti, for example, are nostalgic pastiches, attached to the aristocratic past of European culture, timeless because they are afraid of the passage of time. The opera audience was drawn from the wealthy and distinguished. Such a depersonalisation opened the door to the cultural wealth of the European past; a specific quality of lightness sprang from the obvious obsolescence of the whole menagerie. Detached from the historic pillars of wealth, power, and land ownership, these amusements acquired an insubstantial, frothy, and groundless quality. This includes what we call theatrical magic. It avoids serious notes like the plague, and is inclined to vanish in a moment. Everything which could come from the experience of life, is here replaced by elements from other works of art. Everything seems to take place inside the glass case of a museum display, inside which are bubbles like champagne. This is the atmosphere of *The Dark is Light Enough*, or *Nones*, with their twittering, twinkling, make-believe. The 1950s saw a rising preoccupation with the household: the "baby boom" was between 1946 and 1951, and this is the frame grouping "domestic anecdote" plus "consumer durables" plus "Biedermeier charm"—a formula for the majority of poetry over the 40 years since. I am looking for an art-historical term to cover this. The Biedermeier era, as explained notably by Eda Sagarra, was one of stifling domesticity—the political police had closed down public activity, it was an era of deep conservative repression as the government and Church identified all ideas with the subversion of the barely defeated French Revolution. The preoccupation with domesticity in the '50s was nothing like so sinister, but did produce an atmosphere in which the artist imitates children in order to be charming, or where poets wrote suburban poems which were totally uninteresting. Another comparison would be the Rococo—obviously closely related to Biedermeier, which after all was a regression to late 18th century norms. Rococo, Biedermeier, Viennese operetta—none of these is quite right. Betjeman, Fry, and Auden share a distinctive fluency, a tone just off-pastiche, nostalgia, brightness, calculated pointlessness, avoidance of any grave subjects. Arguably, they are non-priests who think everything important must be said by priests, within the Church. This is different from complete privatisation—but may look like it.

The final example of slight, highly controlled, movements being defined as the culturally good is Close Reading. This was felt to be desirable for over-energetic teenagers. Simply—because it was repressive. The publishing world needed to race into false enthusiasm—because the sheer nastiness represented by Allott just made reading and writing poetry impossible anywhere within earshot. I'm enthusiastic about fake enthusiasm.

Christian heads of household

This book is called the long 1950s because the styles developed in the 1950s ended when the poets came to the end of their creative lives, not punctually in January 1960. Of the various strands within 50s poetry, we can identify (at least) the twirling decorative style, the academic existentialist style, the domestic anecdote, and an exalted style based on religion or spiritualism. This last style is not going to appear here because it is described at length in a previous book of mine, *Origins of the Underground*. John Press' book *Rule and Energy*, which is effectively a history of English poetry in the 1950s, isolates two currents, of which one is something like academic existentialism and the other is this religious style, in which he would include Kathleen Raine, David Gascoyne, Vernon Watkins, and Thomas Blackburn.

The superiority of the work of Logue and Hill inspired certain reflections. We have this double twist, that two '50s poets have dominated the scene of around 1996–2006 and that the death of the main '50s style has liberated the official English poetry. The quality of their verse depended on a finished idea of what goodness and sound politics consist in. Unlike children of a more relativist era, they are not overwhelmed by doubts. They can give an account of social process—of history, which is what social process amounts to over time—which does not simply drown in narcissistic subversions and digressions. As they made the fundamental moral decisions at an early stage, they are integrated personalities and when they speak it comes from a fund of secured knowledge, tried by time and experience, and it is not subject to coming unfastened because its parts are incompatible or flowing at different speeds. This process of self interrogation and commitment is not inside the poems and happened long before they were written. Its nature takes us back to a primal moment when the nucleus of their late work was formed almost in secret: around 1952, or maybe 1954, when they were young and when self interrogation and commitment were things which every writer was practicing and which were within the scope of the times. My reflections, just mentioned, were that *since 1965 no one has developed this kind of moral integrity and sense of pitch* and that *a narcissistic parading of their own moral virtues is the thing which makes most m-stream poetry unbearable but moral integrity is what makes this poetry great* and, less so, *socially critical poetry turned the volume knob on morality up to eleven and perhaps it failed because it was too much in love with condemnation and sonorous judgement and lacked proper foundation.* Logue and Hill actually have an ideology as opposed to a nebula of glittering doubts and tricks. I still think that ejecting from the whole moralising view of the world was the great reason why m-stream English verse got better during the 1980s. It is not enough to narrate the changes of poetry, we have to expand the scope to look at structures as well, and to place the movement of poetic style within the triangle of prestige, morality, and fantasy and the field of force they stretch between them. This chapter tries to grasp some of the contradictions involved here.

The discourse typical of the whole period 1945–65 is existentialism. We can present this as a new variant on the relationship of the Western citizen to large-scale ideas—the grand narratives, to use a term from the 1980s. This has to be combined, in Britain, with the action of Christian values, still decisive for most educated people and for their comprehension of literature.

The rejection of totalitarian ideas, even the rejection of the imperialist idea, was expressed by restricting the poem to the suburban life of the poet, presented with a sociological realism which could also be acutely limiting and negative. The fashion for existentialism identified it with the life of a member of the Resistance, a *resistant*, faced with urgent and personal choices—existential choices, in the jargon. This highly-charged courage could be continued much later in the atmosphere of resistance to the colonial war in Algeria, where left-wing Frenchmen were exposed to danger in helping the Algerians to buy and deliver guns and munitions, and in counteracting the intelligence services who were trying to close these networks down. Far more Frenchmen, of course, were involved in danger while fighting for the other side, in the largest terrorist movement of the Western world since 1945. The abstract level of existentialist philosophy was of dim importance compared to these real life commitments, which were evoked in literature by Camus and Sartre. The relevance of these legends to the life of English academics in the 1950s is now hard to perceive. However, the forcing of focus down to the concrete situation of an individual's life was inspiring, and justifies the writing of poems about life in a suburban marriage as if the great philosophical issues were being resolved in those dining rooms, gardens, family cars and PTA meetings. The closing down to household level is a feature of the 1950s and the transition to a white goods economy as the war economy was demobilised—still focussed on two little people and on moral duty. At that time governments were preoccupied with the equipping of family homes to the extent that poems might well be directed, not at Agincourt or Blenheim, but at the kitchen resplendent with cookers and washing-machines.

Someone who asserted that the abandonment of kings, nobles, saints, as protagonists and their replacement by a middle-class teacher was courageous would be correct. Of course the corollary was that lack of scope, pettiness of scale, the absence of exciting resolutions, became central—to the point where the poetry was *deliberately* boring.

When writers, in the 1950s, came to make generalizations about the task of the writer, the topic of commitment and conscience was always to the fore. There is an exhibit here, being Cruise O'Brien's collection of essays, *Writers and Politics* (1965). O'Brien was Irish, and worked for the United Nations during the '50s. He is an example of the hope that the UN could defuse international conflicts and prevent further wars—the Republic of Ireland being especially hopeful of this, as a country which had no imperialist past, no corporate lobby, and no inclination to war. He was not compromised by being the citizen of a great power. But he had experience of managing international crises and combined this with being a serious student of literature. These are actually great essays. They should be read because they put you right inside the '50s—the whole landscape comes to life. Once you see the ideal which writers were working to, you can understand the rules they struggled with, and understand their failure. It seems odd to look for prose, rather than poetry, to find ideals. What we find in O'Brien is a steady demand on the writer to be the conscience of the modern state. The failure of the priesthood and the intellectuals to prevent the rise of criminal regimes in Germany and Russia had traumatised the educated public. (O'Brien published books during the 1950s—under a pseudonym because, as a teacher at a pious Catholic institution in the Republic of Ireland, he could not be seen to carry out critical thought. What can you say—it was the 1950s. He was a classic writer.)

Something which says a lot about the '50s scene is the movie *High Noon*. There are four desperados coming to town to kill the sheriff, in revenge. He is old and his limbs are stiff and he cannot shoot first; they are athletes. The townspeople are numerous but decline to help him, out of fear. He has the chance of fleeing—but stays, to fulfil his duty. They are arriving on the noon train and Gary Cooper waits for them in the main street. The desperados are poorly co-ordinated and he shoots them all, one by one. A lot of '50s writers saw themselves in the Gary Cooper role. They face the tough decisions. They face down the desperados. They rise above the stress. They know what justice is, and do not conceal this from us. Their power of decision gives them authority. *High Noon* was probably about the Korean War—the use of ultimate force to quell people who break the rules; the aged sheriff doing the right thing despite the anxieties of pinko civilians.

The problem for such writers was how to exhibit Christian values in contemporary life. If we are going to look for the way theology affects poetry, we have to find an invariant. The poem takes place in quite different terms from the theology—it buries the theology in secular existence, where it grows as a harvest, in the same way that the soil affects vegetation. As Eliade says, the sacred is hidden in the mundane, the eternal is hidden in the created world. The invariant is the structure which appears both in the theology and in the poem. A simple example is in the area of self-assertion. We would expect poetry to choose large-scale, high-energy, high-speed, unpredictable events. These are more dramatic. Writing about warships blowing each other up seems obvious—it appeals to children, so it must be simple. Conversely, a Christian is enjoined to be meek. This implies small, low-energy objects, interacting in non-destructive ways. Internal, emotional objects are similarly downscaled. A certain range of imagery may therefore present signifying objects, coded by a Christian aesthetic; they are meek objects. They mirror group interaction in which people do not invade each other's space. This is intimately related to the theme of conflict handling. As we have seen, *High Noon* is about conflict handling—it was a key theme of '50s international politics, where the liberal conscience was preoccupied with how to prevent another world war while also discouraging violent and expansionist regimes. A European might say that *High Noon* is still about the aestheticisation of violence, it is all about the build-up to Gary Cooper shooting four people to death; its work-up aims to smooth away our resistance to violence. The final rule of *High Noon* literature turns out to be: Write boring poems because writing artistic poems is not the act of someone tough and authoritative.

The doctrine that Style was Morality prohibited style from doing other things. The 1950s preoccupation with the family redefined the poem as the acts of the Christian head of household—a retraction of scale and a withdrawal from expression. It moved the site where the key action of the poem took place perilously close to the tests of virtue by which someone could prove their right to middle-class status.

The keyword for the attitude expected of the Cold War intellectual, by the faction committed to the capitalist side in that war, was toughness. Within poetry, this presented itself as the resistance to rhetoric. Whatever excitement exciting language suggested, tough people would say no to. In dealing with ideas, the keyword was empiricism. This in practice meant saying no to ideas. The reasoning, or metaphor complex, was that abstract ideas led to stylised visions of social order which could not adapt to the varying wishes of millions of people and so led to the abolition of civic rights such as the vote. The conclusion was that intellectuals—not psychopaths—were responsible for the Nazi and Bolshevik dictatorships. Empiricism in this sense cluster therefore meant something like involving all adults as citizens in making policy; but in fact letting all citizens have a share of economic power and letting public affairs be directed by that purchasing power. After the Cold War, it is apparent that this idea was the winner. But almost anything interesting in poetry could be written off as non-empirical. In official poetry, concrete details were written up as supreme acts of virtue because they symbolically stood for this empiricism. The Movement poets were in competition with the Marxist (or quasi-Marxist?) poets of the 1930s, still vital and famous in the 1950s, and won by narrowing down the scope of poetry. Documentary had eschewed fantasy, display, and so on, and had been a great feature of the 1930s and 1940s, possibly reaching a peak with the range of films produced for the 1951 Festival of Britain: but the *empiricism* tag was a code-word for documentary which is about one household and ignores the fact that society exists. Older poetry had situated itself largely inside the Church of England's notion of the parish as the local human community, which allowed for a vision including people of all ages and all classes, and this underpinned the poem in its general statements. The poetry of the 1950s has visibly lost this even when it still has a Christian allegiance.

British poets found existentialism after the world war was over, and had no Algerian War to repine over, so their heroic resistance turned out to be domestic in scale. It was a kind of courageous reading of the quality newspapers. A quote from the TLS on the jacket of a 1960 book (by John Holloway) says "These poems display a sensuousness, a feeling for tangs, harnesses, distances, for the muscularity of nature", and this is a kind of boilerplate version of unconscious yearnings of the period. The part about sensuousness was very strange given that almost everyone writing was an academic and wholly involved with words and ideas. I don't see how Nature can be muscular, but I suppose this is a projection of Cold War rhetoric—toughness being set up as the primal virtue, the one that the splendid wilderness is so full of. The preoccupation with solid objects ties in to the practice of reason in separating truth from falsehood, and of course this empiricism has a strong link to politics. Reason as articulated by law is the protector of the fair social order. This toughness is a guarantee against emotional states being raised in a unique and sheltered part of the universe and flowing in a cascade of increasing excitability to produce unique and infectious states of mind. This might actually be how art works, though. I don't think the sensuousness is about the preference for cookers and washing machines over ideas in the discourse of politics—not consciously, anyway.

The ideal of toughness needs to be taken to its classic moments if we are to understand the partial successes of those who followed. It is important to look at Daniel Weissbort's anthology of *The Poetry of Survival. Post-War Poets of Central and Eastern Europe* to see a whole assembly of poets talking tough. This is not acceptable as an overview of post-war European poetry, obviously, but it is a good anthology because all the poets sound like each other. They all talk like a captain of partisans, just out of the Lithuanian woods. This is an image (one of several, no doubt) of what modernity was in 1947.

Another Penguin book, *T Carmi and Dan Pagis. Selected Poems* (translated by Stephen Mitchell, 1976), shows two of these poets at greater length: both writing in Hebrew and both closely related to

Weissbort's artistic conception. This is really important poetry and it makes toughness look like the greatest virtue for a modern poet; I have to say also that it suggests that there was no such thing as a Tough Poet in Britain. I also suspect that the category of cold-war intellectual did not exist in Britain, although they certainly existed in other countries. Dan Pagis was a native of eastern Europe and T. Carmi of New York. The title of Weissbort's anthology is probably taken from a line in ML Rosenthal's introduction: "Pagis is a poet of survival."

The style also had local successes. David Wevill's early volumes are existentialist in the way they pack the drama into animals, with the limits of being savagely inscribed into the basic position. These poems are concise, overtly restricted, but also dramatic and of course artistic successes. The projection into animals once mastered could lead the way towards the creation of a complete world within the poem, in fact to mythical poetry based on anthropological knowledge—which was Wevill's next direction. Through careful and fastidious study of Hopi mythology, Wevill came to write his own myths—grand narratives, of course.

The difficulty of recovering existentialism is that it was a state of mind. This is also why it is so evocative of a period—it vanished like some rare animal. When The Beatles went to Hamburg in 1960, the group they hung out with were called Exis. This was in fact short for existentialist, *Existentialisten* I suppose. Astrid Kirchherr, who invented the Beatles' look, was an Exi, and so was Klaus Voorman. It was much more a way of dressing, a badge of recognition between similar people, a diffuse mood of sophistication and revolt, a choice of cafes and cultural pleasures, than a theory. It was a generational thing—if you were a student in 1955, you couldn't be a Ted or a rocker, but you could join a youth movement which also gave you a credo as a young intellectual. I think I have not been clear about the gap between a *Cold Warrior*, someone who identified with the military-industrial complex because it was the only means of realising the goals on which he (rarely she) had set his heart, and a *fifties academic*, because the people who read modern poetry and supervised its production and reception, etc., were not Cold Warriors and you are not going to find poetry which promotes the Cold War and weaves laurels on its warriors.

Unfortunately, all that talk about courage and commitment was easy to recuperate as enthusiasm for fighting in Korea or in the Canal Zone and for taking a tough stand against communism. But when I talk about existentialist academics the people I mean looked toward Sartre and Camus on one side, and toward Christian idealism and the Prince of Peace on the other. The Cold War was the dominant cultural fact, but the tier of State professionals, say 20,000 people, did not dominate cultural production and in fact lacked a bank of instruments with which to influence that production.

The peculiar formula of the Movement poem involved ideological resistance to various things which were not discussed directly but only rejected codedly through verbal gestures of avoiding rhetoric, softness, subjectivity. The group speaking in poems had a territorial position which had conflicts and ideological tensions on all its borders, but it also had an aspiration to meekness which involved not showing yourself as self-seeking or violent, so that you were *unable* to talk about the sites of real conflict, e.g. Korea, the repression of other political parties in the countries of eastern Europe, or labour unrest. The exit into anecdote followed on from a collective decision not to talk about the decisive issues which were also the interesting ones. *Meekness is better than escalation.*

The Movement poem was low on expressivity, low on ornament, low on fantasy, low on display. There was one level of ornament, that is rhyme as part of the apparatus of regular metre, retained. This was a central feature of the 1950s (and late 1940s) and its disappearance may represent a crisis of the style. The programme of removing rhetoric was bound to clash with the apparatus of rhyme and metre, which is obviously decorative although it also feels like discipline. The shift away from it is very interesting. Perhaps this scraping away of the poem down to the ultimate tough, gritty, unselfdeceiving (etc. ad libitum) essence, or perhaps to a layer of grey sludge, was the move which doomed the Movement by leaving something which was appealing to no one and simply fell flat.

It is important to stress the moral commitment of this stratum of poetry. This is utterly distinct from the supercilious line also known among academics. In fact, the secular quality of this poetry is slightly deceptive, as the pressure to compete with the blatant goodness of

Christian poets is firmly directing it away from artistic values. Stylistic values were constantly functioning as metaphors for an idea of how social duties are carried out. This poetry is anti-individualist and communalist, regarding preoccupation with oneself as perfectly immoral. At the same time the dominant political idea is anti-collectivist and the rule of reason is essentially individual reason. This tension blocked creative activity and more successful poets rather obviously disrupted it.

Fitness for office

Frans de Waal explains in his book *Chimpanzee Politics* that although high rank in chimpanzee troops is dominance and is based on physical strength the vote of the group as a whole is decisive and you cannot rise to the top unless other creatures approve of you. Systematically bad behaviour, the deployment of the strength to hurt other individuals and to take food from them, loses you points and enables your rivals to get ahead of you. This act of justice, so beneficial for the welfare of the group as a whole, is only possible because the troop members relate past actions to individuals and remember which individual carried out bad actions. The correlation between bad behaviour and refusal to give access to higher political status rank is based on a cognitive category of the individual and cannot work without it. That is, the constituent element of human politics, *long* before the origin of a human species, involved the individual as the accounting unit, the unit around which behavioural memory was organised. Literature carries out a function of social record which already existed in primate species before the blessed dawn of the humans. The individual as a gross mystification of bourgeois ideology remains high on the philosophical agenda but cannot be washed away as simply as by announcing that only the collective matters. Rather, the concept of injustice depends on the existence of individual rights and the concept of ethical behaviour by politicians depends on identifying the politicians as individuals who can behave badly or properly as individuals. Notoriously, politicians evade accountability by burying the key decisions and defining them as structural constants of divine law, human nature, statistical patterning, etc. and so *not being decisions at all*. All language articulates the dumb, and the higher practice of language is to break the barrier between conscious and unconscious and have the suppressed parts of the whole burst into shared awareness.

Part of the pattern is the uneasy status of English Literature departments. They had no well-defined product. Separating literature from morality is more likely to work for sea-slugs than for primates but does this mean that scholarship in literature makes you moral? Engineering departments trained engineers, languages departments taught people French or Russian. EngLit staff, with no historical background to make their activity seem normal and indubitable, reached out for forbidden fruit—the claim that they taught morality. Actually, instructors did not pass any exams in morality. No one thinks any longer that literature graduates are more moral than, say, dentists or physics graduates. If anyone was teaching morality, it was the faculties of divinity—the background is the loss of the position dominating the universities which these faculties had once had, and EngLit scheming to take over their territory. If you look at various mid-century addresses, in which senior academics made solemn generalisations about the state of the profession, it is striking how far they believe that studying English literature means moral progress. I don't think we would expect this today. The other thing which these addresses draw attention to is the high proportion of the new graduates who would go abroad to teach their hard-won knowledge—mostly to colonial possessions, current or recently liberated. In a mixture of motives (commonly unacceptable to modern sensibility), this course of instruction was seen as bringing progress to the backward, disseminating Christian values, spreading goodwill towards the British and their way of life (and their export commodities), and preparing the colonies for democracy. The teachers were supposed to embody the values they and the Great Works were transmitting. This major tranche of employment put a strange pressure on the university courses preparing the future teachers. The New Criticism displaced a project, latent or incipient, for making patriotism and imperial history the core values to build literature courses around. The equation between admiring English literature, admiring the values it embodied, and admiring the history of the civil society which expressed those values, was natural and hard to avoid. This core project had gone a long way towards taking over the elementary school syllabus, in History and English Literature. The astringency of the New Criticism, its hostility towards teleologies and mere group-feeling, at least protected the universities from becoming guardians of national values and trophies (which happened in Russia and Germany, for example). The Movement was a group of graduates in English Literature, was individualist in approach and was in this way free of the military-patriotic cycle. This is not to be underestimated. Culture in the 1950s was dominated by memories of the Second World War and by the narrative of success in battle, defiance of foreign enemies. They evaded this levelling and increasingly dull propaganda by refuge into the domestic. Empiricism was a notional threat to the dominant modes of hypocrisy and glorification of authority, but never carried out this promise in Movement poetry.

Status

Another ethological study of primates developed the idea (only a hypothesis, as we write) that there is an instinctive drive to watch high-prestige individuals. Scientists tested this by a set-up in which monkeys exchanged tokens for the right to watch certain images, and showed a preference for finding out what high-status individuals, male or female, were doing. This is intimately linked to the preference of culture throughout recorded history for representing high status individuals in art, which is almost certainly not simply due to the narcissistic display drive of those individuals, with their financial ability to patronise art and influence it. The evolution away from these individuals in 20th century poetry is therefore one of the central questions.

The interest in politics in poetry is inseparable from the biologically given drive to observe high status individuals and also from the preoccupation with morality. The whole area is caught up with the poet's drive for status, where display signals status and status is the intended prize for so much self-display.

The solution reached by certain poets in the 1950s answered the problems raised by these issues of morality and prestige, and the success of that solution over at least the thirty years which followed is a compelling story, brought to an end by shifts in the audience's perception of what was moral and what was prestigious.

The poetry of the long 1950s was deeply invested in the academic world and so in a model of virtuous activity which excluded the imagination in favour of exact knowledge. This was at the conscious level, but at another level the system was there to certify people and to divide them into classes by ability: "In a very real sense the pupil is being judged every time he responds to a piece of literature" (*A Language for Life*, The Bullock Report, 1975, as quoted by Sinfield). How much more intensely was this judgement to be feared when a product of the system wrote a poem of their own. The EngLit system granted status to the A-stream of its pupils and was concerned, as if territorially, to legitimate its right to make non-defective notarisations of status and its fitness to receive public funding. This was the reason for developing rigour at the expense of the imagination, and it has little in common with the documentary movement, for example, which was interested in promoting social change and breaking down barriers of ignorance. It would be unfair to deny that the system was the path of upward mobility for a large number of its successful pupils. However, restricting the way this certificate of status could be awarded was a measure of fiscal control which guaranteed that it kept its value on the market. If we look at the bad poets of the long 1950s, we can see them also as victims of an abusive relationship in which the way they were taught to succeed damaged their imagination.

Fantasy

Something else caught up in the field is fantasy. The absence of this from Movement poetry is a peculiar and distinctive trait. It sounds like legislation if I say that fantasy is a core component of poetry. All the same that is my belief, and the whole English mainstream thing was suffering from a kind of nutritional deficiency which led to abnormality of growth. This no longer has to do with the restriction to the household, but with the institutions where Movement poets typically studied and taught. Their attachment to the English departments of universities was peculiarly and dangerously close. This already offers us the dialectic possibility that as the English departments evolved the basis for Movement poetry would be destroyed and the artistic problems along with it. This evolution was inevitable given the respect for originality burnt into the collective ideology, and given the rate of growth of the Eng Lit professionals. Poetry has evolved *in line with its academic base.* Evidently the liberation of English poetry in the 1980s was directly linked to a newly permissive attitude towards fantasy. Evidently, too, the ban on fantasy in the earlier period was linked to the truth telling function of the poet: you abandon the imagination because you want to be a credible witness so that your testimony on whatever it is is credible.

This area of inhibition has an intimate relationship to status: the anxiety about depicting false experiences is linked to a social machine in which class distinctions are of key importance and in which anxiety leads people to resent any claim to experience which cannot be documented. Fantasy is very likely to involve experiences you have not had and which are not strictly consonant with the social niche you genuinely occupy. That is, fantasy benefits from the solid nature of roles in a society with rigid role ascriptions and the interdicts lend it solidity for its scenarios and a reservoir of unfulfilled wishes.

The idea that there are only two possible poetries, irresponsible fantasy and drab neo-Christian poetry which bans fantasy, is utterly depressing; it cannot be true but for a certain stretch of time it was an accepted fiction, and this was because of the polarisation which the poets of the 1950s, that whole authorised poetic world, had lurched into. It was like the stalemate of superpower confrontation. After the tension has gone the whole set of attitudes seems exaggerated and laughable.

The fantasy which is most recurring and pleasing is likely to be one about changing status and so the challenge to poetry in the period of political optimism was to furnish the possibility of a complete change of status, the dissolution of all inherited status and the rise of everyone to have high status. This was inevitable, but the extent to which poets could actually write about it is doubtful. The m-stream poets came to fill the role of denying anyone's right to change their status, but that was not a feature of the original package, it was rather a consequence of occupying the role of *resisting rhetoric, resisting imagination* in a period when the Imagination was visualising a classless society.

There is this social phenomenon of people not wanting me to distinguish between good poetry and bad, and not being interested in poetry at all, not wanting to read it, except for this dominating expectation that it should level everything and make everyone equal. I want to separate good poetry from bad, always.

Behavioural beauty

The whole argument made by the opponents of the Movement, including myself, has said that their moralism is dull and depressing. This does not follow from a general dislike of religious art, moral art, or art about goodness. I wrote about this topic at some length in the chapter on Denise Riley in *Centre and Periphery*. What we are attracted to in art is related to what we would like to experience in real life. In real life, we would clearly prefer to be among good people, as they will not hurt us and damage our interests, or hurt those we are close to. Goodness gives rise to a behavioural beauty which is fundamentally similar to other kinds of beauty. We want to be close to good people, including good people who write poetry, not only in order to admire them but also *possibly* because we want to be good and we can learn from them. This poetry could be written in a successful way and it is important when assessing the whole genre to look at the best examples of it. This would mean reading Peter Levi and Anthony Thwaite as Christian poets formed in the 1950s, and interested in formal verse, who are a great deal better than the poets in *New Lines*. Looking at the failed examples of a genre is not enough to support a historically valid account.

The phrase about behavioural beauty comes I think from an essay by Andrew Sarris about women's pictures and referred specifically to the films of Frank Borzage. I am a fan of Borzage (women's pics or not) and I am fully in agreement with the idea of behavioural beauty and am convinced that it is one of the bases for liking poetry. We have to take the discussion to another level: the Movement poets do not fail because of their morality but because their attempt to present behavioural beauty is *unconvincing*. This may be because their intent of winning the poem is too obvious and the foregone conclusion of proving themselves moral dominates the construction of the poem so that it is obviously rigged. Further, their idea of seizing authority has too much of gruffness, giving out orders, learning, lack of sympathy, and not enough of kindness, generosity, unselfishness, solicitude, love. Staging behavioural beauty may be as difficult as photographing physical beauty.

The proposal is that some people identify a particular way of writing with morality and that this explains a great deal about their behaviour around poetry. This would not just apply to the Movement but also, and perhaps more, to the Marxist/avant-garde poets. Winning in the stylistic tests imposed by networks of poet-academics was imagined to be a test of morality as well. The need to control the results was so great that it led to a reduction of the tests to rules. This was artificial in the same way that a rhyme-scheme is artificial. The proposition that a certain style displays the quality of your moral imagination and so your fitness to judge other people was unpersuasive.

The problem with the idea of behavioural beauty is that it involves a reference to the author's character, which is not really there in the text, and which can be seen as an unknown. I have no problem with this, since I believe that we are qualified to read someone's character and disposition from their utterances as a consequence of living in the human milieu all our lives. The project requires that the poet should display their character in their poems—hardly a problem when the underlying rules of the poetic genre in this time are to display your character and to make the knowledge available for those who seek it. So being a good person is something that is made visible by the way you write—but not by writing orthodox Movement poetry (or orthodox Cambridge poetry).

Quite evidently carrying this payload dictates many aspects of the design of poetry, and prohibits a number of possibilities which are outside the modern range. Poetry could perfectly well be about other people and depict their behavioural beauty, but the issues of describing and voicing other people are a central problem of poetics in this period. There is also a distinction between egocentricity and offering knowledge to satisfy the wishes of readers as they read, to fill the patterns they draw up to be filled. The issue with avant garde poets is partly, largely even, that the readers are imposing patterns of information seeking and the poets are frustrating these patterns by not supplying the information required. Instead, they offer quite different information, which would fill quite other patterns.

It would be more logical to write a history of the empty patterns which readers impose on poems asking them to be filled than to write the history of the poetry.

If the poem says very little, shuns fantasy, myth, etc., then one of the objects which survives within its depleted boundary is status: the manner of writing makes clear a knowledge of literary standards as installed by university critics of the time, its austerity and self-control exhibit managerial virtues which qualify the speaker for a profession, that is a place in the upper fifth of the income pyramid. It thus arouses solidarity among readers with similar assets—if not necessarily among readers without them. It would not be accurate to say that the status advertisement was the central or express statement made by these poems.

I developed this argument in a previous essay about Logue, in *The Council of Heresy*. What I said about Logue's poems about the Trojan War was that there had been a dramatic narrowing of scope of poetry which his serene staging of events within the royal and noble class of the Greek (and Trojan) polities drew attention to by its stunning artistic success. The image I used for the modern course of poetry was the film of *The Incredible Shrinking Man*: after riding his boat through a cloud of poisoned gas (the product of some Cold War arms experimentation, without doubt) he began to shrink, all the way down to molecular level. At one stage he is of mouse size and the cat tries to catch him. The suburban house where he lives with his nuclear family swells to occupy all his awareness, right past the point where he can only be in part of the house and the horizon of his awareness is smaller than the house. Equally, poetry in the Cold War shrank to a suburban scale, reflecting a building plan where there were endless houses all of the same design and no monumental ideological sites, so that a poem about a house in one suburb somehow "fitted" all houses in all suburbs and yet brought them information which they already had. Meanwhile the Cold War ideological campaign was being fought on the basis that Western freedom brought prosperity at household level and that a weak State was the cause of suburban prosperity, houses stuffed with white goods, and that consumerism as displayed in advertisements was going to win over people everywhere (being offered not only to dissident working classes in the West but also to the dissatisfied masses in the Communist bloc). The part saying, society succeeds because the State is becoming weaker, was especially pushed in Britain, where the rapidly progressing loss of the Empire was being proposed as a good thing for the average consumer within Britain. The government's propaganda voice was thus saying that relinquishing government control is the best thing for everybody. Poets also reduced the scope of the poem to themselves, by slight extension to the suburban house, their wives, the garden, the university where they worked. The proposal was that within the boundaries of the household, the curtilage, the poet-academic is the highest status individual and also represents the moral authority, the equivalent of the priest. Obviously this forebodes conflicts with the wife and children. Privatisation opens an exit from the past in which you successfully expel bishops and lords from your poems but nobody is interested in your poetry except yourself. I want to suggest that the peculiar development of poetry in the main Movement line of around 1948 to 1985 was based on overcompensation for this terrible loss of scale: as the radius of action of the conservative poet became smaller so certain functions became overdeveloped and strained. The function of defending moral standards became overrated. The function of asserting status became overdeveloped, also because it was largely unattractive when applied to the poet, as the historical function of poetry had always been to ascribe and legitimate the status of the top tier, senior nobles if not actually the royal family of whatever state it was. The suburban cell was at one level a sensory deprivation chamber.

The project of poetry which simply builds status for the poet, in which a volume of my poetry simply functions to show what a great guy I am and continues a project about me, was thus of limited interest. Propaganda about Stalin, or Queen Elizabeth, or Augustus Caesar, or 15th century Welsh landowners, was actually more interesting, or at least had a larger and more compelling scope. A project to revive everyone's interest is the project of granting everyone high status, which is helpfully set out for us in *Political Shakespeare*. (This is about the Bard but is also a kind of manifesto for the Left in literature.) Sinfield does not explicitly say that the completion of the task of glorifying royalty leaves poetry as a resource available for giving status to everybody, but that is pretty much the intention. To twist that slightly, the empty space left by getting rid of the kings, peers, dukes, etc. who strut through Shakespeare's plays was filled, or at least plotted out by a planning application for a redevelopment, by a Marxist project in which the whole ranking structure of society was to be razed and re-erected and poetry was going to play a leading role in the re-teaching and the new narrative. I don't think this actually happened—maybe the planning documents are still going through the courts—but I admit that this is more interesting than the scheme of ascribing a meed of acclaim to the achievements of a hundred or so poets, which is what I am actually trying to do.

Although the separation between proving yourself moral and proving yourself fit for high office was radically broken down in this era, the withdrawal into the small scale—the marriage, the PTA meeting, the classroom, finally the individual soul—was also humility. The move into theology was a renunciation of ideologies, recently popular, aimed at controlling the State. The striving to be good was not in itself evidence of badness. However, the general withdrawal to the scale of the household also removed aspects of idealism inherent in nationalism and removed all obstacles to the expansion of individual status and to a bourgeois frame of reference. This is what we now have to address.

Defence of the homestead: domestic anecdote

I may as well quote my own definition of the genre: "The events in the poem are not felt to be important. The domestic setting is a refuge from disturbing ideas and the public realm. The reader is supposed to go along with the poem because to reject it is to reject themselves. The more banal the poem is, the more you are expected to like it." This poetry was very easy to write because it came directly out of everyday life. A lot of people wrote it. I can't point to any classics of the genre. It doesn't run to that. The first poem of domestic anecdote known to me is the 'Ephemeris' of D. Ausonius Magnus, late 4th century. *Ephemeris* means daily and is the Greek equivalent for what in genuine Latin would be a diary; the poem gives an account of his activities for the whole of one day, *id est totius diei negotium*, at his villa near Bordeaux. The poem reads oddly, and Georg Misch in his epic *History of Autobiography* (up to the 12th century) has pointed out that there must be a folio missing, and the line jumps several hours. In the edition I am looking at, it is next to a set of poems called Parentalia, poems about his family, a title which was used by George Herbert for some Latin poems and again by Geoffrey Hill. The most obvious feature of Ausonius is that he's boring.

A book on Egyptian archaeology says that the papyri found in the rubbish-heaps of Oxyrhynchus are important because they are unimportant. They deal with everyday affairs of obscure people and are not written with any literary ambition. They do not deal with affairs of state but with details of wayward pupils and problems with deliveries. So the details of domestic routine become a fit subject for university historians, for popular books of history, and for the government ministries that deal with welfare and education. When looking at Dom An we have also to ask if the poetry is unimportant because it is unimportant.

Moving on a couple of millennia, Roy Fuller published *The Middle of the War* in 1942 with the Hogarth Press. The book has a thematic unity and is appealing because the poet is emotionally frank and the scenes he acquires as symbols are persuasive and clear. I am not positing it as a part of the "mid-century decline", because it has integrity as poetry and its dismal qualities are part of a deliberate political intent and brilliantly stylised.

The objects are disposed: the sky is suitable.
Where the coast curves the waves' blown smoke
Blurs with the city's and the pencilled ships
Lumber like toys. The searchers for coal and driftwood
Bend; and the beach is littered with stones and leaves,
Antlers of seaweed, round gulls, to the belt
Of sand, like macadam, watered by the sea.
  ('November 1941')

(Why are the gulls round? maybe because they have their wings tucked close to reduce wind resistance. But *round*?) They even embody hope, in the specific form of the self-destruction of an outworn society. After describing an idiot "slobbering his thumbs" he says

I have no doubt that night is real which creeps
Over the concrete, that murder is fantasy,
That what should now inform the idiot sleeps
  Frozen and unfree.
  ('November 1939')

The reference is to reason, of course, and to say it sleeps evokes a Goya painting (where "the sleep of reason begets monsters", impersonated by Franco and Hitler in particular) but also implies that it will wake. The central position of the book is a kind of vigilant numbness, where the speaker is magnetically alert to the contours of a scene but has absolutely no way of participating in it. They are as if an alien waiting for the chance to leave the landscape altogether, or a conspirator who has no interest in what is taking place except for the cue which will unleash the political coup in which he is to act. This inability to participate is double: not only is he a weary and partially unwilling participant in the war (serving in the Fleet Air Arm, the airforce organic to the Royal Navy) but also he regards the British society which he is fighting for as bourgeois and corrupt, a scene which is about to be struck. The references to Marxist myths of overcoming and redemption are sparse but repay close attention; 'Soliloquy in an Air Raid' is the most explicit of these and, delicately, raises the tone to the level of history:

> It is good-bye
> To the social life which permitted melancholy
> And madness in the isolation of its writers,
> To a struggle as inconclusive as the Hundred
> Years' War. The air, as welcome as morphia,
> This *rich ambiguous aesthetic air*
> Which now I breathe, is an effective diet
> Only for actors[.]

This is as close to making the fragility of an era which is about to come to a crashing end into something fascinating and theatrical as one can get. The whole concept of domestic anecdote is illuminated by a poem like this: where immediate personal experience—as arresting as "A billion tons of broken glass and rubble" could be—is urgently linked to a huge historical context, the old bourgeois civilisation and the new socialist one. It is as if the demolition of a city cleared a perspective at the end of which something completely different could be glimpsed. Fuller records the "permitted melancholy" but little of the besetting and wonderful idealistic films, running constantly in the imagination, which show socialists the goal of their historical journey; this lack of optimism is appealing, in a way, and persuasive because it asks us to believe in nothing which is hard to believe. The lack of any subscription to the martial virtues is striking: Fuller is frankly longing for peace and not concerned with the military efficiency of himself or his colleagues. Fuller is much more interested in the decline of the bourgeois world than in the overthrow of the Third Reich. The centre of the book is thus the family from which he is separated—the notion of happiness within the family circle, as a prolonged love affair, from which he is cut off by a miscarriage of history. The most powerful poems are the ones where the pattern of the poem is complex enough for us to get a real glimpse of this happiness, despite the labyrinths of historical contingency, of literary "plot", which constantly separate him from his desire. The poems are thus domestic in focus—but not anecdotal. The engines which bring about frustration are of a scale above what we would call anecdotal.

The treatment of the scenery, the human arrangements, which surround this sailor is Kafkaesque—or surrealist, if you like, or alienated. The scenery arranges itself into a parody of a pattern through which a journey is visible, so that by following signs you could travel to where you want to be: it is full of roads which lead nowhere and staircases which lead backwards. The poems are full of material details, giving them a considerable weight and authenticity, but they are not documentary because the poet is not interested in the possibility of us acquiring knowledge of how the social machine, or two or three of the social machines, work. The aesthetic power of the poems is evidently limited by this frustration and disenchantment; the poet is not willing to waste much energy on life in this state of society. The book is obviously only a prelude—its value was not going to emerge into plain sight until the main process had occurred and life could be lived to the full. The atmosphere is also like that of a thriller—in which the protagonists wake from a recurring nightmare to encounter menacing, urban, and yet baffling situations. Physical danger is present throughout these poems, and the hint of an international criminal conspiracy directing the bombs is literally correct. We could hardly miss the emotional pulses of a genre we see so often on screen—since we pay for the cinema tickets we must enjoy the sight of these prominently unenjoyable escapes and adventures. We are being shown the United Kingdom as a kind of small town whose corrupt administration will be brought down and "cleaned up" if the trench-coated hero can evade death for three more days.

The question then was what Fuller would make of a post-war world in which the Communist Republic he obviously hoped for failed to materialise and in which bourgeois society simply continued on its way. Since he never reversed front and proclaimed his enthusiasm for the Welfare State, or for a market economy where the ownership of capital was the decisive thing, his condition of numb vigilance could hardly persist undamaged over three decades in which the thing he was vigilant for failed to arrive. The disappearance of the element of danger gutted his wartime style with its urgency and sophisticated no-saying. In fact, the question is why his heartfelt lack of enthusiasm for daily life in bourgeois society or for the role of the alienated artist did not show up, in the literary world of the 1950s and 1960s, as deviant and pessimistic: the explanation, embarrassingly enough, is that the other poets who were not cocooned by alienation still lacked enthusiasm *either* for the fabric of daily life *or* for the rich private worlds of art *or* for the possibility of social transformation. Even those who did not have Marxist objections to the way British society worked were no more enthusiastic than Fuller: a huge reservoir of inhibition and cynicism and indifference seemed to dominate British poetry and be its only supply of juice. It would be convenient to define this dreariness as the empty space once the belief in a golden Marxist future had faded, but the evidential basis for this is poor and we could just as well conclude that poets produced dismal sounds because they were all imitating an invested and official dismalness. Perhaps Fuller had the more local problem that he was a clever Auden imitator and after 1939 Auden gave up the Marxism and became more interested in consumption, status, and trivial details of his own personality.

We are fortunate to have an example of where Fuller took this problem, in the 1973 volume *Tiny Tears*. This in fact is the type volume for the genre of domestic anecdote. It is not true that all the poems are domestic—they cover a narrow range of themes which do include trips outside the home. "Domestic" is a code-word for something more subjective, like "banal" or "confined". Looking at the title poem, with its astounding weaving of images, makes one reflect that the key to the volume is indifference—most of the poems could simply be thrown away. In 'Tiny Tears' we hear about an ammonite fossil, trapped in layers of crumbling cliff (perhaps at Lyme Regis):

> Pathetic souvenir of a fatal
> Visit, to a world, to the mothering sphere—
>
> Which eternally receives coolly her
> Offspring, who to live have enclosed her wet
> Saltness in membranes of varied splendour
> And complication, truly analogous
> To polythene

and then goes on to discuss a doll made of polythene which has the capacity to urinate (there is a Chuck Berry song which mentions a similar doll) and is called Tiny Tears. The theme is the origin of life in salt water. A passage about Aphrodite, said to have been born from the waves, links our drives to the archaic rules of reproduction. Finally a perverse passage shows the hard (inedible) plastic parts of dolls as part of the detritus on the sea-shore, strewed organs recalling the origin of life in the sea. The whole thing is sarcastic, fluid, paradoxically twisting, archetypal. It also reminds me of the jetsam in an excellent poem, 'November 1941' from his wartime book. Fuller's relationship to his expected audience is close, but the passage of time seems to have emptied it out: there is no longer anything to say. Most of them could probably write similar poems. The frequency with which he remarks on how pointless his poems are makes this almost a trademark of the genre. The expectation of a new society has faded. The anxiety which made every image of his older poems burn has muted into numbness. He addresses a poem to Auden as if Auden's creative ability hadn't vanished years before—as if it were still 1941. I am proposing this book as the type site for the term domestic anecdote and a whole era of inhibited and ineffective poetry by educated people. Especially, the poem 'Georgics'—

> No use to comfort my ordinariness:
> All is a projection from domesticity [.]

He features here as the type site because these poems are slight, pessimistic, set in a situation without offering insight into why it started or how it could end, lack passion, have the figure of the poet everywhere, do not make that figure dramatic or interesting, persistently talk about the garden and routine family events, avoid originality in language, have little interest in political change or the future, have cultured trappings, and frequently describe how insignificant this poetry, or any poetry, is. Other books which share these features are the ones we mean when we talk about the poetry of domestic anecdote. Having said all this, the 81 pages of *Tiny Tears* include a lot of material which does not fit inside this category, and which at least shows the possibility of an exit from a dully unbearable artistic fix.

A surprising poem ('Georgics') says that the passions of the socially powerful are not ennobled by the scope of that power—we might expect this to justify "a fanfare for the common man", or something like that, but the construction appears to be that once society has become egalitarian then poetry too becomes flat and gives up. Really he would do better if he were an orthodox Marxist. A poem to two dead friends (Swingler and Rawsthorne), respectively poet and composer, fails to record the fact that both were communists and that this was presumably part of the shared friendship. This is truly a reduction—I suppose the audience for the book would have been bored by the communism, but its absence is almost frightening. This poem ends up with an attack on modernity in the arts. Fuller doesn't want to remember the past and is afraid of the future.

Auden, who had a more deliberate view of the diminution of scale and impact, was from perhaps 1940 following a personalist line, a branch of Christian thought rather than Marxist. It is easy to believe that goodness is disseminated through a million washing machines, that goods are goodness indeed. It is very easy to justify the idea that the goodness of a society is not in the souls of a few dozen politicians or bishops but *disseminated at cellular level* among millions of good individuals whose right decisions produce a moral fabric where children can flourish and security and comfort can flourish. Enemies of this idea have to pass through the dark and narrow passage where you say, families don't work, fathers can't father, mothers can't be mothers, sisters can't be sisters, teachers can't teach, prosperity is bad for you, etc. etc. and generally dwell in the wilderness with the squirrels. You could write about relations within a middle-class family and still capture something momentous happening. The problem of writing interesting poems about ordinary people is related to a problem in writing history. When someone titles a book "Louis XIV and twenty million French people", the point that everyone matters is made so forcefully that there is no point denying it. Everything is history—so what can you really write about. We avoid the powerful to find the typical, and to write tediously about them. Pierre Goubert's book came out in 1966 reflecting a shift of attitude among historians which dates to the 1940s—poetry was coming late to the feast. A basic issue is how you deal with a town with no important buildings, a suburb with all its small status symbols, its endless flat symmetry, its modularity. You can never go anywhere. The Second World War, with its heroic narrative filling every horizon, hid this problem.

If we can do without ideas, speculation and grand narratives, we can very well do without books. Is it all like an eighty foot wide bowl filled with rainwater and old newsprint? or can we find some domestic poetry that reaches the status of art? The merit of the basic product is in doubt. The political argument is quite convincing. The artistic argument is deeply unconvincing and is not frequently sustained by the very large numbers of poems written inside this style—which is now unfashionable.

We have to glance at the future arrival of feminism, which also treated events within individual families as the great events of history. It posed itself in one guise as an attack on male heads of family, men as moral authorities, and not least on men as poets. It is conspicuous that such powerful currents of poetry as academic existentialism were already aimed at reducing the position of these male figures, from within the corps as it were. The tactic of domestic anecdote was supposed to cut poetry down to a small scale, to an art of the real. A glance at social history shows the rise in the prosperity and claim to equality of women already in the 1950s, long before large numbers of women poets made their presence felt. No doubt the dislike, between say 1950 and 1970, of any form of self-projection or self-aggrandisement in poetic expression was connected with this weakening of male authority and superiority. It shows up the fact that the academic line was *also* a way of attacking and undermining rivals—constraining them to stay within the suburban grind. Perhaps this whole line is not the expression of any egalitarian ideals but of a suburban status competition which has been so successful as to destroy anything which could impress.

This White Goods poetry is related to a new kind of history which was interested in the details of ordinary people's lives and in structures which changed little over a long period. All this social history was a loss of interest in the State. An example of the renewed interest in the existence of obscure and uninfluential people is a volume by Brian Jones. *Family Album* (originally 1968) immerses hopelessly in domestic anecdote and yet expands it by going back into Jones' family history as if several generations of the ordinary could become extraordinary by cumulation—destroying its supporting or restraining structures. This aspiration to the history of the banal does actually relate to the Marxism which Fuller came out of and the departure of which tinged his late poetry so much. The important people are being disqualified as the rightful subject of important poetry. The chronicler is expressing a view of his noble patrons by returning his fee and chucking them out of the poem. But what is to replace them? We seem to be looking at an endless series of wrong answers.

This alliance with new history, at its most compelling in Braudel and the *Annales* school, is not a guarantee of being artistically interesting. The idea of replacing events with structures involves a kind of symbolic camera that takes five years to make an exposure. Situations we are in involve us because we see them over hundreds of days. This slow build-up is known to work in novels and TV series. Poetry has not got that leisure. It must mutate into flash experiences that instantly lock you in. We are looking at poems that say this texture may be tedious but if for 300 pages you will identify with me and persist with the other characters, it will become significant. I am just saying: *this is boring right here right now and I am leaving here and now.* Poets need a theory of time that suits poetry; Jones seems to have fundamentally misunderstood something.

Andrew Crozier has cruelly summed this line up as the poetry of domestic anecdote. This verdict will stand. Much of this poetry is soggy and undistinguished. A significant point about Jones' poem is that it is all written in the present, as if it were a camera looking past a scene. This is a new feature of the 1960s. The organised knowledge which Jones jettisons is part of education and literate culture, and his book is about a working-class family. Another point is that there are poems in Jones' 1966 volume *Poems* which tell the same stories much more effectively—*Family Album* is apparently something more aggressive and larger scale but it is inhibited by his sense of guilt, it is too slow, and its impact is slight. So after tedious poems about middle class domesticity we move on to Jones' poems about working class domesticity and discover that no real advance is visible. Important pressure groups have, since 1968, urged poetry to go down this route of describing the lives of the poor and inarticulate, irrespective of the merits of the product.

Something which sedulously accepts the prevailing social ideas of what is realistic, real, and credible faces a charge of being unnecessary: what we expect is all we can possibly hear from it. Someone who eliminates fantasy and even imagination as derelictions of duty and then proposes to write *poetry* on this basis is likely to be forgotten by history *more thoroughly than a passing fantasy.*

There is a dirty little secret—that domestic anecdote came on stage in the '50s and spread remorselessly in the '60s and that when feminist poetry came along, after a few false starts, its belief that "the personal is political" found artistic form in a current of domestic anecdote which could not enrich the poetic repertoire by adding what was already there. In this grey flow of tiresomely concrete detail, the artistic achievement was left up to a few intellectuals whose ability to reflect a revolutionary creed and original states of mind was seen in startling and alien language. So runs the legend, for most people I know. Can we outrun it?

The older poems of merely domestic scope had as the loudest component of their message the argument that the (male) author was morally fit. The concrete implication of this was that he was fit to occupy social roles, certainly including roles of teacher, moral adviser, husband, and father. These were monologues which showed females in silent complementary roles as pupil, moral ward, wife and daughter. There is a moment of referral to this—George MacBeth says in a review of a book by David Holbrook: "His best poems tend to present an etching of himself as the virile paterfamilias [...] This is a pretty common attitude among the potent young domestics of the early sixties. What about Anthony Thwaite and Peter Redgrove?" (*London Magazine*, April 1961, p.81) The word *tough* turns out to mean *stiff* and this means *virile*. Wives (and daughters) were already there inside the poem, and so feminism was already there *without a voice*; when the voice arrived, it produced feminist poetry. Saying at first, *o no I'm not.* The monologue is broken open by adding a second voice raising doubts. Dom An is continued by non-theoretical feminists, so feminism did not close the landscape but stayed essentially within inherited confines. This account implies a continuity in English poetry since the 1950s which expels the poetry of the underground as an alternative, artistically superior to be sure, which failed to consolidate its grip on the territory.

The early stages of the feminist movement in Britain were integrally tied to the New Left and were quite clearly Marxist-feminist. The liberation of women was expected to follow from the collapse of corporate power and the rich, and could not come first; the expectations of dominance held by the male leaders of the radical Left were the particular sound which outraged these feminists. After the revolution, they felt, there should not be a system in which women were thoroughly offstage because the glamour of male revolutionaries/ warriors had won undying gratitude (viz. *submissiveness*) in fighting for the revolution (like Yugoslavia after 1945). Examples of feminism as a form of radical exploration in poetry are Denise Riley, Grace Lake, and Maggie O'Sullivan. Feminist poetry gets going in the mid '70s, although the individual volumes are few enough to count. Brian Jones is again a part of the transition. Much of his volume, *Interior*, is about marriage. The sequence is written in the wife's voice (but still *written* by the man) and the man is seen as the manager of what happens. The title refers obliquely to a Dutch still life, a genre of painting which is already about domestic and non-noble subjects, and can be seen as an anticipation (or justification?) of domestic anecdote in the 1960s. This is pre-feminist poetry by a man. It seems alien now because things changed so fast afterwards, but it is closer to the new thing than the academic existentialism we have been talking about.

The 1970s were taken up with shared theoretical shifts which are bewildering in their number and rapidity. A revolutionary process dissolved the original positions of revolutionary intent. From a starting-point which placed Marx and Freud as patron saints in a campaign to change the bases of the economy and of personal life, the movement then rather thoroughly unseated those characters, with their patriarchal assumptions, schematism, and authoritarian attitude to knowledge, to debouch into a great delta of modern revolutionary attitudes. The notion of a small party which seized control of the State in a moment of crisis was refuted in favour of change at the roots with (more or less) everyone participating. The Anglo-Leninist cadres who had provoked the original crisis of self-definition were rather thoroughly reduced to insignificance. As an unemployed ruling elite they were seen as all too similar to the ruling elite in post. The military metaphor of the Leninist redemption myth was deprived of force, bringing more traditionally female virtues to centre stage and allowing a real alliance with pacifism—another mass movement. The image of a state-owning group imposing revolution from above on a large mass of defeated and sullen conservatives (clinging to male supremacy, capitalism, militarism, imperialism) and effectively making war on its own people via the State apparatus, was replaced with a notion of peaceful, irreversible change to structures of feeling, of custom, and of moral perception. This corresponded to processes of *longue durée* as recovered by *Annales* type historians.

These proposed changes were going to be slow, local, and undramatic, but irreversible. In the context of Conservative dominance of politics during the '80s and '90s, the movement gave up most of the anti-capitalist project and absorbed conservative feminist elements to the point of being taken over (or, just beyond?). Another way of putting this is that the gap between Leninism and Christianity was largely traversed—the radical dislike of the State was not a new thing on the English Left.

What seems to have happened with all this is a move within women's poetry from experimentalism to casual egocentricity (a form of cultural modesty?). The radius of the poem is startlingly decreased. Expectations of radical political change are made slender to the point of vanishing. The idea that the personal is political can be rewritten to say that a poem should be a domestic anecdote. The egocentric plan is presented as the fruit of a revolution. Collectivism, and the exploration of a mysterious future, and theorising, disappear. Individualism, with a charge of consumerism, is presented, within the limits of domestic anecdote, with a notion of linguistic realism which inhibits any novelty. Representing a personality is felt to be enough. This poetry is written in bulk. Whereas poetry of the feminist-Marxist stage had a strong flavour of not being domestic life as lived, but rather something risky, insecure, steeped in theory, driven by the will, this later poetry was quite the reverse—the impression of realism and ponderous self-certainty was quite oppressive. This is a new type of m-stream which is vaguely feminist but also domestic and self-aggrandizing rather than political. The change from a previous generation is that the poets are not identified with academic existentialism.

An example of the transitional stage is a 1982 volume, *Touch Papers*, subtitled 'three women poets', who are Michèle Roberts, Judith Kazantzis, and Michelene Wandor. This was published by Allison and Busby, who at the time had a certain association with communist politics and did not publish poetry unless there was an agitprop angle to it. The packaging does not include the word "feminist" but the biological sign for "female" is on the front cover with a lit touchpaper beneath it. All three poets were quite prominent in feminist journalism at the time, writing for *Spare Rib* or *City Limits* for example, and in fact a note by Wandor on the last page of text says "[…] our poetry is in motion in two senses. First, we are all feminists". The title overtly refers to the fuses of rockets—light the blue touch paper— which would cast the poems as tinder to light the fire under perishing patriarchy, but we are supposed to look for double meanings and this phrase may also refer to touching—touching the reader, perhaps, or even "a woman's touch" as in the song sung by Doris Day in *Calamity Jane*. Wandor and Roberts edited the pamphlet *Cutlass and Earrings* (1976), the first British feminist poetry anthology I have been able to locate. "Second, we are all poets for whom the usage of language and imagery in poetry is a primary concern." This draws attention to critical weaknesses of the poems. Wandor refers to a file she keeps labelled "Poetry in Motion", which is the title of a song by Johnny Tillotson about watching his girlfriend walk—she is "poetry in motion". This is one of the great songs of the era (around 1960) but it is very sexist. Wandor's jokey approach limits the impact of her moral protest. She offers a poem called 'Office Party' which is not in fact domestic in subject but which could be put in a dictionary as an example of banality and loss of ambition. She editorialises on the need to make the poetry accessible, while implying that she has the treasure of literary capital which demands aspiration and self-sacrifice, but it is very hard to agree with her about this. This poetry is not a thrilling exit from the mid-century decline of British poetry, it is clearly part of that decline and falls under the same strictures.

Two of the poems are about films and make as if to uncover unconscious structures of fantasy which direct the films and which seem ridiculous to the poet. These are very similar to the kind of film reviews which were appearing, in 1982, every week in *City Limits* (where Roberts worked) and *Time Out* (where Wandor worked). The poems are developments of defacing posters, taken as "ideology made visible". The problem with these is that the films offer highly wrought subjectivity which the poets are ticking off and reducing to order. The idea that in the film *Earthquake* the emotional behaviour of the Ava Gardner character is the cause of the geological earthquake which comes later in the film is rewarding, and it does offer an example of fantasy becoming ideology, which would license new fantasy within which to reconstruct social norms—but it says No to the imagination and is also, in Kazantzis' poem, unpersuasive. Roberts' poem on Nic Roeg's film *Walkabout* is more tentative but still underlines the fact that the poems are obviously miniature in scale and do not have the complexity of meaning and the engulfing depth of the films. While these are not interesting poems, Roberts does a lot better, and comes a lot closer to intense first-person experience. Kazantzis then supplies political poems which link the personal to affairs of state and to foreign policy and transcend the anecdotal altogether.

The change in the civil and economic status of women over the last 40 years is a project of a magnitude comparable to the industrial revolution or the Second World War. It is a decentralised change and lacks monumental or photogenic symbols of its intensity or success. So many million ants can build, together, a huge building, but it is easy to end up with a picture of an ant carrying a crumb and looking like nothing very much. Roberts' poem 'to a male intellectual' illustrates the problem: the sociological classification implicit in the title deprives the poem of reality and reduces the actual person to a symbol, yet at the same time gives the poem a heroic capacity to be generalised, a door onto the place where the rules are kept. The depersonalisation carries it out of the anecdotal and tedious realm. Basically he gets contradicted but we don't find out what he said.

This poetry often stays within the bounds of anecdote because it is unwilling to get into politics. The desire to be glib and pacy overwhelms the interest in staging and resolving problems. There is such a thing as throwing away the poem to avoid giving it weight: *you're too thin to be a feminist poem*. It is hard to see poems about a female protagonist moving through the world of journalism in North London as political. The concept patriarchy is no more substantial or true to everyday life than the thinning abstraction of "a male intellectual". I can see that there is a problem finding patriarchy, given its hegemonic, deeply instituted, and internalised status, but surely that is what political poets have to do: make power visible, make its end palpable. *Touch Papers* still has the sound of classical Left poetry but is visibly on the path towards a poetry where the female protagonist writes about her shopping feats.

These poems suffer from the absence of a villain. I saw a slow film about gay politics in San Francisco which became exciting when Anita Bryant popped up and gave us a good quality villain. Roberts' admission of having fallen for deceit raises the spectre that the only poets who were willing to write convincingly about the internalisation of norms that humiliate you were ones who did not want the political status which the appearance of coolness, intelligence and control bestows. That is, that the didactic role, with its not easily avoidable currents of smugness and routine, is like being a public official and incompatible with writing about bad experiences or at least deep bad experiences. But other kinds of experience do not carry a burden of evidence tending to prove feminism right. The said journalists led rather pleasant lives and were no doubt going out with (male) left-wing intellectuals also involved in academia or radical journalism, possibly the media. They were "new men" and for that reason only second-rate villains. They may not have been the world's nicest people, but journalists sauntering between Upper Street and Clerkenwell are not victims like 18-year-olds in Hackney. If you aren't deceived, where is your oppression?

Show me your oppression. I was trying to think of monumental canvases for feminism, to avoid the "ant with crumb" problem. Maybe the strike of the match girls at Bryant and May in around 1900? Or a fire in a firetrap factory at around the same time—a female workforce trapped out of reach of ladders. Since 1976 or so any image of a nuclear submarine or of the installations which support nuclear missiles has had a latent feminist cover text silently imprinted on it. These could be feminist monuments—plans of *destroyed cities*. Kazantzis' poem 'Progenitor 1979' takes the domestic and makes it a symbol of the life we are not going to lead if the Cold War gets hot. This is no longer anecdotal.

> I was born in war
> a day the pilots burnt and rampaged in mid-air.
>
> February 1979. Among other flourishes,
> other border wars, China invades Vietnam.
> the newscaster essays casually,
> seriously. Will the Chinese

use tactical nuclear
if so will the Russians, and if so.
One week.
Winter halts in our streets.

February '79. I was born in war
and grew up ignorant.

She has found the way to write about international politics in a personal and emotional way. This recalls Fuller's '40s poems—he was missing family life and this is his way of expressing why war is bad. Writing about longing for home is a way of making an emotional attack on militarism, agreed to be the core value of Nazism. Kazantzis writes about imminent danger which, at the moment of Reagan abandoning detente and launching the so-called Second Cold War, around 1982, was present and pervasive. The progenitor is the bomb: "We didn't know we had a third parent/a godfather at every baby's christening,/ henceforth; a progenitor." The poem stretches to about 300 lines and covers a big slice of contemporary foreign affairs without losing the solidity of daily experience.

Suppose we accept that domestic anecdote is a necessary mode. The problem then is how could it possibly work. How do you get the mundane to glow and become significant? with its overload of sensory data and rules.

Reality is much more involving than it seems in literature. The confessional mode is evidently one way in which domestic life can become dramatic, as relationships within the family emerge as tense, damaged, and perverse even though they are monumental within the life of one individual. It may be forgotten today, but was well known in the 1960s, that Alvarez had proclaimed (in a Penguin anthology) that confessional poetry was the future for Britain and that the extremes of neurosis were where modern art had to happen. (J.G. Ballard, now accepted as a classic, accepted this view of the imperative to go to the border. Alvarez's friends Plath and Hughes also bear out his theory— which works for very few other poets.) The rejection of the confessional mode in favour of the disengaged and moralising is accepted to be the story for Britain. The category of "confessional poetry" is very nearly empty. Where the domestic becomes pathological it also becomes material for high drama (this was the basis for much Gothic literature, and this line has tended to have recourse to Gothic schemas).

One simple way of describing the expansion of British poetry after 1960 is the arrival of archaeology and anthropology as subjects. Both of these are prominently to do with the structures of everyday life and with ordinary people—not with the State and the State elite. Archaeology, where human agents are silent, is a way of *making the homestead the hero of the story*, where examination of huts and household equipment allows us to reach out to revolutionary changes and to engage with highflying speculation and with the testing of complex ideas. They would expose the household of the 1960s, or even the 1980s, as the product of complex historical processes, something which reveals long spans of time and which may be very unstable. Archaeology in fact was the equivalent in the past of what revolution promised for the future: Marxism wanted to show the instability of currently normal arrangements, archaeology showed them as unknown in the deep past and even as the product of domestic revolutions in the untraced past. So many times in this work I have talked about when structure becomes narrative. Domestic drama is more interesting than domestic anecdote; structural change is more significant than personal crises which rarely resolve anything.

Underneath the Literary

Outsider Poetry

Why are you not a fish or a frog? The elemental vertebrate genetic material is still in your cells, but it is directed by a program which is in a complex way negative, it sorts and eliminates almost all the possibilities for tissues and proportions. In poetry, too, the knowledge of the expert is of what is impossible—narrative, verse drama, metre, are the easiest blocks to define. The injunctions cover a vast territory, it seems. The slight shifts in them help to date a poem, and their dissemination points to an invisible crowd of Cultured Opinion. The substream certainly includes poets who ignore those blocks and so includes a wider range of stylistic possibilities than the mainstream. We can compare it to the unconscious, which contains everything, is prepersonal, and escapes attention. Most of it escapes my attention, too.

The selectiveness has also to do with the avoidance of ambiguity: a poem avoids prosaic self-evidence but is completely clear to someone trained in modern poetry (not necessarily to all those who try to read poetry). The restraint can go too far. Unsuccessful poetry may have the buoyant quality we associate with naive paintings or the art of children. It is good that there are people who think they can write in the manner of Shakespeare or Blake or Tennyson or Prynne, and others who think they can write about galleons, dreadnoughts, luggers, flags, pennants, and billowing canvas, too.

The possibilities for amateur poetry would seem to be (a) that there is a great fund of optimism and innocence which gives rise to something like naive painting, unrestrained by the cynicism of the educated; (b) that amateur poetry is essentially like "official" poetry except for the greater commitment of official poets, and in fact is mainly written by educated people who don't read poetry all the time. There is a variant, (c), that unpublished poets are dominated by literary conventions but are out of date in what they take as binding artistic rules and are repeating effects worn out in a previous era. My vote goes for variant (b). The "accepted" poetry is a thorough mixture and if you try to separate it out stylistically you find that it includes poets who can write naively and successfully, such as George Mackay Brown, and that elements of the naive, the infantile, the folky, are deployed by a very wide range of the poets who get mainstream visibility. In the avant-garde, the recursion to the infantile, the unconscious, and to folk modes is quite central. I would argue that status is attached to poets who have given pleasure and who are familiar on the scene, rather than to particular registers of language or conducts of artistic ornament.

The idea of a reservoir beneath our feet was tapped into by the Festival of Britain. Along with so many other examples of the obscure, eccentric, and charming, they drilled for the wellspring of amateur poets, using the simple method of offering a prize for the unknowns. (To be exact the known were only excluded by the need for the poems to be unpublished.) The judges were an awesome battery of old-fashioned taste and connoisseurship. The scripts were either a long poem or a collection of short poems and 2,093 of them rolled in. Most of the scripts have long since been burnt and restored to the Elements. However, John Hayward's emotive summary survives: "There was [...] a great deal of very bad verse, ranging in ineptitude from the expanded cracker-motto to grandiloquent failure to imitate *Paradise Lost*. There were the great Imperial sagas from the first week of the Creation to VE Day; the sacred oratorios and the patriotic hymns; the epics of rural life and odes to British Industry. There were the oddities which relieved the monotony of the judges' task—poems written on cardboard, or in coloured chalks, or on scraps of paper, or in block capitals; poems engrossed on vellum with illuminated capitals, or with calligraphic title-pages, and bound with loving care, complete with leather thongs or silk ties. There were the eccentrics and the moonstruck, bemused and halting followers of Blake and Smart, with their obscure cosmic visions and their fearful prophecies of imminent damnations underscored in blood-red ink. And above all, there was the vast chorus of those content to chant in monotonous unison the joys of love and springtime, with special emphasis on bird-song at morning and starshine at night." Hayward sounds a bit battered. Maybe there is no wonderful reservoir of bashfully authentic naive poetry? He observes that the entries showed a remarkable lack of response to the prestige of Hopkins, Eliot and Yeats: "Their sources, if any, would seem to have been [...] entirely of nineteenth century origin, and principally of the Romantic period."

The Hid Cisterns of Eternity, or, The Naïve Sublime

It is a strange thing that there is no equivalent in poetry of *outsider art*. By this I mean the gaudy and uninstructed art which is represented in the paintings of Henri "Douanier" Rousseau and the buildings of le facteur Cheval, or which is shown in Oto Bihalji-Merin's *Primitive Artists of Yugoslavia*. This art is a compelling example of artists untouched by urban opinions moving into the empty spectrum of visual possibilities. It is much more interesting to think about than to look at. The talents it draws on are the mentally ill, the untaught and unreachable, children, and artists from colonised societies with (supposedly) no access to lessons in anatomy and perspective. Exposure to quantities of such art, for example by regularly reading the specialist publication *Raw Art* (translation of Jean Dubuffet's phrase *Art Brut*) produces total disillusion.

The two countries most associated with the movement are Switzerland and Yugoslavia. We do not normally associate the cultures of these two countries, but after all they are in close proximity and share the Alps. Both regions share the massive strength of peasant culture, conditioned by the weakness or absence of a nobility. Bihalji mentions the influence of Austrian painting on glass on Yugoslavian peasant painting, which often uses glass. Slovenia and Croatia will have drawn on the Catholic visual culture which was available at village level in Bavaria and Austria. This whole area has a great fascination which, due to profound ignorance, I am quite unable to explore.

I am going to wheel on a completely wonderful book of which I am very fond: *Visionäre Schweiz* (Visionary Switzerland), by the great exhibition organiser Harald Szeemann. Szeemann's father was Hungarian, and I think the name is pronounced zeemann. He produces numerous Swiss visual artists whose methods were naïve and whose message was optimistic, humanitarian and idealistic. They do not have any element of close psychological observation and character recording, but are vague and focussed on an allegorical no-place where everyone is noble and benign. He tells us that Armand Schulthess bought two plots of unproductive land and then devoted his life to writing down items of knowledge, in a careful block script, and pinning them to tree trunks, branches, walls, fences in these plots. "Schulthess covered thousands of sheets of tin, cardboard or carton paper with knowledge in the form of headwords, tables, references to books in many areas: physics, chemistry, economics, history, astrology, psychology, cybernetics [.]" There was a curatorial problem with the inscriptions, especially as his family were embarrassed after his death about his eccentricity, and tried to destroy the groves—or "installations" as new jargon would have it. The project, titled 'Encyclopaedia in the woods', has exactly the same design as the *Encyclopédie* and is inevitably connected with the Enlightenment and its whole apparatus of liberation through knowledge; but Schulthess was working between 1951 and 1972. Of Werner Hertig we read that "Via a coordinate system developed by himself Werner Hertig locates, temporally differentiated according to the position of the sun, stars, seasons and times of day, the various influences of cosmic rays on the terrestrial ones, which in their joint effects announce places which cause sickness, future earthquakes, and volcanic eruptions." His graphics are extraordinarily complex and symmetrical diagrams seemingly drawn by a rotary program rather than by a human hand. The use of a pendulum was basic to his ability to tap these rays. A common urge among these visionaries is to shatter the bounds of a two-dimensional discrete (and commodifiable) visual object and to create a sacred space, willingly extending out into other forms, such as music and language. This is hardly separable from the wish to create an ideal society and to live in it, and at this point we realise that the impulses which created the Red Cross and the League of Nations in Switzerland were parallel to these visions. Johann Michael Bossard (1874–1950) created a *Kunststäthe*, a complex of buildings surrounded by a sculpture garden. This wish to expand the merely symbolic space of art into a robust, three dimensional, external space, was not uncommon in that period. I view it as integral to late Symbolism, the last decades of the 19th century, but evidently the building at Dornach dates to around 1910 and the impulse to erect these buildings was slow to stop, may in fact be still persisting. Bossard was born in Zug, Switzerland, but worked in Hamburg as a teacher of sculpture and built his *Gesamtkunstwerk* on the Lüneburg Heath, in Hanover. "The more a man grows upwards, the smaller his earthly home becomes, but the larger his home of ideas..." He was not a "naïf" but an academic with public acknowledgement. He designed the buildings of his complex himself, in an idiom based on North German farmhouses (and now referred to as "North German brick Expressionism"), designed the glass and furniture in them, and painted the cycle of murals himself. See http://www.bossard.de/ for some pictures of his cult site. The saga of the Volsungs, the *Bhagavad-Gita*, the Silesian mystic Jakob Boehme, were important to him. He dedicated painted rooms notably to the Edda, to Eros, and to Orpheus. Bossard was one-eyed and identified himself with Odin, who in the Edda gives an eye to Mimir in exchange for knowledge.

I found Szeemann unbearably exciting. Obviously I wanted to find something similar that I could write about. I was wondering why there were no outsider poets in Britain and then, possibly in a momentary lapse of reason, I decided that we could grandiosely relabel religious epics by J Redwood Anderson and Sir William Watson as comparable to the idealistic extravaganzas of Szeemann's book. They stand on a mountain with a plateau where everything is noble and visible.

John Redwood Anderson published a triptych of three volumes in 1946–7: *Approach, Fugue of Time, The Ascent.* I have not located a copy of the third. His cover note says "The Triptych consists of three volumes (...) The first deals with the approach of the soul to God by each of the three traditional paths: that of mystical love ('Radha'), that of action ('Heracles') and that of Thought ('Odin'). [...] The *Fugue of Time* is an imaginative presentation of the World-Process seen, as it were, from the inside: that is, as the self-realization of the Divine Activity and the content of the Divine Experience. The treatment is, in part, symbolical[.]" Almost the whole set is a dialogue between gods. It is couched throughout in a kind of Inane Sublime. It is a stream *from the hid cisterns of Eternity.* It is set "in this tumultuous being that, face to face,/ kisses its challenge, and passes, and cries *Ahoy!*" In 'Odin', Thor returns from killing someone called Hrungnir, as part of the eternal struggle of good and evil—much as in Watson. The lead character, Odin, chief of the Norse gods, "mood-rapt in foreboded futures", makes a speech to Thor and then goes on a journey where he meets Mimir, who embodies the memory of everything that has happened in the world (name cognate with memory), who directs him to an older, even less personal figure, Ymir, an ice giant from whose body the world was made. They engage in long solemn speeches. The bit with Ymir is almost good, as we see Odin's mind collapsing, ego projections vanishing and the landscape disintegrating to a featureless, blasted waste as he does so. Anderson adds to the inevitable vantage point from which everything in the cosmos is visible ("rock-towered above the orbic scope of sense") an interest in the dissolution of knowledge as it is proved to be projective. He derives partly from German idealist philosophy (which itself had absorbed Buddhism in a refracted form). The poems seem to fit almost perfectly into the visual world of Bossard.

I am claiming that these highly educated and successful men were writing as quasi-primitives. I have to concede that they go back to an era of late Symbolism or the realms of Tennyson and Henry Irving, that they were writing in around 1914 and are nothing like an instance of outsider poets from our own period.

Anderson (1883 to 1964) had most of his books published by Oxford University Press, so someone thought he was significant and official. Watson had the insight to write a panegyric to Lloyd George at the height of the Great War and got a baronetcy for his pains. These were not peasant outsiders. I have an uneasy feeling that Szeemann's outsiders are different from cultured artists because they are reproducing modules which came from the cultured world but which had fallen out of fashion. We have mentioned the Irving/Faust style which was used by Stephen Phillips and Watson among others. We see this habit of conferring with the great figures of history and piercing the secrets of destiny as naive because of a shift of perspective: these privileges belonged to the high art of a particular period of time and while high art has moved on the naïve have loyally persisted with the beloved pattern.

The rejection of idealistic and boundless casts of writing in favour of empirical pessimism, suburban realism, or light verse is both a sign of austerity and a renunciation of literary power.

There is something abidingly attractive about Szeemann's artists— not only the willingness to spend their lives imagining beauty but the cheerfulness with which they swing into their favourite creative activity, the belief in wholeness which fills every corner of their consecrated spaces. Anderson and Watson are not only outside my period but also utterly terrible poets and not worthy of our interest. Their style seems to have hit a chronological expiry zone, as the examples Hayward fabulously cites, the "great Imperial sagas from the first week of the

Creation to VE Day" do not exist in the period I am looking at. So to sum up I have a vivid idea of the Naïve Sublime but I can't actually give any examples of it. Taking a certain leap in the lurch, we can name Marxism as the survivor of bombastic high-calorie 19th-century German idealism and look for the grandiose and World-Historical in relict form in the variants of Marxism which were florid in the '60s and 70s. Maybe we can see Randall Swingler's pompous and quasi-religious poem of about 1957 ("'Come ye' said the Bishop, 'to the waters of life/ And they shall be radio-active'"), on the atomic bomb, with its leaning on Blake and allegiance to Marx, as the Naïve Sublime.

Formalism

Eric Homberger, in *Art of the Real*, identifies Formalism as the dominant style in Anglo-American poetry between roughly 1947 and 1961: "By 1962 (in America at least) poetry in the formalist mode seemed a little dated." Anyone using it today would sound like a derivative of that period and not like a voice of their own. This clearly overlaps with other strands, but it has a strong profile simply because it vanished from the scene and so captures the flavour of a time now unfashionable. Formalist means most simply using regular metre and rhyme, including tricky use of syllabics, internal rhymes, ornate and grand rhyme schemes. An example would be this poem by Audrey Beecham:

> The rootless, fastly bound to the rounded earth
> Are dragged by tides and shoulder-glancing moon.
> In childhood they renounce the tarnished spoon
> And dance upon a howling rim of mirth.
> By centrifugal force spinning from birth
> Taunted and driven by a half-learnt tune
> They spill their sands out for the singing dune
> Or wander through uncharted wastes of dearth.
> > (from poem 1 of the 'Sonnets of the Twelfth House' section
> > of *The Coast of Barbary*, 1957)

However, it also carried strong implications of a view of life as something chaotic which has to be mediated by forms, in an ambitious scheme which assigned to law the task of defending against totalitarian forms, Nazi and Communist to be exact. The critique took place at the level of the individual because it was individual persuasion which recruited the dark forces of those anti-democratic parties.

John Holloway's long poem *The Landfallers* (1962) is about a country occupied by British forces where refugees from the Soviet lands turn up after crossing deadly cold mountains and are processed by military bureaucracy. The poem is about 1800 lines long, pentameters each close to ten syllables, rhyming ABABACDCDCDE. The introduction is octosyllabics rhyming AABB to show that it is less serious. The drama of the poem is the responsibility of officers acting as lawyers to decide on the survival of humans who are in the aspect of *cases*. Logically enough he evokes an older Inner Asian bureaucracy which may be in part the origin of Soviet despotism:

> The Mongols had a paper money, dark
> As charcoal biscuits, that they squeezed and snipped
> In varying shapes from Chinese mulberry bark;
> And wrote, at first in borrowed Uighur script,
> The values on it that the Khans decreed;
> Sealing it with their fuming dragon, dipped
> In alizarion crushed from madder seed.
> Right from the rice-plains to the sandy hills
> The couriers bridge with their unfaltering speed,
> Their bodies strung with ropes of ringing bells
> (The music trails all night across the cold,
> Kindling the land-long darkness as it swells)
> That money circulates like solid gold.

Holloway goes on immediately to describe the administration of Charlemagne, with Western Europe trying to start an economy based on literacy, central government, and money. When he describes, a few lines further down "These mute, archaic continuities,/ But constituting and traditional,/ Run about such routine work as his,/ Sustaining lines of life that hold it fast", he makes it very clear that education is there to produce fair bureaucrats and that this is the basis of good government. The convergences are illustrated in the comforting and regulated repetition of the rhyme scheme. This is art which promotes good order and which does not claim to channel chaos. Holloway's ability to process and set out information in this non-personal style is quite extraordinary. This sort of *Eric Ambler novel in verse* was little read at the time.

The political metaphor charging the style is that the *formalities* of the way the State deals with the citizens and the way laws are made defend freedom and so the good society; the restraints of verse stand for the limits to be placed on the power of Parties (and corporations?). This emphasizes the mediating powers of language, standing for the organ of reason which simultaneously reflects other people's wishes and exercises control over our own drives by anticipating those wishes. The overthrow of the style came from poets recognising chaos as fertile, subjective, and accepting, and swimming out into it.

G.S. Fraser's anthology *Poetry Now* of 1956 claimed the best anchorage in the harbour for the new style; his defection from the New Romantic group, of which he was one of the leaders, is especially striking. Homberger lists *The Beautiful Changes* (1947) by Richard Wilbur, and *Heart's Needle* (1959), by W.D. Snodgrass, as significant examples of the genre. Unmentioned but there are *Lord Weary's Castle* (1947) by Robert Lowell and several books by Roy Fuller. This list underlines the fact that the key exponents of the style gave it up and moved on—this reinforces its period flavour. It belongs in a glass case or "special room" of objects redolent of the 1950s. He specifies that this whole way of carrying yourself in poetry belongs to a generation born in the 1920s, which would tie in with my observation that the New Romantics were mostly born between 1908 and 1920. He also mentions *Exiles and Marriages*, by Donald Hall (1955), *Home Truths*, by Anthony Thwaite (1957), *For the Unfallen*, by Geoffrey Hill (1959), *The Colossus* (1960), by Sylvia Plath, *Nude Descending a Staircase* by X.J. Kennedy (1961). Other partisans or victims of the manner would be Donald Davie and Elizabeth Jennings. A significant reoccupation of older poets gathered up Robert Graves and William Empson as elective ancestors; Auden's new poetry of the 1950s, with its preoccupation with metrical cleverness and neatness, is presumably the achievement which most represented the ideals of these younger poets; his editorship (1947 to 1959) of the prestigious book series of Yale Younger Poets put the tangible resources into the links of affection or respect. Edward Brunner's *Cold War Poetry* has an entire chapter on the sestina, which has a fetish value as the hardest verse form. His list of swathes of sestinas in American magazines includes English poets John Holloway and Patrick Anderson.

I should point out that the "twelfth house" is an astrological term glossed by the poet as "The twelfth house signifies secret or private enemies, prisons, captivity, bondage, evil spirits, torments... this is a Cadent falling house". Beecham was part of the New Romantic movement, and her first book did not appear until 1957 partly, we suspect, because of that affinity. Her new guise as a Formalist made the work acceptable. The originality of *The Coast of Barbary* is its extreme negativity, a sense of chaos which brings her close to Plath and Hughes. For example

> In times of death men are compelled to sign
> Their entity in terms of violent sense:
> With melting flesh they strangely recompense
> The dissolution of their life's design.
> Their desolations on the night air whine
> With fear—ammonia sweet—the air is dense
> But they, within a timelessness immense
> Of bounding instant, know themselves divine.
> (from 'Sonnets on the Theme of Love', III)

Thus, sexual activity becomes more reckless and intense in wartime; air raid sirens are a sort of mating call. The sextet then has the newly dead hovering near sexual acts, fascinated. The "melting flesh", an echo of *Hamlet*, signals the literary nature of all this verse. Is the formalism a way of smuggling perverse and highly personal imagery past a Christian censor, or a series of muffles which prevent the poems from a personal impact? I am not sure.

The named poets gave up formalism. The shared language changed—to write *vers libre* is now conventional. My own consciousness post-dates this shift of the shared rules and I cannot relate to rhymed modern poetry except as a chore which I have to work through before something more interesting comes along. Like most people, I was familiar with rhymed poetry and song as a child and there was a perceptible shock when I came across free verse at around 16. I can't make the transition conscious—it was sufficiently total for that.

Regular verse was historically tied to music, but the rule that music has to have a repetitive metre has now collapsed, and perhaps free verse is now supported by the way we hear music. The sixties saw the collapse of a regime, which like other collapses seemed natural as soon as it had happened, so that recovery of the previous position of loyalties and unconscious attitudes seems impossible. In a general way, the end of the formalist style came with the rise of a new subjectivity in which the sound of the poet's voice was felt to be crucial, and *vers libre* was felt to express that; while mediation came to be identified with a wages and incomes policy and sexual repression. I have looked at poets who moved from metrical to free and the artistic nature of their poems did not change a great deal. So I do not want to put free verse at the centre of everything. If it is a revolution it should change everything. Verse lines tend to drift towards an average of eight syllables.

Homberger is a wonderfully sensitive observer of the shared attitudes and projections of poets, the codings of gestures: the coding of formalism in 1956 may be quite different from the coding of regular metre in 1996. The background of English poetry from the 12th century up to the early twentieth involves rhyme and regular metre rather consistently: anyone who reads historic poetry and fails to notice the twentieth century is likely to come out writing with these weapons in 1996 or at any time. If they fail to notice contemporary currents they may be unable to use coding. I am aware that there was a self-conscious movement of New Formalism in the USA in the 1980s, which was rather tightly coupled to neo-conservatism and the roll-back of the libertarian advances of the second third of the century. The recent neo-formalists have badged themselves as populists, with the argument that a wide audience could be reached for poetry only by writing in rhyme and in even lines. Evidently there is a world of people who live with poetry and who legislate for it unconsciously and collectively. They are under attack both from right-wing radicals and from anarchist radicals, and this attack is generally linked to a rejection of the kind of people who teach English Literature, who go to university, who support the permissive society, secularism, and so on.

It is unkind to speak of "retarded" formalism in Scotland and in Welsh. The line defined by Homberger was the property of young university poets in England and the USA, a keen and fashionable lot equipped to dominate and to lead other poets to imitate them. How exactly would we distinguish this lot from people who had simply failed to adapt when the 19th century ended, writing in the manner of hymns and popular songs, indulging their cravings in what we could call *palaeoformalism*? I am unwilling to provide an answer. I do not think that we can identify *cynghanedd* writers in rural Wales with bow-tie wearing sestina writers in Harvard or Oxford. *Continuity* formalism perhaps.

Pop starts: Christopher Logue, *Songs* (1959)

> I came among you in a time of hunger,
> Born at daybreak in a dockyard suburb
> Gunboats like grey scum lay on the water.

In the 1950s, Logue and Barker were the rakehells of English poetry, giving off a hot breath of sexuality which revealed the grey pallor of virtually everything else. A whole new world of sensibility was opened up by forgetting the rules of middle-class exclusiveness and literary propriety. Investigating the gap between song and poetry. Dropping pebbles into that abyss brought the individual back on stage—out of the grey fog of theological and existentialist abstractions. If existentialism did not mean the surfacing of sexual feelings and economic facts into the position of the writer, it did not mean very much. Logue and Barker were perhaps the only authentic poets of the 1950s. Because life is full of contradictions, authenticity also brought up many paradoxes— and the ability to convey psychological conflict was therefore crucial. Producing poems free from conflict did not amount to authenticity. The evolution of Logue (1926–2011) from his first neo-romantic volume towards simple, rhythmically-bound forms parallels the evolution from neo-romanticism to the stilted regularity of The Movement. His model was Brecht's songs; of course Brecht's model was Kipling. *Songs*, full of riddles, drinking songs, sexual puns, and ballads, still contains interesting neo-romantic gestures, as in this story of the training of recruits for a colonial war:

> So twenty weeks went by and by,
> My back was straightened out, my eye
> Dead true as any button shone,
> And nine white-bellied porpoise led
> Our ship of shillings through the sun.
>
> (...)
> And three by three through our curfew,
> Mother we marched like black and tan,
> Singing to match our captain's cheers,

Then I drank my eyes out of my head
And wet Her shilling with my fears.
      ('The Song of the Dead Soldier')

but is also full of committed poems; the playing-card world is by now the whole bourgeois social order, admittedly shaky at that time. (The "shillings" are the recruits, who have taken the Queen's shilling. The war was in Cyprus.) Neither faction—left-wing satirists or The Movement—can have realised that the jingling efficiency of rhyme and stanzaic form was about to be exploited by the new English pop song, drowning them both. Although Logue anticipated almost everything about the 1960s, his recycling of old English folk songs is rather overshadowed by Bob Dylan's. Song, rebellion, lechery, immediacy: this formula was about to be taken up by people whose surnames were Jagger or Morrison. Brechtian populism was outbid and bought up. His natural environment was political cabaret; something which probably reached its peak in the twenties: although he wrote the songs for The Establishment, a satirical nightclub flourishing around 1962.

Our volume is full of the presence of Brecht, Neruda, and Homer—three false moves as far as the Hanging Bishops were concerned. Titles include 'The Song of the Outsider' 'Lord Christopher's Goodnight' 'Drunk as drunk on turpentine' 'The Thief's Story'. Sections include twenty translations from Neruda's first volume, and a substantial extract from Book XXI of the *Iliad* (the combat of Achilles and the Scamander), a translation project that occupied him for the rest of his life. The logical development into narrative verse, capable of depicting a society rather than just a few images, took this form, of a Bronze Age translation. The extended version, a masterpiece, now occupies several volumes. The book does not quite give us lyrical poetry—except as translations from Neruda. Logue dislikes the autobiographical touch; not out of repression, but perhaps out of a dislike for introspection—he prefers action; his irony has a sharp point. Looking at his ballads about patriotic soldiers dying, such as 'The Song of the Imperial Carrion', one is tempted to link his *Iliad* to the irony of his modern-day poetry: the bourgeois hero fulfils social obligations, apparently wins, but finds his real wishes flouted. But the connection is strained. It is but a short step from Logue's ironic dialectic around the slip between purpose and outcome to the structurally discrepant montage effect of the 1960s, which also had an anti-bourgeois tendency at its outset.

The juxtaposition could take three forms: the uncovering of absurd positions (the USA bombs Vietnam to protect it, Wilson's socialist government fights to defend capitalism); the moment of dissociation and drift, letting go of rationality; and the arduous and far-reaching building-up of new poetic associations, replacing collapsed systems with a journey into the unknown.

His poems, too, are perhaps closer to Greek anecdotes of the philosophers, as in the well-known book by Diogenes Laertius, than to the knock-down late-night communist cellar cabaret they superficially resemble. If we envisage the sophist as someone who wandered around, gathering audiences at crossroads or in marketplaces by wit and verbal skill, naturally in compressed and salty form, then Logue is a sophist. The crossroads harangue is close to the parable and the comic tale. He is a bright and tireless disputer, always close to the actual.

The Mad Tom songs ('The Song of Mad Tom's Dog' and 'Song of Mad Tom's Dog's Best Flea'), "a bright-eyed/ Clayboned beggarman mad O", are interesting because they represent a continuity on the Left. Jack Lindsay, a communist at this point, had edited a volume of bedlamite poetry of the 17th century, in 1927. Sean Bonney, in 2002, wrote extensively on Tom O'Bedlam in his work *Notes on Heresy*. They reveal a structural link between left-wing poetry (any effective left-wing poetry) and the New Romantics. The irrational is also a critique of the real. The Bedlam poems resemble both nonsense poetry and William Blake.

By chance I have a copy of a magazine where one of these poems was first published—*The New Reasoner*, for Autumn, 1957, edited by the Marxist historian E.P. Thompson. Most of the contributors—except Logue—have something to do with the Communist Party. Six pages are given up to Randall Swingler's leaden and pseudo-religious dirge on the atomic bomb. *Songs* puts on the table the question whether the onrush into song form, into parataxis, bold colours, and the immediate present, which made the Sixties, came out of the Communists—and was the fruit of the heavy pressure they'd put on poets, for so long, to get back to popular and social forms. And to realise human freedom by stepping out of acquired structures, of course. Maybe intelligence entered popular song (for the first time), via Dylan, because he was able to draw, at the beginning of his career, on the riches of political folk song, as developed by the American Left. Poetry was revolutionised because the pop song was revolutionised—and we know fairly well why this happened.

Logue, representing in so many ways the destruction of the Fifties and the arrival of Sixties ideals, is also a formalist. In order to understand the new informality which came along quite shortly after *Songs*, we have to consider the relationship of poetry to song and how the idea that song pressed poetry towards rhyme and regularity was replaced by the feeling that the new song culture demanded informality. This is a confusing shift of position but if we grasp it we may also understand the demise of rhyme and metre.

Oral Poetry

The '60s, especially the second half, saw a great expansion in the variety of styles on offer and in the number of poets writing and being published. This was a revolution. It could not be reversed. There arrived a new basic style for modern times—not the elaborate and difficult forms used for display by a minority of the exceptionally gifted, but the conventions which several thousand (counts vary!) amateur or limited poets deploy. This was an informal, free verse poetry, and its pervasive spread is the main change in the period. It seems likely that amateurs in 1952, if they wrote poetry at all, wrote it in rather a formal, elevated way, generally involving a rhyme scheme and regular metre. We can see some of these poems in the anthology of "non-professional" poets produced for the Festival of Britain in 1951. Looking across the whole spectrum, we find something in 1970 that wasn't really there in the '50s: the idea of a spontaneous poem, completely broken down in linguistic form and "transparent" to the immediate impulses of consciousness. My guess would be that it's really good for people to have access to this style with no rules. It favours self-expression and removes the idea of a schoolmaster peering over your shoulder and criticising what you write—as if he owned the poem and not you. This is of course a break with English poetry as we can see it going back to 700 AD, and probably much further too. An observation: the *bareness* of recent poetry. Modern poetry is remarkably prosaic. Traditional forms of ornament have broken off and have not been replaced. With modern poetry you have to figure out the problem, that "it's direct because it is linguistically bare" while simultaneously "it's only interesting for other people if it's linguistically rich and original".

Logue's 1959 volume is the start of the Sixties in poetry; its title seems to challenge poetry to become like song. Indeed, in order to grasp the changes in poetry around 1960, it is helpful to listen to songs, and to wonder about the relationship between different genres of song, in particular: the new Pop song; the Anglo-Celtic folk song; the more learned Elizabethan song, for example Campion; the protest song as written by Brecht and Weill; "ethnographic" music; poetry and jazz. What often seems to be at stake is the idea that the Renaissance saw a basic split of poetry from song, through introspection and analysis;

and that the disruption around 1960 saw the break of poetry out of this acquired superstructure of self-awareness and complication, and that the Folk boom was in part a recovery of a pre-Renaissance song tradition with all its rigidity and directness.

Pop

One style in use in the 1960s was Pop poetry. Almost anything I say about it will be too much, because it is so permissive—the spontaneous tone can go in any direction. The act of under-specifying produces the under-specified. It is as fair to claim that it is insouciant and anti-political, as that its disregard for regulations is tacitly critical of the social system, the government, and their anti-spontaneous rules. Its quality of "presence" reflects a fear of routine—equally, I suppose, of academic moralising poetry and of the dead skin texture of avant-garde procedures. It is the lifting out of the rhythms of suggestion and instruction.

The wide spread of this style can be dated, with great probability, to the dissemination of *The Mersey Sound*, a Penguin book of three Liverpool poets, of 1967, which sold a quarter of a million copies. This volume of sales makes it likely that it reached virtually everywhere. Of course this manner had been available to poets well before 1967.

The idea that the simple style is connected to the arrival of a mass of people active in literature but not emanating from the traditional middle class is more credible. The source they were tapping might be surrealism. We have to mention Soupault and Prévert, who were writing such poems already in the 1920s.

The constant attack on rhetoric in '50s criticism was bound to conduce towards the idea that abolishing any kind of linguistic organisation was even better.

The reaction inside the Church against fine language, as something which divided the community between linguistic experts and the uninterested, and as their chief problem in reaching a working-class audience, also conduced towards a simplicity and spontaneity of language. This continues the Protestant revolt—it is a revolt in favour of secular life, and of the pleasures of secular life. It continues the attack on the institutional sublime which saw the monasteries close. It says, let the sacred and the everyday come together! It follows the Rhineland mystics, writing well before the Reformation, in the search for the personal, the unstructured, the everyday.

Or, we can see it as an extension of the light verse so dominant in the '50s—light verse lite. Or, we can point to the influence of the photograph, something fixed in the instantaneous present where everything is tentative, spontaneous, direct, yet interrelated.

We have to add a new factor into the model here: the demon of orality, something haunting poetry in a difficult and only partly voluntary love affair.

A feature cluster involving (restricted vocabulary; sympathetic circularity; repetitive syntactic patterns; lack of abstraction; preference for solidarity over originality; simple rhythms; lack of introspection; egoism; the continuous present; lack of ambiguity) defines the low oral. It is fair to say that this cluster is restrictive—and, I personally, find poetry defined by it to be uninteresting. We can call it undertainment—as something radically simplified but without sparkle. *That's undertainment.*

Does Larkin lead on to pop poetry? Roger McGough once said to me, around 1973, how much he was inspired by Larkin, when he was a student at Hull where Larkin was librarian. I remember it because I was 16 and not used to adults saying anything to me except "shut up". The point is not whether Larkin despised Pop poetry. Instead it's about Larkin evacuating the poem of significant experiences and the Pop poets taking that and extending it further.

Brian Patten was one of the more gifted Pop poets of the 1960s. His work has been collected and offers a tangible record of an elusive movement. It is hard to dislike but shows no development over several decades. It's acutely similar to advertisements—a scenario where an ordinary consumer is raised to a vague spiritual high by a special experience, for example eating a Mars Bar. This enlists a binary notion, of the *special people* and the *soulless,* and is pleasurable in the way that ads are. It is heavily dependent on the flesh of young girls—like a million ad directors of the '60s. Poetry might go further into all this but not Patten, he never lets things develop. At some points he identifies the soulless with people who dislike his poetry. Do we identify Patten with the Special People? Hardly so. His procedures are repetitive and prudent in rather a bureaucratic way. He stays with school kids, teenagers prone to elevated dreams but also egocentric and poorly informed. His work is different from Beat poetry because it is so predictable and minimal.

The notably simple poems of the Mersey Sound were interpreted as a rejection of middle-class values, and an upholding of the North as the place of the future. However, given that there was already a long established line of working-class poetry in dialect, we can also see this new Beat poetry as a rejection of traditional working-class culture. The new poetry bore a striking resemblance to the language and style of advertisements, with its reliance on fantasy and its evasion into a mid-Atlantic manner. The dialect poetry which Ken Smith writes about seems to have come to an end in the 1960s, a moment when the old working class culture was being wound up. The last Lancashire dialect verse is part of the long nineteenth century, and of a certain version of northernness.

Pete Roche

Edward Lucie-Smith pointed out in his review of a bad 1969 anthology of "underground" poetry that the best source for that kind of poetry was the 1967 anthology *Love Love Love. The New Love Poetry*, edited by Pete Roche. I found Roche's book and, yes, this is the one to go to if you want to study the virtues of Pop poetry. The book is from Corgi and comes in a gold cover with Hindu deities (referring to the Kama Sutra, undoubtedly) and some '90s-ish fairies, also felt to be erotic. Design by Hapshash and the Coloured Coat, a name of the time. A quote from marbled endpapers as backdrop. Lush and meaningless textures code for drugs and the Hindu look codes for sex. The look was used for other books in the same series, I am sure my father had some. The cover design obviously stuck in my mind. I wasn't interested in pop poetry as a teenager so I didn't read them. The title obviously came with a melodic fragment, at that time: the chorus to The Beatles' 'All You Need is Love'.

Pop poetry has been notoriously fickle over the last 50 years, and the word Pop therefore has no value unless you can be precise about time and flavour. Roche's book can be compared to the pop songs of 1967, precisely. I can remember almost every song that was a hit in that year, but I recognise that to people born since 1970 the comparison may not be enlightening at all. However, let me compare these fragile poems to 'Paper Sun', by Traffic, a single of that year. (Even more floaty and mysterious was 'No face no name and no number', also on *Dear Mr Fantasy*, their first album, 1967.) 'Paper Sun' says everything in 3 minutes, even giving an opening onto something vast and undefined just outside the plane of the music. At that time English pop was completely about three-minute singles and had a wonderful lightness. Roche found poems which have that light, floating, high quality, empty and complete at the same time. Heavy music came along sometime in 1968. The poetry Roche collects under the rubric of "love" is not so much about love, more about casual sex. I don't mean that badly, the lack of a serious investment in the Other Person means also the lack of compulsion and is the key to a lightness and freedom rare in modern poetry. Indeed, this is the pastoral quality: the shepherds and shepherdesses are dallying with each other rather than worrying about their long-term economic future. The mood of the poems seems to be thinking about the person you were with last night, enjoying the mystery, enjoying the few vivid things you can remember about them, but actually knowing almost nothing about them. When I say "casual" I am implying "relaxed" "undemanding" and even "ego-free". The writers, equally, have no strong sense of their own identity, they are ready to improvise as you must be with someone you don't know, ready to abandon any positions that might close off the relationship.

It may well be that a sense of their own importance prevents heavy poets from writing lyrical, pastoral, dreamy, pleasurable verse. Roche's poets have a weak sense of identity. It's very attractive. They were all under 25 in 1967. It's me who is ridiculous looking back after 40 years, not them. Poets can get too important to take the Other person seriously and even to give the poem freedom. The contrast with the insistent Character Testing of '50s-style English poetry was entrancing. Moments were simply not being taken as tests for how well you were going to behave over the next 50 years. The style in Roche's chosen poems is not a weapon for demonstrating status: it is underdefined, almost not there, yet with a unique flavour.

The flavour is charm. The intoxicated textural mix of the cover—
Art Nouveau and Hinduism?—is not yet reflected in montage within
the poems. Spike Hawkins is the strangest poet here, a hint that
disorientation was going to lead all the way out. 'Let me take you away
from all this.'

If this kind of poetry slipped away from view it is not unconnected
with changes in the pop world. Pop music was about to become very
pretentious, and the phrase heavy music became important in 1968.
Strikingly, the same word meant "pressurised, sad, authoritarian,
depressing". The idealised 1967 music I am talking about does not
cover everything happening in music in 1967, far from it. Traffic were
distinctive because they had so thoroughly abandoned the basis in
Black American music, especially the blues. The model of an emotive
male figure, intense in feelings and often feeling betrayed, projecting
sexual dominance, had been stealthily removed from their music. A
musical aesthetic based on a loud repetitive beat with a heavy bass
register, in which insistence stood for "strength", was also missing from
their creation. Their music floated and relied on your intuition. Traffic
slipped away into long musical "jams", making them very popular with
a drug-oriented American audience. The jam allowed for the floating
and ego-free qualities. Drifting and shifting moods could be captured
on tape: permanent evanescence. But the ideal three-minute pop song
vanished from the landscape as they did this. (The jams were 100%
derivative of Black jazz ensembles who did it far better.) The possibility
either of dissipated meandering (as on their albums of the 1970s) or
of heavy-handed pretentiousness (which in other bands could make
monumental length and complexity seem justified) stalked on stage,
hateful and yet destined to stay around and to generate millions of
pounds of revenue. People just forgot how to write three-minute pop
songs. Pretentious concerts and heavy albums made far more money.
It's amazing that Pop poetry stopped and yet that was predestined by
the link to Pop music. Writers like Lee Harwood and Tom Raworth
coincided with Pop but took its unrefined qualities much further into
the realm of pure freedom, making the transition into long form and
deep originality—as some pop groups did, I suppose.

If Roche's anthology is so poignant this is evidence that the Pop style
did not altogether take over. The set of assumptions which took over

as the norm for British poets, and replaced the 1950s, was significantly different and allowed for considerably more linguistic complexity. To find the source of the new set of norms we have to look beyond the Pop song and its innocence or indifference.

Folksong and poetry

We can hardly miss the fact that the new simplicity in poetry was arriving at much the same time as a radical move towards simplicity in music, namely the Folk Boom. It is marginal in poetry, obviously the stalwarts see words primarily as parts of songs. It is something pervasive in the culture which has mainly failed when applied to poetry. Folk is the prehistory of Pop but around 1960 "folk" singers hated pop music. Folk poetry is more patterned than pop poetry. Take this example of a narrative feature from a folk song:

> You set one foot on the platform
> the other one on the train

which continues a much older:

> He set his ae fit on the grund,
> The tither on the steed;

This is not the most concise way of describing a journey but it has the formal property of symmetry and avoids banality. The resources of folk poetry are restricted in quantity and generously repeated, but they do work. The metrical rules being followed by poets like Beecham carry the same genes as those used by folk songs and by Welsh poets: symmetry, emphasis, regularity. Whatever force decreed that humble production should make folk songs in AD 1450 had emigrated by 1950: amateur poetry is not like folk songs.

The closest marriage between folk poetry and art poetry was in the heyday of Housman, Hardy and Kipling, which we would place around 1890 to 1920. The whole Georgian movement (peak 1912 to 1920) was in their shadow. Actually the folk movement is most closely related to the movement to revive Shakespeare, with people singing Tudor songs as a variant of actors delivering Shakespearean verse in the broad-based preoccupation with the national past. Logue and Dylan drew on folk song which communist theory said was collective and superior to all individualist poetry as produced since the 15th century, but they were both individualists.

There was a folk boom in 1958–65 (roughly). This was an all-over thing which resists logical analysis. I would happily divide white blues, folk, and protest songs, and they are very different, but from contemporary sources it is quite obvious that a singer starting out in 1960 did not have to decide that they belonged to one and not the others. With folk, there was a "feeling in the air" that it was the music of the uneducated people, but the songs recovered clearly included those beloved by the court and by professional musicians. If you hear Martin Carthy's storming 'The Famous Flower of Serving Men', one of the great recordings of the 1960s, it may not stand out that it's about being a servitor of the King. Being "low culture" is an elusive thing, so it's really the archaism which is decisive for the "folk" element in poetry. The appeal of half-timbered cottages, tithe barns, painted carvings in the roofs of old churches, Tudor embroidery, old cider presses, etc., is part of the box of beautiful things. I suspect that the folk element in poetry has more to do with this than with class consciousness.

Elektra recorded, in the 1950s, a lot of Appalachian folk songs—famous for preserving Elizabethan English. The folk movement can be compared with young academics of the 1950s writing poems in Renaissance metres (and even styles) as a reflection of the literature they were teaching all day. The comparison should not be stretched too far, but academic poetry too was engaged in a deep recreation project which went back to stanzaic forms and favoured stylisation. In both cases, the path which people followed as they moved back out of the "recreation project" into original material which gradually incorporated elements of "modernity" is of great interest. England is covered with various "recreation projects" and of course the nations of Wales and Scotland as constitutional entities can be described as "recreation projects" which have reached a climax. The failure of the stanzaic neo-Formalism of the 1950s can be compared with the failure of the Folk movement. What they gave rise to ate up their resources.

We can pencil in as the origin of "folk" the rise of a set of cultivated stylemes from roughly 1540 on which left behind an archaic and rigid stratum of song and folk poetry. One index would be the pentameter versus octosyllabics, the longer line being more fluid and sophisticated, inherently beautiful because removed from ordinary speech. The older stratum could not disappear and had built into it devices which were even more formal, if more coarse, than the new courtly diction. This stratum was familiar to all because of its persistence in "low" verse such as playground rhymes and riddles, and unsophisticated songs. It was always open to 20th century poets to relapse into it, a deliberate shedding of sophistication, self consciousness and ego. There was a certain cult of John Skelton (1460–1529) and his awkward and lumbering if occasionally jolly and grotesquely animated verse. We have the spectre of a historicism in which everything that has developed in poetry since 1540 or so was added to an archaic but perfect conduct of verbal affairs and destroyed it while creating successive flights of modernity, so that a predestined move for poets is to go back to that archival conduct, robust in that it can be easily memorized and is easily understood by anyone who speaks English, and crawl inside it to be sheltered from change and discontent. This can be an anti-capitalist gesture; it can be a Christian and anti-capitalist gesture. As a variant, in the "Atlantic periphery", it can be an anti-English gesture.

The way back to myth ran via folklore. Charles Causley wrote poems in a ballad style. George Mackay Brown is a poet without a modern voice, who has drawn on folk elements very extensively, without using its versification. Mackay Brown exploits archaic modes of perception which are flattening but also integrative and continuous, and with powers of assimilation proportionate to their inability to reproduce difference. A comparison would be with textiles, where the limits of the stitch are compensated for by the richness of patterning and the willingness to abandon realism in favour of incorporation as a principle. Language can be complex and "modern" but can have another stratum where it is like textile, rigid and patterned. The "folk" manner is flattened by stilted language into a stiff and rich pattern which is blocked in every direction except what is preordained and a fulfilment. It is Gothic, pre-modern, pre-Renaissance. His theory of time is based on recurrence, with charged numbers as the keepers of significance, while progress is frozen out. Quite a few poets have adapted elements of folklore in their poetry. Peter Levi imitating Nikos Gatsos gets snatches from the Greek ballads which Gatsos drew on.

There is a lower stratum of poetry in Welsh, by the so-called *Beirdd y bro* (*bro* meaning "neighbourhood"). This uses the difficult and formal rules of *cynghanedd* and is so in great contrast to Pop poetry. It belongs with a rural world where there were many tasks surrounded by ways of being wrong, with in the middle a right way of doing it. Skill was much valued, and there was a competitive approach to poetry like ploughing competitions. One well-known *bardd y bro* is Dic Jones, who comes from an area where they're all at it. I came across a book by Dic Jones, *Caneuon Cynhaeaf*. Books are not necessarily the way to enjoy his poetry. The poems were amazingly anti-literary but followed formal rules. Someone emailed me info about a recent book of Jones' where the poems were printed as prose. Dic Jones *arbrofwr*? Dic Jones experimentalist? Dic Jones typographical Futurist? Jones' poetry is completely oral and so the typography is irrelevant.

Oral style

It has been pointed out that the plays of Shakespeare and the sermons of John Donne are both oral literature. To make the field of play visible, we have to refine our terms and distinguish *low oral* from *high oral*. The former is in fact sub-literary and need not claim much of our time. It looks more like a form of under-achievement than something specific to any ethnic group or set of groups.

If "performance poetry" in this country has been unnaturally simple, this is because of a will to simplicity which is independent of the live situation, and which continues into the printed form. The problem which restricts the interest of Low Oral poetry for me is the low rate at which information flows. Stereotyped constructions, simple vocabulary, sticking to the immediate present, all combine to give a text which captures very little information and which goes nowhere if it is collected in large quantities. It lacks social memory and is unable to cope with the complex experiences of daily life which add up to political knowledge. The egocentricity, charming in a child or a pop singer, becomes wearing and irritating when exposed by the print medium. It looks as if the high flow of information typical of print poetry wraps up egocentricity and makes it tolerable. We experience the world as selves and our awareness is egocentric as, probably, a biological given. But the world is complex, we have a refined nervous system and brain, and the rate of flow of non-self information contextualises the selfishness inside a complex web of relationships. When language is dumbed down so that it can't take any of this on, the surviving egoism, like flotsam after a literary shipwreck, is unsatisfying and so irritating.

It is hard to write the history of the m-stream because of its conservatism and its peculiar relationship to the topic of innovation. It is even harder writing the history of oral poetry. The avant-garde has a continuous consciousness and documents itself. So does academic poetry of the legitimate line. But there is another poetic world which is too fluid to have any institutional memory, which therefore lives in the shadow of repetition and of historical myths. Live events essentially leave no trace. This becomes an issue when you want to establish where anything started: at every point you find people saying "no one ever had poetry readings before me", "no one ever wrote spontaneous & colloquial poetry before me", "no one ever wrote left-wing poetry before me", "no one ever set poetry to music before me". These things get forgotten very quickly. Political poetry also loses its charge very quickly. There are hucksters around actively forgetting the past on our behalf, replacing it with legends designed to promote the poetic commodity they're selling. So I think dating the start of any of the contemporary currents has a value.

Clearly there were moments in 1958 or 1965 when you could go to a poetry and jazz event on the Friday and to a folk club on the Saturday. We are fortunate to have in Martin Booth's *Driving Through the Barricades: British Poetry 1964 to 1984* a written account of the boom in readings. He thinks the boom collapsed in 1974–5. This account of a revolution in about 1965 is probably good history and draws attention because it is not compatible with other people who claim the same revolution was happening in 1985 or 1995 or 2005 and that they owned and managed it. I believe Christopher Logue founded the "jazz with poetry" idea in about 1958. There is an anthology, *Jazz Poems,* of 1963 which captures something of these events. The poems are unrelated to jazz. Obviously you could play a kind of chamber jazz while they were being read, and that is what happened.

The singer-songwriter genre

We can think about modern poetry through the atmosphere of poetry sections in High Street bookshops. This is the poetry *market*. It reveals a world of delicate and cultured people, low on aggression and high on conscience. The keyword is sensitivity, implying a nebula of fine structures which cannot thrive in an environment of coarse surfaces. The value is in the slight and easily damaged wisps of atmospheres, not the big and powerful feelings. The language is quiet enough for small and rare sounds to be heard. The inclination is towards personality and not towards analytical intelligence, which is more readily to be had in adjacent departments. It leans towards the small scale and organic. The customers identify with the personalities of poets, relate to them as friends, rather than identifying with techniques and ideas. People who actually buy poetry approve of this atmosphere. It has the warmth and intimacy of a student house, the mixture of hope, naivety and deep interiority of a teenager's bedroom. This poetry seems to favour the personal to the exclusion of anything else. When I look at the poetry in shops, the present dispensation is recognizably similar to what was being written in the 1960s, and even in the first half of that decade. But something has changed since the 1950s. It is not that the poets of that time (generically Christian and academic) fell silent, but that there was a change of mood which defined them as less than wholly modern already from the early sixties. The 1960s saw a swathe of conservative polemics warning against the new style of poetry and so, reluctantly, giving a description of it when it still seemed strange. The new thing must come out of music, must come out of youth culture, and must satisfy student taste. So, the following essay takes on the modern period in terms of an approximation of poetry to the singer-songwriter genre.

The conventions of an age are not visible to most people living in that age. In our age, poetry has staked its identity so completely on egocentricity and simplicity that it is hard for poets to realise that they can fail because of those traits. Yet most poets fail. The failure is normally *linked* to the central features. The modern manner is remarkably bounded by the self of the poet; narrative and drama are almost absent from poetry because, as it seems, having several characters gets in the way of presenting the central character, The Poet I. This intimacy is related to the bareness. There may be other explanations.

The intimacy seemed possible only in an informal social and linguistic context, closeness abolishing distance. It has been like acting over a microphone: large oratorical gestures seem ridiculous, and you don't have to use a big voice to reach the back row. This closeness and bareness (or being natural, we could call it) is hardly there in the 1950s, and we could ask where the poets learnt it from. Because it is so much the basic condition for the crowd of poets, most original poets noticeably depart from it. That is the nature of norms.

University critics may have produced texts and methods which many pupils have to struggle with, and the poetry audience may consist largely of people who specialised in English at school and university, I don't think the rank and file of people who write poetry have any understanding of all that or even like it. The norms of writing poetry do not correspond with the university ideals, and the taste for close reading, post-structuralist theory, new historicism, and what have you is not central to the living poetry world and could not have produced its typical values and standards. Instead the change has to do with a fuller presentation of the self, combined with the dropping of formality, seen as a set of procedures which blocked off the desired mood of casual intimacy. So State education reaches every town but the "modernist reform" was not like that, it defined a place which is optional and where the self-selected inhabitants even have a shared flavour.

The singer songwriter influence has been around for a long time, and this matches a degree of stability in poetry since the 1960s, as I have claimed. If you look at 85 poets in an acclaimed survey anthology such as *Identity Parade* (2010), almost all of them are very easy to read in terms of personalising experience, and it is hard to find features in them that really weren't there in the 1960s. The staging of poetry readings still has that coffeehouse atmosphere—a basket of cultural piety on every table. In poetry, the stability of this line of appeal demonstrates that the audience like it. The scene is amazingly stable. The constant arrival of new names disguises this, but new names don't necessarily mean that the rules of the game change. It doesn't mean that if you listen to an evening of poetry in 2010 it is going to be strikingly different from an evening of poetry in 1975. I want to emphasize how much the audience *likes* the poets who make identification possible. Most poets may fail but it is the popular ones who count. This *liking* is the most important part of the game. It would be hard to destabilise this situation, supposing that you wanted to. So much contentment is not lightly to be dismissed. Of course someone could argue that things have changed radically—just that it is not obvious to me how.

The upper limit on this kind of poetry is that a personality cannot be attractive beyond a certain point. This is an elementary kind of poetry, and anyone more ambitious has treated it virtually as a starting point, the comfort world before anything interesting happens. The bareness can then be traded for complexity.

I regret that I can't point to a book about the history of singer-songwriters in order to summarise the point I am trying to make, which after all will be unilluminating for people who have no knowledge of popular music. Let me mention Mark Brend, *American Troubadours*, as an excellent book on a key period for the genre, the Sixties, which also sheds light on the English or Scottish scene. It is wonderful in biographical and artistic insight, but does not offer a theory which we could take and map onto poetry. (The word "troubadour" is popular but based on a misunderstanding. The poor poets who wandered around with no home, finding an audience wherever they found themselves on a given day, were *vagantes*. The troubadours were part of court culture and wrote sophisticated courtly poetry for aristocrats.)

Comparing (modern) poetry with singer songwriters was a "lightbulb moment" for me. That is because I know quite a lot about popular music, and I have the analogy present in my mind. If I now list some of the "names in the frame", I am doing this with the proviso that sinking into the concrete works of art will probably distract you from the theoretical point. Here goes: Bob Dylan, Phil Ochs, Bert Jansch, Donovan Leitch, Scott Walker, Janis Ian, Tim Buckley, David Ackles, Paul Siebel, Fred Neil, Tim Hardin, Judy Collins, Joni Mitchell, Richard Thompson, Nick Drake, Tom Rapp. Let me suggest that you spend a few weeks listening to the albums. I think you are going to enjoy this. This is why the comparison is not an attack.

Historically, the coffeehouse singers developed out of folk. A big change was the change of expectation, away from demanding traditional material with a thick ethnic signature and towards expecting the singer to be singing their own material. (Why did this happen in 1963 and not in 1953 or 1943? Could we say that bareness also meant paring away the tradition?) The folky idea that the song gave you access to the profound nature of a people seems to have given rise to the belief that the song or poem gives you access to the sociologically defined profound identity of a person. If you think, what you say is not typical any more. The sociological approach to poetry presupposes that the poetry presents a person literally and artlessly and so that poetry has as its principal component the nature of those people, as middle-class, white, male, heterosexual, female, working-class, and so forth. This approach, which ignores the artistic quality of poems altogether, seems only possible in a context of bareness and intimacy, where all poems echo a self and are servile to it. *Everything means me.* A trade fair of identities. I take exception to these assumptions. I don't think an anthology of poems is like an album of hundreds of snap-shots of people's faces. I think that theory is deeply flawed. I don't think a history which assumes that the only things allowed to change in poetry are the social origins, class, gender, region, etc. of the practitioners has anything to tell us.

The academic criticism which triumphed in the 1950s and laid down the norms for a long time after that frequently attacked rhetoric. This is what close reading seemed to culminate with. But without rhetoric you have bareness, already. You have removed the main distinction between poetry and everyday speech. If you add in authenticity, as the quality of an individual conscience, you are just about to invent the singer-songwriter genre: the acoustic guitar and solo voice as music without rhetoric, the voice of the committed individual. What people were learning in the classroom actually reinforced their inclination to write in a bare and committed way.

Some of the rules of the singer-songwriter genre are: egocentricity, the subordination of the whole product to the singer and their personality; intelligence, in comparison to the rest of popular music; simplicity, as the voice and the acoustic guitar are so important; essentially White traditions; introspection (as opposed to being dance music); less definably, the singer is presented as a sensitive person full of compassion and low on selfishness. Less essentially, the genre is middle class and of the Left; it is strong on protest songs and has an inheritance from the Folk tradition. Relative to the rest of popular music, it is strongly verbal, and by extension literary; it is hard to write advanced song lyrics without intelligence, and intelligence is at the core of the product. It can easily become didactic and is not high on hedonism; it sings for a sort of Puritan Bohemia. Biographically, most of its practitioners began with folk songs and started writing their own material later on. It favours small venues, preferring a coffeehouse where a rather homogeneous audience feel very close to the singer (and close to each other). Whatever musical techniques are deployed tend towards transparency, to let the singer's personality shine through. Even in recording, different techniques are used than for rock music; close miking allows as much of the singer's voice to reach the tape as possible; this also goes along with a singing style of intimacy, without high volume and brilliance. The emphasis is on the voice itself and not on tonal purity, ornament, or even metrical perfection. The packaging of the records has a strong emphasis on the image of the singer and their face. We move between the voice and the face, and back. Many of the songs are about "relationships" and the listener is encouraged to enter into a quasi relationship with the songwriter. The records are named after the individual in charge of them, and remembering names is crucial; the production succeeds by displaying as much of the personality as possible, the personality and "talent" are the payload. As this implies, it is a competitive genre and originality is a favoured means: verbal invention is prized. Yet the almost documentary stress on the quality of a voice, with subordinate backing, makes it difficult to differentiate successive records by the same person; the product tends to converge on its payload, a person.

The genre shows no signs of going away and one could list hundreds of significant albums from its history. Its spread was led by Bob Dylan but it's not true that he invented it: rather, when he came to Greenwich Village in January 1961 there were already dozens of folkies there, playing in coffeehouses and starting to write their own material. He learnt from them. (In one version, he had not written *any* songs before 1961.) This scene changed incredibly fast over the following three years, partly because so many talented people were there listening to each other. However, the genre was still there 50 years later.

The singer songwriter genre (SSG) has thrived because its home was in the world of students. This world has grown continuously since 1960 or so, and is in some ways conservative, even if the personnel turn over quickly. Even if the coffeehouse troubadours were living on their wits or on a few coppers payment for gigs, there was a large student presence in the audience and that kind of folk club has thrived in university towns. British poetry has also had a very close association with the student world, even if that milieu has also been re-created or preserved by individuals who have long ceased to be students. It seems natural to look for the formative factors of a specifically modern poetry in the conditions of student night life. To put it crudely, the *typical* individual who writes poetry travels at 18 to receive higher education, writes while a student, and gives it up on leaving university, and so we can see the "serious" poet at the age of 30 or 40 as atypical of poets—someone who *clings on* to an earlier condition or attitude. The students are part of youth culture but are in a sense at the edge of it, its effects are wearing off. Of course someone from "youth culture" who moves into poetry has to adapt and change. Youth culture barely ever includes poetry at all. It has song lyrics but not poetry. This is why the singer songwriter genre remodelled poetry, because other genres were far less compatible with a purely verbal approach. Because it was almost entirely White, and also arguably linked to Anglo-Scottish and Protestant strands in American culture, it was less challenging for White British poets than the rest of American song creativity. (I say arguably because the Jewish and Central European strand was also vital at every step.)

The bareness of recent poetry bears striking, and I think significant, links to the bareness of early singer-songwriters. Early Elektra records were made without a studio: label founder Jac Holzman took a tape recorder round to the singer's house (actually, funky Bohemian type Greenwich Village cold water apartment) and recorded the albums *in situ*. Holzman was better than anybody else at designing a sound within these limits. The guitar or banjo (rarely, piano) was present chiefly as an accompaniment to the voice. The close-up miking emphasized the accidental features of the singer's voice; the closeness of focus suited the sparseness, usually guitar plus voice, and valorised this as a style: intimacy. This is surely suggestive of why British poets *want* a simple style. Adding more features would leave less cognitive space for the ones already present. Expanding to a large ensemble was felt to mean formality, making decisions which became restrictions, reducing authenticity. The coffeehouse scene got into virtuosity very early. This seems incompatible with the "simplicity is authenticity" ideal of folk, but the contradiction is very important. The containment of innovation in British poetry has to do with a belief that ideas get in the way of displaying the personality so that people can develop affection for it. This can be compared with the organisation of a song: if the guitar is there as an accompaniment to a voice, normally an untrained voice, then virtuosity has to be reined in, it can only show in tight little windows.

The singer-songwriter genre began in tiny cafe rooms with a half-dozen tables with candles stuck in wine bottles, but it spread worldwide through television, and probably couldn't have spread as it did before television. The TV studio recreated the intimate space of the Greenwich Village coffee house, that almost frightening lack of gap. The singer's face was a large percentage of the information being sent. The worst thing the performer can do is to make themselves unavailable to the audience. The empty channel will dominate the room. The singer-songwriter is well advised to play simple songs, and not ones where they focus on the music and forget about the audience and the camera on their faces.

A vital part of SSG technique is to have the singer present in every song. If the voice and the face of the singer are central, you cannot have a song where they are blank. The performer has to be present for the audience. *Hit the presence button.* Only songs are possible which allow a direct emotional link between singer and audience. The audience like the performer and have feelings of loss and blankness if the performer is absent or blank. (Alternatively: out of all performers the only successful ones are the ones the public likes.) The singer has to present the situations which develop trust and liking in the audience, and has to hark back, constantly, to those situations. The performance is trapped in the moment of now: neither side wanders off into the broad and generous spaces of thought, because they have to be thinking about the same thing at the same moment, and this is the fuel, beaming out warmth and comfort. They are thinking about each other.

This oneness is not *uncritical.* The whole genre began in a Left milieu, even the old folk material was being heard in those cafes because American Leftists saw it as the testimony of the rural poor—"the people, yes". You didn't get an entire evening of protest songs (to judge by the albums that trap part of the scene), but the protest songs were high points. But the staging was not critical of the relationship between the singer and the audience. That bond was part of the unity of the Left. At the Chicago Conspiracy Trial, Judy Collins wanted to go into the witness box and sing. The judge, Julius Hoffman, wasn't having it, but possibly Collins' voice was stronger than the government's shaky case.

The "folk" thing analysed a great deal of the apparatus of art as simply hiding the primary impulse, blurring the fundamental Now moment of the utterance. The folk singer was naked, deliberately, so that what you were seeing was actually there. This was very strongly related to the existentialist mood of intellectuals at that time, and can be related to abstract art, seen then as doing away with "illusionism" and laying bare the basic gesture of painting. The human voice and face were seen as laying bare an entire structure of alienation, the whole organisation of capitalist society in fact. The movement had much more to do with student existentialism than with peasants of the Tudor era.

This whole cultural strand is not part of privatisation: it has benefited from the advance of privatisation but contains obstinate elements of protest, conscience, rejection of commerce, etc., which lead in just the opposite direction. The English and British poetry I am talking about is not formally uncritical, is not based on ignorance of the history of art. What it doesn't have is a critique which is regarded as legitimate by the post-Marxist, post-Conceptual main line of highly theorised reflection. (When I say "main line", "underground" might be a more accurate term.) I have implied that the egocentricity of the personal poet is linked to privatisation, but no doubt the personal poet would retort that developing a radical and theoretically based style is inherently a withdrawal from the public domain. Indeed, this disagreement might be a significant dividing line.

If we develop the idea that modern poetry showcases the personality in the way that a car advertisement showcases a car, that must be too simple, but we can see that it would impose a whole set of interlocking requirements and limitations, and that there might be a powerful logic, underlying poems at a deep structural level, which follows from this primary idea. Poets might simply be unwilling to write about subjects where they could not shine and where they were not the centre of attention. The market seems quite happy with the poet's personality as commodity number one. Because children in our Western culture are daily and subliminally taught how to process art based on personality, they are expert in it by mid adolescence and so find it easy to process poetry with the same rules. This would seem to minimise the area of what is unique to poetry, while also making poems accessible. We could argue that pursuing poetry without a personality at its centre is purist and admirably elevated, the essence of "high" in cultural level. Poetry not based on the personality arguably has "height" and we can locate the "high-low" axis from it. The prevalence of the personality suggests also that if we are going to become conscious about how poetry is structured, this is the main thing we have to become conscious about.

The value of the "framing norm" is also that it pinpoints where people are breaching that norm. Surely the status of figures like Prynne, Raworth, Allen Fisher, is that they have insistently ignored the rule about foregrounding the personality. The landscape seems to demand a mass of people behaving in a similar way and then a few who do not conform and who achieve higher status by not conforming. We may find it useful to have a frame *against* which we can define what is original in poetry, and how original it is.

The distinction between personality and originality is part of the zone of combat. To be unoriginal is to lack a personality, to be unmemorable to an audience which wants to remember and cherish gifted people. Yet the whole genre of *me sensitive person* is old-fashioned and conservative. In short the poetry world is haunted by the ghost of a time line of stylistic progression invalidating legacy styles, by the hangover from an existentialist and Late Protestant past, and by the spectre of an intellectual, political, and avant-garde art which may have peaked in the 1970s but which still makes conventional poets uneasy.

The framing norm of the poetry world does not have anything to do with political or religious or class values. It resides in the feelings of the people involved about each other, something which can change all the time without changing very much. Art as the vehicle for a personality is its central dogma, and anything which challenges that will cause alarm and a corresponding negative reaction. The stock in trade of the industry is the liking of, and memory of, certain personalities by the market, which tells them to buy the product. Any defensive action will be directed to defend these asset personalities. However, their commercial power does not have to be invoked via poems, and it may be easier to market the personality in another way. Having become a media personality, you can give up the poetry.

I am not pitching the idea that poets are more gifted than singer-songwriters. This is so far from being true that we have to ask the reverse question, namely, why am I writing about poets only and not about the words from the songs of the troubadours? The reply has to be evasive, but then I may write about song lyrics at an unspecified future date. Many of the songwriters are highly intelligent, and this is the most literary of popular genres. It is striking that the singers who have gone the farthest towards achieving literary values in their songs have also been the least popular and most marginal to the music business— Scott Walker and David Ackles spring to mind here. We could say that "poetry is defined by the elements that make it more intelligent than coffeehouse songs", and so demarcate a region which covers only the extent of this difference. Presumably poetry which does not have any advantages over song lyrics is unnecessary, even if arts managers want it to be the only kind of poetry.

The stripped-down quality of the musical texture pointed originally to closeness to the people, the rejection of virtuosity was a symbolic approaching to income group E, the deprived seen as the most folkish of the folk. The fact that this and the romantic intimacy of the coffeehouse left almost nothing to compete with the singer's person, so that the prospect of the audience falling in love with and otherwise admiring the singer formed a very smooth path away from the political intent, was not designed but affected the whole genre, virtually wherever it was happening. Making the personality available as a romantic object involves a certain discipline, and if a poet inspires liking and affection that has to be taken as a success which justifies the artistic decisions which sustained it, even if they imply a certain banality and lack of experiment as minor features. Conversely, the laying bare of the self makes sure that if a poet inspires dislike the dislike is going to be of maximum intensity. Poetic politics stem mostly from people disliking one poet or another and from the excessive personalisation of that failure by the poet. It is hard to write intelligently about the effects of this, but some selves are irritating and out of tune in the way that some people play the guitar badly.

One can see the "core" of art as selective attention, focus, something like a landscape in which all the water flows in one stream bed and not scattered equally over the whole area. Given all the terrible or meaningless features of the world, it is a stream protected by invisible walls from straying off the path to the core signal, which is meaningful and beautiful. The poetry which focuses on one personality has something like this as its ideal. The difficulty of writing such poetry is to be consistent and narratively rich, to deploy the voice and the face (or their poetic equivalents) in a sustained way, without becoming tired or phony. There is a good case for thinking that even the most "data rich" and conceptually ambitious art still relies on invisible walls which protect the steadiness of focus. There is a problem in combining "art" and "inattentiveness".

In considering extremely personal art, we should bring on stage arguments about depersonalisation, alienation, and in general the inhuman aspects of mass society and large organisations. The build-up to this clipping poems to the boundaries of the person was existentialism, as the pre-eminent philosophical fashion for students in Western Europe between, say, 1945 and 1960. Going back in time, we can observe that the norm I have proposed either was not in place in around 1955–60, or that poets were not conforming to it. There is something to be credited to the poets who wanted to be existentialist and austere, unforgivingly exposing moral choices rather than offering their personalities as objects of contemplation. The result of this austerity was that few of them have been retained in the memory of a public which wants personalities. The new pop culture, then, scrapped most elements of existentialism, but perhaps something was also carried over into the seething new world of the 1960s. "Authenticity" was evidently what people were seeking in stripping poetry bare. The jettison of rhetoric by young people, from say 1963 on, was a carrying into action of attacks on "rhetoric" built into the New Criticism by academics from the early 1930s on. When we seek authenticity we must be able to find it. To find it we must have tests of it which we accept as valid. This acceptance in art seems to be subject to change every few years. Its location at any point is of great interest. It represents the freedom of the collective, but not a freedom owned by individuals.

To reiterate, the most original poets rejected this "framing norm". Also, there certainly are poets retaining a style from an earlier dispensation, before Dylan, and Carcanet has been the citadel trying to collect and defend them. And there is the "British Poetry Revival" (or its successors), which no one supposes to account for more than 1 or 2 per cent of retail poetry sales. Because the bulk of the market defined elaborate technique as inauthenticity, it is not in the frame as the "central thing" for modern poetry—but it is not going away.

It would be wrong to sign off without noting some of the weaknesses in this generalisation. You could certainly argue that the genre "singer songwriter" has too much artistic breadth to be useful as a comparison for a style of poetry. Then, even if you peel away a large number of poets who are conscious and therefore atypical, it is arguable that there is no "fundamental signal" shared by the bulk of modern poets. You could argue that amateur poetry as a corpus is full of random gestures, and that poets skilled enough to reach for a definite effect, even one of tremulous naivety, are already an exception.

Virtuosity

Having said that bareness was central to the new poetry, we have to concede that a great feature of the live art of the 1960s was virtuosity. This is a contradiction which we cannot resolve but plan to talk about. It is striking, in "pop culture", how the strands which most succumbed to a romanticism of poverty, authenticity, "peasant-centric", i.e. (white) blues and folk, were susceptible, almost from the first week, to the lure of virtuosi, and how they produced virtuosi: Davey Graham, Jansch, Renbourn, etc. in the case of folk, and Clapton, Page, Beck, etc. in the case of blues. With Jansch, the audience simultaneously saw his mumbling singing and his brilliant guitar playing as signs of authenticity—even though they pointed in different directions. While it would be a gross exaggeration to say that most famous pop musicians were virtuosi, all the same a significant part of the experience of that decade was the awesome freedom attained by musicians like Coleman, Coltrane, Hendrix, to some extent also by blues guitarists. Their virtuosity belonged in a live situation and with that total acceptance of liveness which we call improvisation. If we look at oral poetry through this perspective, we find the low attainment of the nether oral quite puzzling; but we can recognise virtuosity and improvisation if we look a little more closely at some other poets.

The fate of techniques identified with Outsider Art, the landless rural poor, the illiterate, is to be identified as authenticity and spontaneity and then to be copied brilliantly by the most gifted and the most cultured. The era of the 1960s was marked by a counter-culture, in which these signs of authenticity were, comprehensively, occupied and separated from their primary context. The cultured do not view themselves as official or as the oppressors. The use of these techniques is powerfully analogous to the use of folk music and "pastoral" by Ralph Vaughan Williams and other English "nationalist" composers, half a century earlier. None of these strands favours clumsiness and it seems likely that each of them favours high verbal skills and education.

Edwin Morgan's mature style (as showcased in his 1968 volume *The Second Life: Selected Poems*) comes out of the continuous present as discovered by '60s artists. The increased prominence of electronic and audio-visual arts, with their miraculous capacity for delivering all-over data surfaces, raised the stakes for poetry: the presence of the past, as a key component in any page of poetry, was seen as slowing down the text and destroying its present, immediate quality. At the same time poetry somehow acquired the ability for total memory which photographs so richly offered and illustrated. Now, what poetry cannot copy audio-visual media in is rapid transmission of huge amounts of data. Words tend to serial depiction, and so complexity becomes strung out—it extends in the time axis. It is not allover. What words can do is imply a whole situation very quickly—inducing the reader to rearrange their assumptions, in a cognitively complex act which is triggered by a few characters on the page. This very exciting method was radically incompatible with the conventions of the 1950s, where the restriction of subject to the poet's autobiography, of theme to the rightness of the Christian laws, made the unexpected unlikely.

The subtitle is *Selected Poems*, but only one poem is from before 1962—compare the large amount of poems from the 1950s in his *Collected Poems*. Titles include 'The White Rhinoceros', 'The Third Day of the Wolf', 'In the Snack-Bar', 'Siesta of a Hungarian Snake', 'The Chaffinch Map of Scotland', 'From the Domain of Arnheim'. The volume title refers (according to his interviews) to a rebirth which the poet experienced during the 1960s. The 1950s had repressed him and made it hard for him to feel free or enjoy himself, but the new cultural atmosphere of the 1960s (he was already 40 in 1960) loosened the clamps and gave him a new life. This was partly to do with the legalisation of homosexual acts, and the weakening of Christian puritanical attitudes, partly to do with a new freedom in poetic expression—but really it was three dimensional, everything changed. The structural metaphor of the poems is the connection between the avant-garde game—and being plunged into a new situation, with new friends and new rules. Both have a mandate of improvisation. The new field has a full emptiness —nothing is there which we already know, but the cleared space is full of possibilities. The artificial rules of an avant-garde word game—for example, the rule of instancy of *Instamatic Poems*—are a metaphor for a new situation—and this realises our basic wish, to be free and to be excited by what is happening to us. The pivot is the self, which is quite redefined—away from traumatically repeating, involuntary, inflexible, behaviour patterns, and towards a capacity for response—an open system which is cooperative with other people, which does not panic and clench up, and which believes in its ability to perceive and learn. What I most enjoy about Morgan is his willingness to jettison knowledge from the self in favour of a simpler and more capacious set-up. The artificial verbal world is allover because it is all new—as we enter it we have to adjust all our frame of reference. The title poem is also about the rebuilding of Glasgow in the '60s—the clearance of some of the most famous slums in Europe. A whole city has had its physical setting smashed and dissipated—like Morgan's poems themselves.

In this frame the fertility of the poet becomes a demonstration—and Morgan's continued productivity and brilliance are heartening proofs of what makes life good. He defines himself by activity—rejecting the old restrictions, where the poem was confined by the poet's social self, and the self was confined by class society, made so many new worlds possible. Extracting the poet from bound and aged situations, to re-insert him in transparent, "empty" situations, actually made personal qualities far more vivid, far more visible. Using artificial rules actually drove the unconscious rules into consciousness—an unexpected scene which is where this critic started. Morgan identified authenticity with *freedom*.

Procedures include shape poems; running-on sound echoes, the physical shape of the word coming before the sense; name catalogues; serial phonic variations; poems with missing information or with certain moves forbidden. There are 24 pages of sound poems—including process poems, magical acrostics, Doric fantasies. Place-names are turned into a sound poem: "from fogo to fada from gigha to gogo". The shape—of a row of small worlds, generated during the poem, unrestricted by time and space, and self-contained—is oddly reminiscent of *Crow*. There was a certain shared artistic syntax at the time—which made conventional poets seem dim and old-fashioned.

Musical improvisation relies on a mixture of constraint and of the freedom of the pure present. Translated into verbal terms, this combination gives rise, repeatedly and logically, to the ludic. The type-site for Ludic Poetry would be *The Second Life* and the 1965 volume *A Doomsday Book* by George MacBeth (mostly gathered in *Collected Poems 1958–82*). *A Doomsday Book* is credited on the cover as "a book of poems and poem-games", and much of the material is presented as a kind of role-playing game. The same blurb refers to Johan Huizinga's seminal *Homo ludens*, which suggests play as the basis of culture. Example:

> **Castelvetrano**. *Millicent to Sir Lucas Crowther.*
> I am reading the sonnets of Gertrude Thimbleby. There is nothing like them in English. Father, I know you are off to Mangalore. Let Amber advance one reason why this koati should die. I am ill with hate.

> **Conway Castle**. Lieutenant Flyte to Commander Singal.
> We are down to the last barrel of apples. Bartholomew has fled. The men are living on dead mice. I have tested the lifebelts but even the rubber has perished. I am emptied of everything except the desire to hold out for another day.
> (from 'Fin du Globe', from *A Doomsday Book*, 1965)

'Fin du Globe' is equivalent to 'Doomsday', and this is a game about the end of things.

If Morgan and Peter Finch have one thing in common, it is that they are highly oriented towards live performance. So it seems that some of the most prominently performance oriented poets are also the most avant-garde. In fact, the most arbitrary features of their poetry are directly related to the arbitrary rules of games—which are one of the most ancient forms of oral creativity, and which are positively demanded by the spontaneity of live events. We can equate the autonomy so often claimed for avant-garde art with games and puzzles—pre-eminent forms of oral culture. Perhaps we can describe one bloc of the avant-garde as surrendering to games and spontaneity—and as being difficult only because we are not part of the excitement which produced them, or because we look for statements about the world and a self where none exists. So the features of underground poetry that people have most difficulty derive from its origins in the social excitement of a night-club or cellar bar where people are improvising and reaching out beyond the norms of speech?

These poets have the virtuosity we so completely miss in the "nether oral". The virtuoso thing in music involves ornamentalism displacing efficiency and slowing down normal information flow. In language, this corresponds to games, in which language stops carrying out a task, efficiently or not, and becomes autonomous. Fantasy is the form of improvisation which operates here. Whereas Morgan works with fragments of vanished languages stuck in Scottish place-names, Finch starts with finished poems and dissolves their substance into something liquid and opaque.

No one would think of separating Finch and Morgan from the pop culture of the 1960s which so obviously inspired and excited them. They play experimental games, which give rise to, sometimes, obscure poems or passages. This means that the link between pop culture and obscurity is direct and frequently travelled. This is as obvious as the avant-garde methods co-opted for 'A Day in the Life' or 'Tomorrow Never Knows'—or the use of Coltrane in the Byrds' 'Eight Miles High'. More—where a conservative critic sees an arbitrary and anti-aesthetic system, the modern-style poet sees a game.

Shared Genres

The Oxford Line

The visible face of English poetry is Oxford poetry. The problem I have is less that of uncovering the Oxford thing than of writing up something which will eventually be recognised by the reader as nothing curious but simply the poetry (and prose) which they have been familiar with all their lives. It's not secret because the key episodes are published and available to anybody to read. You may want to take advantage of this. If you stop reading this and go out and buy a set of books by the following [Auden Betjeman MacNeice Larkin Mitchell MacBeth Fuller Fenton Maxwell Shapcott] you will have got the mainstream of English poetry over those years, say 1950 on. The artistic quality of this poetry leaves something to be desired. As a collection, it leaves an aggregate impression of being sluggish, apathetic, complacent, comfortable, immobile. Full of shyness hiding self-esteem.

We discussed, in an earlier volume, Philip Toynbee's book *Pantaloon.* There is a key relationship between *Pantaloon* and John Betjeman's *Summoned by Bells,* almost the best-selling poetry book of the 1960s. Betjeman also is deliberately immature, futile, in need of subsidy, engaging. Toynbee was born in 1915, Betjeman in 1906, and both share in an inter-war Oxford atmosphere which floated a great deal of English literature right up until the 1970s. (The best account of this is Martin Green's *Children of the Sun: a narrative of decadence,* a wonderful interpretation of mid-century English cultural history.) Toynbee is not an isolate, but part of a whole literary conspiracy— an enormously popular one. Toynbee's four-volume verse novel only takes its hero as far as just after he leaves Oxford. (This is not quite true, because there is a flash-forward to him in his twenties, in Egypt.) During this time he achieved nothing except the inner changes of development and growth. Privilege and infantility are positively being offered up as the sources of the work's appeal—as the chocolate rather than the wrapper. It is hard to believe that any other culture in history has been quite so interested in the details of immaturity and certified unfitness to take part in adult life. The expertise of these Oxford writers at winning the reader's participation sums up the whole current of Biedermeier sentimentality about children but also takes it too far:

Shared Genres

the modern solution has recovered rather, to become significantly less infantile, less narcissistic.

Green, a grammar-school boy heavily influenced by his teacher F.R. Leavis, might well have wondered, while researching his book (published in 1982), how a set of aesthetic and conversational attitudes invented in one university in the 1920s could still be so central in the 1970s. This important question has lost some of its importance since, as the steel-hard dandies died and were carried from the scene. New currents have flowed in from the oceanic reaches.

Betjeman and Toynbee were writing as part of a programme of resistance to the Newbolt hero and patriotic literature of the 'Fights for the Flag' type, developed as part of the great-power naval and colonial rivalry with Germany. This would seem to limit the infantility we have pointed out to a specific historical era—once the militarist programme had lost its credibility, satire on it would lose its momentum. Newbolt wrote no poetry after a certain point because he was engaged in writing the official naval history of the Great War—he had taken the State into the heart of his poetry with 'Admirals All' and had in return been taken into the heart of the State. When I tried to dig up this work in the British Library, it was listed as "special availability"—something one step above being thrown away. The deliberate parody of the legends of warriors and Empire-builders which was developed in 1920s Oxford—among the survivors of the sacrificial rite, as it were—had lost much of its relevance by 1939, but continued because the writers who had been formed by it kept coming up with the goods and had popular followings. That is—they weren't really futile and they weren't exclusive.

The Oxford network which Martin Green describes dominated mid-century English literature, and has been documented in many biographies—perhaps too many—which make it clear that the style it used did not belong to any individual, and that it embodied an approach to social manners, not a code conceived in a vacuum. It is logical that they would supply intimacy as a preferred literary quality, because the close range was reaching out to fill the territory evacuated by the dismissal of Empire, monarchy, and war as subjects. The warm conversational tone expresses a view of politics.

159

Readers believed they were joining a symbolic group by reading—and they were. Some witnesses have said that they felt they didn't belong to this social sound, and so couldn't get into the books—but from another point of view the books were making intimacy available to everybody. We have to point out that the new broadcast media, as well as leisure journalism, marketed a similar intimacy and casualness as a staple—this manner has had success in mass production. Betjeman was a broadcasting genius.

A trawl through the entries for British poets in *The Oxford Companion to Twentieth Century Poetry in English*, edited by Ian Hamilton (1994), hauls up 367 names of whom 111 studied at Oxford University. That is, about 30% of the poets felt to matter for the 20th century. This is an impressive record, and suggests to us that to grasp Oxford poetry is to grasp modern English poetry. I don't want to suggest that counting and doing arithmetic helps us to understand even one poem, and I don't think the sociology of poets is interesting enough to devote time to, but we have to ask whether the group identity of Oxford students, first and foremost students doing English, is strong enough for a social and verbal style to emerge among them, which we could then consider as a constituent of poetry.

I am not one of those people who do a set of counts and find that all the talent comes from a few sources and then concludes that some kind of conspiracy has taken place. If so many poets have to do with Oxford the appropriate response comprises gratitude and admiration, it seems to me. The generation of cultural meaning is itself like a conspiracy insofar as its vital information is transmitted largely face to face and outsiders do not understand what is going on. Poetry has many insides, and is for insiders.

Is it true that having studied at Oxford University is a bad thing and a source of inauthenticity, ignorance of real life, lack of talent? On the basis of all these poets, the hundred and eleven collected by Hamilton, the conclusion is rather that time at Oxford focuses people on poetry, brings them close to people enthusiastic about reading poetry, close also to people who have thought about the issues of writing poetry in the contemporary situation, and is beneficial. Furthermore, the people focussed enough to get into Oxford at the age of eighteen, especially to do English, have *before arriving* many of the qualities needed to write poetry, which is also a learning activity and to some extent an act of scholarship. Conversely, if you are focussed on television and pop music during those formative years, your chances of writing great poetry are slender.

If someone wanted to seize this list of 367 names and essentially rebuild it, they would obviously need not just a knowledge of the work of those poets but also of the general field of the omitted, say 750 names in all. This is obviously more data than one person can crunch. A cheaper approach is to take a list similar in basic principles and see how much it deviates from Hamilton's attempt. A suitable candidate is the *Anthology of Twentieth Century British and Irish Poetry*, from the same publisher, seven years later, edited by Keith Tuma. I took out the Irish poets and did a count, fallible at some points, which yields a figure of 15.4%, of the 106 poets picked by Tuma, who went to Oxford University. That is, just about half as high as for Hamilton. It might still seem like a high figure for a single university with a limited intake. (Another not perfectly reliable count shows 20.2% of Tuma's hit-list as having studied at Cambridge University; the corresponding figure for Hamilton is 13.4%.)

It looks rather as if Hamilton had picked a lot of people who had the right cultural credentials but who were so smitten with being top people and knowing who they were that they were disinclined to try hard and so wrote apathetic if cultured verse. Tuma on the other hand has gone for people who had something to prove and were willing to do work in the poem, and who therefore were drawn more from the malcontent and those without secure livings. Their energy is displayed on the page. Hamilton seem to partake both of the massive energy of identification with people who basically resembled him and of the myth of calm and mildness, so that everything takes place like a tea-party and no unregulated urges are permitted to ruffle the social surface. Both these inclinations are deeply anti-aesthetic, and it is just as well to have someone who takes a quite different approach. Hamilton's own poetry is faint and negligible, but he had a career as a literary journalist and good network connections, so people acted as if he were a poet.

The aesthetic decisions are essentially silent. Reconstruction can only be an act of imagination. One wonders if there was such a primitive egoistic projection by Hamilton on people like him that he really felt as if a slight on any Oxford poet were a slight on him. Thus English poetry would be completely hidden behind his ego. In developing this line of reasoning, we are going to be pulled up short by the reflection that, if you ban identification, you prohibit the pursuit of art anyway—since it is firmly based on that. However, Hamilton's egoism is part of a group egoism which is *definitive* (so invested in a standard reference work) because he belongs to the dominant fraction—the one which legitimates and delegitimises other people. He learnt most of his style as an editor and perimeter guard from Geoffrey Grigson. Whereas Grigson notoriously voted Auden as Best New Poet for 35 years in succession, Hamilton was boss during the amazing "British Poetry Revival" and pretended it wasn't happening. Neither of them liked poets younger than themselves. Hamilton invested heavily in *The New Review*, which he edited, and in the stable of faint young men it ran as featured poets. The key to Hamilton is that "no one younger than me and talented gets a mention or recognition", and this was less important in 1968 but pretty obtrusive by 1994.

So Hamilton had this *positive ego investment* of liking anyone from Oxford and the *negative* one of disliking anyone innovative or talented except if they were older than him. Do the two failings balance each other out?

What was invisible to Tuma, at the University of Ohio at Miami, may have been a kind of social prestige which is not genuinely present in the poems at all. I like the sound of this—a social illusion, a trick done with mirrors behind locked doors, which isn't visible across the sea because it isn't really there. When Tuma was over here, hanging out with the London underground poets, largely, he made striking remarks about the torn carpets in the upstairs rooms above pubs where readings by that group had to take place. This was a matter of indifference to us. It seems to me that he was horrified by the implied lack of money and prestige which the squalid circumstances represented. This sheds indirect light on what kind of signal is buried in the Oxford self-validation: prestige, power, and, at one remove, money. You can see that this might influence some people a great deal. It's an attractive décor. I would be unhappy to think that the pleasure of poetry is a kind of unfocused fantasy about being part of the elite—and walking on carpets that didn't have great big holes in them. I am aware that I can't hang out in those expensive rooms because I don't have favours to swap and that is really *what it's all about*. This zone of elite exchange is also relevant to the artistic ideal of suavity, which is rather important to the mainstream. Dissident poetry is not suave.

I can't prove that the trick done with mirrors ever happened. It doesn't have that status of visibility. We are on brittle ground here. Maybe there is something subtle and Tuma just didn't get it. I doubt it—he seemed pretty astute to me. We could say "prestige is something that doesn't exist"—this doesn't work, unfortunately. Art and prestige live in very much the same realm, too bright to see.

The tilt away from Oxford towards Cambridge in Tuma's collection may be accepted as a sign that different aesthetics have been reproducing at these two major universities. This is not quite certain, but it does need to be borne in mind. If I say *the Oxford line* that is distinct from saying "the upper middle class line" or "the educated line" or even "the literary line". If we can see some poetry as *not* being literary. But why would we accept that one lot of 18-year-olds come out, roughly three years later, with artistic beliefs distinct from another lot who went to a different university (and studied the same texts)?

An interview with the playwright Christopher Hampton, published in a Cambridge poetry magazine when I was a student, told that during the student uprisings which ran round the whole world after 1967 Oxford had no demonstrations of any kind. This is not surprising. If you feel that you are going to enjoy a position of privilege and influence and esteem in adult society, why smash the arrangements in that society which control privilege etc.? If you are sure of where the path to luxury and status lies, why go to so much effort to protest an outcome which is already safely rigged in your benefit? Oxford people were not asking themselves "am I left-wing enough". (This need not be literally true, but let myth stand in for history this once.) The contrast between the behaviour of 19-year-olds at Oxford and their peers at, say, Cambridge, Glasgow or the London School of Economics, was startling. The corollary was that the whole "British Poetry Revival", with its reckless investment in the headiest of left-wing theories and raids into a liberated lifestyle, would pass Oxford by. Further, that the cultural managers of the new generation would maintain their founding links with patron institutions and have no place for the new poetry.

It was profoundly natural that these worldly wise teenagers should regard their peers, the protesters, as uncouth. Their efforts were practiced, reliable, as smooth as only traditional acts can be. The Left was cannoning into an unpredictable future, where the excitement was that turbulent principle which meant that most effort would, inevitably, be wasted. Equally in poetry, the possessors felt no urge to experiment—to surrender to chance and speculation, to throw away prime position in favour of unbounded possibilities (and too many outcomes where they *did not win*). The antique quality of this poetry for the affluent would be instantly recognizable to any left-liberal reader, like Tuma, or anyone who had accepted the changes of the 40 years after 1960; equally recognizable to a kind of ally in whom the Oxford person would not wish to recognise themselves reflected. The anglophiles in the USA are divided between the Left and the Right—who can really be a problem. Narcissism has such surprises waiting for its gaze.

We claimed that the dominant line within 20th century English poetry was the Oxford line. The nature of this domination is not wholly visible in the poems. It has also to do, quite crucially, with networking, media manipulation, fashion, and the ability to please the powerful. Notoriously, power over poetry rests with people who have no knowledge of modern poetry, and who judge poets and cultural managers by quite non-artistic, external, criteria. Evidence offered to me shows the Oxford ethos as laying great stress on making a career, on pleasing the powerful, on giving an impression of being perfectly smooth and in control, on marketing—a trade which starts with marketing yourself. The ability to create a stir around a poem is like making a restaurant fashionable. The issue about creating an image is not about inflation; the propaganda around avant-garde poetry is designed to create a vast imaginary territory and proclaim ownership of it, to assert the inferiority of other poets, to manage opinion and discussion. The issue is that the Oxford style propaganda is far more effective, producing stories which the media actually want to run. It is tempting and amusing rather than abstract, subversive, and seeking domination. Charm is a feature of these smart cultural operators, but they value their time—if you aren't important then their attitude is one of humiliation, and anxiety in case they become associated with you. People who believe in the principle of patronage have a sense of hierarchy so mighty that all their social perceptions are coloured by it. Other poets are more egalitarian and have a sense of comradeship. The Oxford line does not have any role for artists who withdraw in order to experiment and go through a stage of failure before their innovations become recognised. At certain points it would seem that the reaction against this conservative line was the main emotion on the scene—and that the main policy of the cultural managers was to eliminate their critics. The charm ran out here. But being within the double mirror system of prestige is unconscionably seductive: where precious gifts are consonant with high social standing and high social standing exalts the price of the gifts. The patrons are keen on talent-spotting; the lure of being recruited because of overwhelming talent, of being acknowledged, produces a euphoria which is only to be envied. It radiates outwards as a state of group narcissism which offers people membership as long as they acquire the underlying values. Impressionable 18-year-olds who are drawn into all this are given symbolic "permission" to use a set of stylemes which are at least able to produce significant poems, and which simultaneously support a way of conversing and a technique for going about the culture business. Oxford poetry is continuous with a social stance, a social life that many people lead; this skill set makes prize pupils, on graduating, better equipped to acquire assets like jobs and public appearances than other 23-year-olds who have developed no technique at all. The least we can say about this machine is that it works as well for the future authors of masterpieces as for self-regarding *dilettanti*.

Mary-Sue was intimidated by her first term at Oxford, in 1953, after growing up as the daughter of a goose-girl on a farm in East Volhynia. Everyone is so *intelligent*, she lisped, while crying in a pew in the 11th-century college chapel. After early *faux pas* she dazzled everyone with her paper on the influence of Jesuit interior decoration on Walter Pater. In 1954 she was arrested for after-hours drinking at a fashionable club by a Constable Morse, with whom she kept in touch after the court appearance. She soon rose to be secretary of the Poetry Society and editor of *Poetry Oxford*, a role she shared with Martin Seymour-Smith, George MacBeth, and Michael Horovitz. After a dizzying year at Georgetown on a Cold War Culture scholarship to write a dissertation on 'The pronunciation of Anglo-Latin 1800–1950', she went to a job at the National Trust in the team with special responsibility for the care and upkeep of venerable literati. In 1956, **Mary-Sue** encouraged Sandy Wilson to telegraph Bert Brecht in East Berlin to suggest a pastiche musical set in the '20s in which happy-go-lucky young communists in Wedding have a surprise box office hit. Later, she collaborated with Wilson in the first trial production of 'Valmouth', his Firbank musical, in which she played Walter Pater. In 1970 Geoffrey Hill told **Mary-Sue** that he was having problems with two poems he was writing. After a few minutes she explained to him that he could splice the two poems together to create a montage tilting modernistically to and fro between a Worcestershire childhood in the 1940s and the kingdom of Offa in the early ninth century. Hill was very dubious, pointing out that there are no montages in the Bible. Anyway the double-header sounded too much like Ornette's Double Quartet whereas he was more of a Sonny Rollins man. **Mary-Sue** had not lectured at the Anglo-Catholic seminary in Iffley on 'A textual enigma in the sermons of Bellarmine' for nothing. After rapid thought she pointed out that Matthew Paris—or the pseudo-Paris Continuator Verulamensis—had written the *Vitae Duorum Offarum*, lives of the two Offas, juxtaposing the 5th-century Angle and the 9th-century Mercian, so that the bifocal depth had unquestionable support. She gave him the name "Vespasian Interlinear" which in the final version became *Mercian Hymns*.

It is not a random incident that **Ian Hamilton** was in a position to control this reference book, nor that he had a managerial career in poetry for more than thirty years without having any ability as a poet. He had acquired the ability to form alliances both with his peers and with potential patrons, willing for example to subsidise his magazine. I don't want to close the door on these abilities; the game has to be played, before it starts you can't predict if it will go well. Also, given the possibilities for rage and contention the scene is going to work better if you have notably smooth, suave, sociable people doing the negotiation and making the arrangements, with an obvious stake in affable relations rather than in immovable values. Detachment minimises conflict—if you are dealing with dozens of poets most of whom really have no talent then it's going to work better if you aren't too up front about your artistic beliefs, if you can be charming to anybody who turns up. As for the outside patrons, it's inevitable that poetry is dependent on the Arts Council, the BBC, on large circulation magazines which occasionally run poetry reviews, on High Street shops, and so on. You can't make this go away by replacing all the poetry managers.

Narcissism is infantile and yet there is no satisfying replacement for it. Its natural home is in networks where it reverberates and catches itself always in its own nets—a rare bird in a forest made of birds. As the glass enclosure closes up the last gaps in its self, it suddenly emerges that status is also narcissism, newly instated as property and as the custom of the country.

The Oxford insider, I take it, is simultaneously wrapped around a core of narcissism like chocolate around a dollop of liqueur, and is at the core of a network which wraps him around like a shell of chocolate. There is nothing esoteric about this success, which is public in its nature. The majority of people you encounter will after all concede that what they have in the way of social charms and prestige is not successful. The impression of effortlessness is what persuades most people that they admire this style and truly do not want to put obstacles in its way. This ease makes every social contact so easy. The young people are so very worthy of being spoilt and rewarded and the old people are so dignified by the act of spoiling and rewarding them. Why argue about the arbitrary quality of this investment with prestige and the key to all the walled gardens when we live in England and this investiture is not potential but actual? Why have a command of language unless what you have to say is something which excites other people and which they want to repeat, and what you have to hear is also something splendidly flattering to you?

There is no point in developing an artificial and original style of language when the pattern of speech you already share says perfectly clearly what kind of person you are. That is to say, Why would someone inside this park ever want to be anywhere else?

Walter Pater (1839–94)

Pater did not invent the state of rapturous group narcissism, but his conception of it as the basis for every great era in the past of Western culture, and as a design for living, was and is irresistible. Pater's point of departure is very simple, in view of the evidence collected by Michael Levey in his biography. He had no money, and planned to become a priest despite his agnosticism: he told his best friend that it would be fun to be ordained and not believe a single word of what one said (p.85). Later, still agnostic, he could only express his belief in earthly pleasures above piety if speaking cautiously. The stirrings of homosexual desire are widely agreed, in the absence of documentary support, to have called for further discretion. This cluster of coincidences came together to produce a quality of distantiation and obliquity, even of hypocrisy and ambivalence, which appealed to anyone who wanted to hide their face: everything profound loves a mask, as Nietzsche said. Not every mask is hiding anything sophisticated or exotic.

Pater went up to Oxford intending to become an Anglican priest. At the end of his life, he was supposedly contemplating joining the priesthood anyway—the Unitarian church, a minor sect hardly even inside the broad spectrum of Dissent. He never lost his spiritual intensity, and that combination of spirituality, deep Classical learning, and obsession with the intricate details of language, makes him close to his pupil Gerard Manley Hopkins. Most of his published work is about visual art, and his most famous book is *Studies in the History of the Renaissance*. He is not to any great extent interested in the available facts about the Renaissance, and his essays are not designed to recover historic realities. Theology, relations with patrons, the game of prestige, mean little to him. The point of his work is not obvious, and is certainly never overtly stated. It would be easy to summarise it in a quite misleading way: it is oblique and intricate and the message is embedded in that receding and distancing structure.

One of his first published essays was on Johann Winckelmann (1717–68), a German scholar who founded the scientific study of art history, but who also represented in its pure form the homoerotic approach to Greek art, with the appreciation of beautifully proportioned male nudes being more than an academic duty. Plato was known to be part of a homosocial group of male intellectuals, which is the story told in the incidental staging of the dialogues; the Renaissance added the shocking intensity of pride and self-regard of nobles with great artists in their pay. Pater's inclinations were no secret to those of his contemporaries who could read the code of discourse about Platonic love, the beauty of male statues, and so forth. His inclinations were shared by enough of the products of the public schools and universities for his aesthetic line to be part of a cultural movement rather than a private escape into a Greek world, and he was sufficient of a public figure to be satirised in W.H. Mallock's novel *The New Republic* (1876). The *only* published essay where he spoke directly about undue admiration for the male form was the one on Winckelmann, to whom the admiration is attributed; moreover this essay was published anonymously. Pater is the prelate of uplifting chastity, not of carnal homosexuality. The endless recession which gives his work its dizzying depth is also the steady remoteness from carnal fulfilment and release of tension. Although his work has the ability to make anyone who partakes of it feel part of an aristocratic elite, he did not come from money, and the intensity of his aesthetic dedication is not the product of privilege or moneyed leisure.

His work is notoriously little read today, but many of the texts are available here: http://www.gutenberg.org/browse/authors/p#a1367

The four imaginary portraits express the most suggestive aspect of his work. The extreme stylisation of these four figures who are "live" but barely seem to have left the paintings they come from suggests the possibility of a whole life of narcissistic self-cultivation. His portraits are also erotic projections. The frozen scenes are rigid—perhaps because they are about to vanish back into smoke, perhaps because they are about to evolve into something more basically erotic and tumescent. The suggestion of life as a screen on which the imagination projects strange and essential impulses deeply influenced Proust and Huizinga. They lack reality—they are never allowed to become more than projections. Art itself is shown as something subject to the will of the beholder. The implication that in erotic relations the other person can also be used as a projection, a stylised depiction of exotic and occult forces, is unstated. The important feature is not that Pater is captured by the images he dedicates himself to nor that he feels apart from them but the exact quality of his reflexive immersion in them, its resemblance to a voluntary dream in which we wish for a scene and then see it. There is no attempt to give the imaginary portraits three-dimensional reality; rather a whole landscape is stylised so that they can move through it as if through the scenery of a ballet, everything wrung through a sieve of stylisation until it is homogeneous and dreamlike. We are not supposed to think that 15th-century Flanders looked like a painting; the figures are autonomous from physics or sociology but have no wills of their own. There are four tales in *Imaginary Portraits*, but to these we can add four more: 'A Child in the House' 'Emerald Uthwart', *Gaston de Latour*, and 'Apollo in Picardy', as well as the novel *Marius the Epicurean*. 'Apollo in Picardy' is the story where Apollo simply turns up in Picardy, hair and all, and re-enacts the myth involving him and the boy Hyacinth. (It's in *Miscellaneous Studies*, which is there on the Internet.) The formula was decoration and repression.

Pater is close to the *Symboliste* movement, and it would be hard to define something in his approach to art which is really missing from Symbolisme. Yet, his influence was so great that the specific ways in which English 20th-century writing misses modernism can be attributed to him. He was not Baudelaire. He had a key influence on the development of the horror novel in English, and his work has a recurring climactic violence replacing the missing sexuality. Both the myth and the ritualised death anticipate *The Waste Land*, which includes "the hyacinth girl" in a bit part.

He wrote a great deal for large-circulation magazines, and was able to reach a wide educated public; he was the equivalent of a modern television don, not an obscure cultist content to speak to a dozen effete acolytes. Yet, I find Pater's prose unreadable. Something is alive in there but only like a fish moving beneath a hundred feet of only partially transparent water. This is consistent with intensive reworking of a surface to eliminate every sign of the deep impulses, with their pressure of criminality and impiety or heresy. He did not want martyrdom, and the mixture of prominence and sibylline clarity brought him close to it at every step. Pater's journey into distantiation and alienation was revolutionary and foresaw a new age in which those qualities would rule, but did not make for warmth or openness. This is quite different from the effect of thinking about his prose—something a thousand times more rewarding than actually reading it. The concept of *Imaginary Portraits* is wonderful. This is just underlined by reading Ronald Firbank and Sacheverell Sitwell, two writers obviously much influenced by Pater, whose work is warm, emotionally direct, and light in touch. He was known for rewriting his prose endlessly, producing a marmoreal, completely controlled, surface, a wondrously opulent thing, a hollow gleam. Probably, every rewrite dropped the temperature and hid the true motives more thoroughly. Consider this passage, set in 16th century France, from the opening of *Gaston de Latour*:

> They had set out on foot, after a votive mass said early in the old chapel of the manor, to assist at the ceremony of the day. Distinguishable from afar by unusual height in proportion to its breadth within, the church of Saint Hubert had an atmosphere, a daylight, to itself. Its stained glass, work of the same hands that had wrought for the cathedral of Chartres, admitted only an almost angry ray of purple or crimson, here or there, across the dark, roomy spaces. The heart, the heart of youth at least, sank, as one entered, stepping warily out of the sunshine over the sepulchral stones which formed the entire pavement of the church, a great blazonry of family history from age to age for indefatigable eyes. An abundance of almost life-sized sculpture clung to the pillars, lurked in the angles, seemed, with those symbolical gestures, and mystic faces ready to speak their parts, to be almost in motion through the gloom. Many years after, Gaston de Latour, an enemy of all Gothic darkness or heaviness, returning to his home full of a later taste, changed all that. A thicket of airy spires rose above the sanctuary; the blind triforium broke into one continuous window; the heavy masses of stone were pared down with wonderful dexterity of hand, till not a hand's-breadth remained uncovered by delicate tracery, as from the fair white roof, touched sparingly with gold, down to the subterranean chapel of Saint Taurin, where the peasants of La Beauce came to pray for rain, not a space was left unsearched by cheerful daylight, refined, but hardly dimmed at all, by painted glass mimicking the clearness of the open sky. In the sombre old church all was in stately order now: the dusky, jewelled reliquaries, the ancient devotional ornaments from the manor—much-prized family possessions, sufficient to furnish the whole array of a great ecclesiastical function

like this—the lights burning, flowers everywhere, gathered amid the last handfuls of the harvest by the peasant-women, who came to present their children for the happy chance of an episcopal blessing.

This is extremely stylised, but the motive is not obvious; we have to guess at it. This is a work of art dedicated to evoking another work of art, and yet reducing it to a tool in some hidden design. The style is unctuous, Latinate, almost ecclesiastical. De Latour is not described from the inside at all. We are only told about his passion for architecture, as a total expression of the man. On the second page of the romance we discover that he has decided to become a monk. Again, we find out nothing about his motives; the romance takes a firm path away from worldly interests, and the building project, the realm of aesthetic choice, strides further towards totality.

Pater was a deeply spiritual man. He was an art connoisseur who did *not* hang out with millionaires and take their money. He was hardly aware that this ejection of every ounce of personality into an object, the ability to deify a work of human hands, was wonderfully capable of being taken over by a class dedicated to conspicuous consumption, that it fitted so well into the pockets of those who would believe that their possession of elaborate and exclusive objects, such as buildings or cars, made them the winners in life's contest. It was hardly a deviation from artistic ambition when he made his heroes so superior and admirable and indifferent to others, but in combination with their aristocratic train of life this was creating objects of envy which would fit into less exalted daydreams. We can easily take on the idea that other men have unfeasibly large amounts of money, but the idea that their fetish commodities are imaginary portraits of their austere will to form and to spiritual triumph, with every detail showing an almost secret refinement of impulse and knowledge, is less easy to snuggle up to.

The combination of secretiveness and egocentricity will always attract the proud. If we see something very smooth, emotionally cold, glittering but almost unmotivated, in the 1980s, we could attribute it to Postmodernism, but there is another possible attribution— to something much older and more native, the lingering and de-spiritualised influence of Pater.

W.H. Auden and the hegemony of light verse

Auden's prestige in the '50s and '60s, and the influence he exerted on hundreds of young poets in favour of infantilism, domesticity, and triviality, cannot be exaggerated. I have written on Auden (1907–73) but that piece cannot find space here, first because he did not do anything significant in the period after 1960, and secondly because everyone already has their opinion of Auden and there is no point bringing the matter up. The question of his influence is more important. I will extract two points from the essay.

"Auden is in fact entirely self-centred, his sentiments (under whatever cover) are personal lamentations." (Garrett Jones) This remark in a letter written in 1934 is astonishingly prophetic about Auden's whole career. Egoism is his speciality. But the Western public prefers to see events through one person's eyes, and this is true over all media, not just in poetry.

If Auden anticipated something, it was not committed art, but the new cultural consumer product which we call the middlebrow, being developed on radio while he wrote, and already groping towards becoming television. The travelogue is a typical product for this market. His infernal fluency, like the incessant images of television, distracts us from the lack of high points in his work. Especially important is the star phenomenon: we would not tolerate banalities from an idiot, but we find banality flattering when it is rolled out by a professor, or a famous poet. Clearly, he could say something we would find it hard to understand: so that his avoidance of intelligence appears as generosity. The points which the middlebrow listener finds exhausting are thought and emotion: Auden was popular, and indeed made a living, not despite avoiding these but because of it.

D.S. Savage, in *The Personal Principle*, his 1944 Personalist book on modern poetry, had already identified Auden as having made an epochal swerve into light verse, and undemanding entertainment: "The first sign of literal disintegration in Auden's poetry took the form of a fissure between the solemn and the farcical elements in his work. (…) In the early poems, as we know, seriousness and satire combined. But as Auden developed into the poet of the pontifical solemnity of

Look, Stranger…" a mutilated and uninteresting light verse separated out. "An ominous interest in 'light verse' was apparent as early as 1935. (…) Later he began to write verse which was self-consciously 'light' in character. (…) He became, in other words, a 'light' verse specialist or expert." No doubt this switch, which Savage locates around 1939, was influential in shaping a very wide sector of publicly visible English poetry, and in legitimating a tone of slick ninny inanity. We are going to suggest that this *sprezzatura* was bound to be attractive to any group involved with intellectual endeavour.

The chief quality of the early verse is to be enigmatic. This is the direct link to Pater; if Auden simply wanted to be evasive, local literary heritage encouraged that. We can imagine the narrative pictures which would connect all the enigmatic and silent images of so many of his early books: like Pater he writes secondary texts to primary pictures *which may however be imaginary*. Familiarity has not made his poems cease to be enigmatic; they are merely overlaid by an assumption about what the real meaning is, which time and apathy have allowed to appear solid. His imitators have reproduced the ambiguity—thus linking poetry of the 1980s back to Pater.

John Betjeman

I recorded that Radio 4 broadcast on 28/8/06 that 2 ½ million copies sold of Betjeman's *Collected Poems*. This dwarfs the sales of any book of poetry around it. Betjeman dominated Auden over 20 years, as Auden progressively imitated his manner and tone. He also spent much of his career in broadcasting, being one of the very first to deliver the appreciation of architecture into a mass medium. The odd mixture of speech and written forms which broadcasting came up with was something Betjeman understood very well. His peculiar lack of intensity was unbelievably influential on English poetry. His relaxed tones made people feel they were part of a conversation around a pub table—the nature of the conversation made revolutionary resentment of the old high culture seem ridiculous.

There is also a direct link between Pater and Betjeman, and I chose the passage from *Gaston de Latour* to illustrate how they were interested in the same information but wrote about it in completely different moods. Betjeman spent his whole career relating architectural style to spiritual qualities, as Pater did for his high-ranking monk; his knowledge of church design and of all the accoutrements (achievements, reredoses, rood-screens, what have you) came out of a notoriously Oxonian aestheticism, an exit into objects. No one was more witty, superficial, and stylised than the undergraduate Betjeman. Yet, what he ended up with was full of warmth and emotion: his knowledge of church furniture let him capture the spiritual life of middle class Anglicans caught in objects, the worn, shabby, culturally derivative bric à brac of the parish church. Their relation to these objects was of profound significance to them.

Although I do not like any of his poetry, I keep coming back to Betjeman because his vision of the status-conscious individual, as an ego surrounded by a bric à brac of words and pride-objects as a nucleus is surrounded by electrons, is so persuasive; especially for dealing with poets. Poems, notoriously, acquire objects and succeed or fail via their skill in doing so. The history of poetry includes a catalogue of objects flowing through the poems. His vision of a country moving from Anglicanism to consumerism (and the relic soteriology and bliss lurking inside the latter) is too good to resist. Today, all accept that consuming is something people do, rather than a betrayal of sound socialist ideals. People are defined by their objects, and constantly striving to redefine themselves through acquiring new ones or battering the old ones. The tones which Betjeman left out have been left out of popular English poetry ever since.

His conception of the ego's pet objects as small-scale and comic is the one I like best. Let's not try to punish people for writing bad poetry or for being upwardly mobile (a movement which only conservatives dislike). Forty years ago, books spoke of literature and life as if the substantive reality outside human vagary could be used as a measure to disqualify bad and deviant poems. Betjeman was writing under the assumption that human activity is mainly self-referential. This is where he is closest to Pater.

The archaeologist P.V. Glob remarks that, around 200 AD, a fireplace was built in Denmark (where the Angles came from) with glazed pottery surround: clearly in imitation of a Roman mosaic, which the purchaser had heard of, but could not get local technologists to reproduce. An enemy of all Balticdom and of *terre pisée* floors, he returned to the land of his birth full of a new taste. Ever since, we have been seeing the decentralisation of elite domestic objects and manners; and we have to sympathise with this trend and not apply conservative criteria like authenticity. Instead, let us speak excitably of stratified diffusion, elite innovation within rules that generate innovation, sites of tuition in elite value scales, curves of leads and lags, flotation of styles, public tribunals of taste. Betjeman, prepared for this sort of activity by his father's background running a furniture manufacturer's, was a past master at it: he gave millions of people an experience of Oxford which they had not had, and injected a share of the old elite culture into the new broadcasting culture. He shows linguistic expertise as an elite attainment which allows him to speak to the radio audience as a whole rather than to an elite only. No, you can't live by the barbarian Baltic and pretend it's the Mediterranean. But you can imitate Roman décors and dream. Enough of seeing the barbarians as mainly warriors: time to regard them as the inventors of tourism and the greatest shoppers of all time. There's just no stopping those Angles from shopping.

Speech is a form of consumption (and reading poetry is an act of consuming speech). Once we accept this, we can compare speech patterns with the purchasing patterns analysed by historians of furniture and clothes. Poems too are filled with speech patterns. As individuals are upwardly mobile, the forms are downwardly mobile, being successfully imitated. How can we look at irony, insouciance, narcissism, posing, evasiveness, etc. and not realise that they have been features of writing from Oxford since the 1920s at the very least? How can someone dissolve away all seriousness in order to create an artificial aesthetic order in which to carry out cherished and fantastic acts and avoid being connected back to Walter Pater and a whole tradition of Oxford aesthetes doing exactly that?

Where did two and a half million people come from to buy this alarmingly middle-class verse? Over a generation after 1960, the middle class grew from 20% of the population to 50% of it, a social revolution which could not be repeated but which expressed all of its phases in art. Education played a pivotal role in this. In the years after the first great expansion of the universities, say 1960 to 1978, the students were aware of their dependence on the working masses from whom they were growing more distinct, and invested heavily in left-wing politics at least partly out of guilt. The realisation that they were a new affluent class was dodged until the very last minute, people were as if surprised that they wore suits and worked indoors in the warm. Later, and most especially in the Thatcher years, students were eager to become more distinct, and had no thoughts for anything but the new affluent class they intended to join. They were quite conscious of being the new middle class, and with that wanted the traditional privileges of the middle class, of which going to Oxford and having the Oxford manner were hardly the smallest. We have already spoken of this *upward mobility of individuals* and *downward mobility of forms*. The leisure patterns of the privileged few in the 1920s become some of the favoured patterns of the affluent many in the 1980s, and this included shallow and suave poetry. I can't really believe that insouciance is not the *direct product of affluence*, but is something worked out after years of philosophical searching and disproving of grand intellectual structures.

Personally I feel that it would be more heinous to deny to the new bourgeois masses the cultural equipment of the old middle class minority than to acquire those assets. Teasing people a little about the imitative status of their cultural white goods does not mean that I want everyone to write like Alan Sillitoe. It is a constitutive quality of culture to be participative and to allow imitation and adoption. This is no less true of English middle class culture, or upper middle class culture, than of a religion or of surrealism or *cynghanedd*. The precious cultural acts are simultaneously difficult and free for all. The link with status is no hindrance: when millions of people were acquiring the status, it was logical for them to acquire the cultural patter that goes with it. Further, the experiment with demolishing inherited aristocratic and bourgeois culture had a free run in the sixties and seventies, and by all accounts was not successful. It would be perverse to reject the alternative as well. A key opposition here is between intellectual activity as work and intellectual activity as irony, detachment, leisure, game, in fact *anything but labour*. Mottram had all too clearly identified the kind of poetry he liked with *hard work*, both in acquiring the cultural code and in reading the exalted texts. The leisurely line had been developed to perfection in Oxford, and had probably already reached modern perfection in the figures of Pater and Firbank. Perhaps we have a puritan class licensed to live by hard work, austerity, rigorous self examination, who are masquerading as negligent aesthetes. In a community of intellectuals, social conversation is only going to be possible if there is a taboo on going into your work in too much detail. The company was based on taking intellectual pains and on the hard intellectual professions which such exercises prepared for, so that advertising hard work and obscure knowledge was the most depressing thing. Such work was not apt to make people happy. People engaged in it admired a style of not overworking and worrying but being natural and drawing on the whole-brain faculties which are inhibited by reflexivity. The ability to do things quickly and naturally was the very object of envy; a pattern of the mind which could be advertised by qualities in verse. *Sprezzatura*, the habit of doing things with an air of ease and negligence, was the keyword. Eric Mottram, significantly, was a product of Cambridge. He admired dumbfoundingly original and effortful projects in which the intellect could stretch over vast spaces.

Oxford took on Pater for the long run. The most obvious feature of the adaptation is the decline in intensity. You could unplug the homosexuality, the displaced Greek spirituality, the exaltation, and end up with just the superciliousness and the smooth finish. The way of reaching sophistication by becoming completely detached from the situation you are depicting, disconnecting from it so that you could focus on the tiny details of transition between planes and sentence structure, worked too well not to be endlessly re-used. In English culture, emotional intensity is a lower class trait, because the goal of the upper middle class to reach the wished-for level of distantiation and self-control has been achieved so pervasively by those able to observe the behaviour codes close up. A whole stratum of English writers is unable to write directly about emotion—cut off from lyric poetry.

The question of the Oxford influence is one of the major questions about 20th-century English literature, and is not one I can claim to have resolved or even fully set out. I would like to see a book about Oxford poetry, as also one about the London school. Even if you accept that a house style exists for poets at Oxford, it is clear that many people react against it after leaving and that many others find it incompatible with their own character even as student poets. The subject comprises dozens of gifted figures whose work calls for imaginative appreciation rather than complacent dismissal.

Cerddi Hir and communalist poetry

An individualist can't be attractive because they care about themselves and not you. They can't be a good person. The more poetry they write, the more you find out about them. But they can offer you the same bet that they made: if you go with them you can in their place be as selfish as they are and also make experience centre on you.

We are going to talk now about a book called *Cerddi Hir* (long poems), an anthology of ten poems in Welsh made by Islwyn Jones and Gwilym Rees Hughes. The dates of the poems are between 1941 and 1969. Seven of these poems are in *vers libre*, although not of a strident sort, and they owe their nature to commissions for the radio, which wanted poems of a certain length to provide a big, continuous focus for the listeners. There was also a legitimated genre of *pryddest*, a poem of unspecified length which could include unrhymed and irregular verse. I don't have enough Welsh to read poetry in large quantities, so the normal pattern of grasping a context and then relating individual poems to it does not work for me. These poems have to stand by themselves. These long poems were chosen because discussion of thematic lines and construction can be carried out in English, in contrast to details of metrical/semantic interaction which can only be brought over with great effort. These poems are forced to make explicit statements of shared symbolism where short poems may simply refer back to and enact complexes shared implicitly. Insofar as the poems are not short and not built into intricate and formal phonetic patterning, we can probably say they are atypical of Welsh poetry.

The contribution of this chapter to the book is to demonstrate the existence of another mainstream within the island, which will simultaneously naturalise the London/Oxford m-stream which we are often discussing and give indications that there are other centres of cultural attraction which compete with it and which may equally well give the poet feelings of belonging, of security, of carrying out a shared and predestined pattern.

Poetry in *Cymraeg* has been chosen because of the well known collapse and prone position of Scottish and Anglo-Welsh and North English poetry in the mid-century. *Cymraeg* poetry was certainly not going through a bad patch in the 1950s. Including Welsh poems is an ideological gesture which is not a solid structure because I don't have the knowledge. To clarify, I do think Wales is complete without England but I don't think a book on British poetry is complete without that high-value P-Celtic component. I am not the best commentator on these poems—the Welsh-speaking critics are the best source—so I will keep it short.

It is normal to have a mainstream, a set of limits within which poetry is usually, normally, written. The experience of boredom at familiar patterns, even, is normal. We are looking at a m-stream which resembles the Oxford m-stream but the key assets appear in different forms or marques of design. Terms like *Christian, formalist, moralising, conservative* are applicable in both areas looked at but on analysis they are deployed in quite different ways. If we get into the fine detail the data start to get too thin to support the generalisations. The simplest difference might be that between communalism and individualism.

I want to suggest (as mentioned in *The Council of Heresy*) that there is a communalist pole or party in poetry and that while this qualifies as part of the m-stream it is in great contrast to other parts of the centre which are severely privatised and invested in the sovereign individual. These poems can stand as a "type-site" for communalism. Because of its serene attitude towards style, this area is not narrowly part of "the 1950s". It is much more like "timeless". You may notice that these are original poems and not obviously m-stream in any restrictive sense. This is because I would rather write about interesting poems.

I propose to use the introduction by R. Gerallt Jones as a definition of communalist, where he says, "But although nation and nationalism throw a heavy shadow across the poetry of the period, although the perishing of a nation is the framework for the tragedy and the faintness of the Language is deepening the lack of communication, yet the crisis is personal and individual at its root. This is a century which has seen the individual become isolated in his own world. In a society which has become crushingly over-ordered and oppressive in its interest in the private world of each individual, the individual has turned inside for security in his own thought and soul. And as an increasing degeneration has come over the world of belief, and on the firm foundations of the old rural society, there has been less and less security to be found, even in the womb of the individual. In the words of Professor J.R. Jones, a "crisis of evacuation of meaning" has come over a society which once succeeded quite well in papering over the cracks in creation. Despair in this situation and the evident need to regain creed and direction have come to the surface in this volume[.]" [*my translation*] This is a negative definition but makes clear the investment which communalist poets have: they do not take this isolation as a fact and are writing against it even where it impinges on their world. I presume that you recognise these sentiments and that they have been expressed hundreds of times, are in fact widespread enough to nourish a whole genre. (I discussed J.R. Jones and his work *Bychanfyd* or microcosm in *Centre-Periphery*.) The communalist poet speaks from inside a community and the information supplied in the poem draws on a rich imaginative knowledge of the subjective experience of a great range of people within that community. Its subject is the fate of the community as an entity rather than the fate of individuals who are a temporary part of it.

This communalist strand is noticeably bound to particular regions within the United Kingdom. I want to suggest, and this is less clear, that the project of close reading, elimination of rhetoric, elimination of what cannot be tested empirically, is not communalist and that the Communalist Matter is pinpointed and resident precisely in the rhetorical flight with its potent symbolism and billowing offer of an exalted and shared identity. Empiricism is allied in the United Kingdom with the triumph of private property and of possessive individualism. The line of reflexive critique tends to eliminate shared symbolism at every step.

I want to distinguish communalism from collectivism. Although many such writers have a Left political view and might not dislike the word "collectivism", many others have a Christian view of the human community based on faith and the parish. George Crabbe springs to mind here. Also, many writers with a theoretical Marxist affiliation are quite unable to write about the community and spend their lives chasing incomprehensible theoretical points and staging games in which they verbally defeat their rivals.

I have had difficulty in listing English writers, as opposed to Scottish or Welsh ones, who are clearly communalist. John Masefield and Wilfred Gibson spring to mind. Did it really stop with them, the alarming and super-productive stars of around 1912? This is a question which could easily occupy a whole book. Only one moment seems clear. The *documentary style* was a feature of mid-century English poetry. It promised to write about ordinary people, but it also needed to outdo Masefield and Gibson, who were still writing in the 1930s and whose claims to be outstanding writers about the common people were irrefutable. We can see it as replacing a communalist manner, tied also to a shift in the knowledge base of welfare politics, in which statistics and objective observation replaced sympathetic attention and personal intuition (which itself was like holiness, like religious insight). This new manner was structurally commensurate with the activities of central government, which had replaced the parish as the source of schools and welfare services. It was like legislation which deals with the typical and which for that reason works for the entire country. The picture is composite. However, it is fair to say that the documentary of Auden, MacNeice, and Day Lewis had too great a gap between the poet and the subjects, and had the poet as too much the central figure. There is no fusion between the poet and the human subjects. A huge share of the poem's claim to cultural significance is that the poet is an exceptional and virtuosic figure. His decisive connections are with other important cultural figures, *not* with the miners, village labourers, housewives, and so on. Meanwhile poets without those connections do not get written into literary history.

In order to get at the dominance of domestic anecdote, and why the documentary petered out into "empiricism" on a domestic scale, we have to understand the passion of the documentary, which lasted from at least 1930 to the middle 1950s. I discussed the passion in *Origins of the Underground*. All I will say is that it was a great idea and that the outcome was not simply failure and withdrawal. The romance between poetry, sociology, and the camera has had many episodes and is not over.

Evidently these poems are not strenuously original and their linguistic register is such that they were expected to reach a wide audience, within the cymrophone community. I mentioned that several of them were written for radio broadcast. It would be perverse to deny that they are *mainstream* poems, and this is part of their strength. To make that clearer, we have Euros Bowen's poem 'Difodiant' which falls outside the Welsh mainstream because it uses an unconventional metrical pattern and because the way it is written is difficult, if also connected to Welsh classicism.

W.J. Gruffydd's poem *Ffenestri* was an entry in competition in the 1955 national eisteddfod. It is about the decay of a small community, perhaps just a hamlet, called Pen Cwm Bach and sited on some hill in Cardiganshire. It starts with the ruins, and we feel that the place is deserted in around 1950 and the writer is remembering it as it was in perhaps 1910.

> There is yonder the skeleton of a cowshed in the yard
> Where someone stuffed friend-to-the-calf hay
> Into the foot-square window, when the muck
> Was concrete round the dung-heap of horn, and the wind
> Was scorching the hair of the greybeard. I see through
> The crinkled armful of the hay, the day-and-night's distant
> Wild paradise of the peacock, and their pride
> In pulling-dropping a hand across the broad back
> Of animals.

The whole history of the place is encompassed: the poem recalls the foundation, as a *ty unnos*, in a Welsh customary right that, if you went onto the common land and set up a house which was built between dusk and dawn, you had the right to live in it. This implies that the land is not especially good: the poet stresses the quality of the vegetation (gorse, broom, heather) which marks the soil out unmistakeably as thin and acid, probably leached because it is on a slope. The place name element *pen* means head, so we are in hills. The title means windows. We see them in ruined houses, offering a view into empty rooms as if we were looking in on a family scene: "You can see beyond the solid shoulder of the Bank/ Sockets in its wall without glass or pane/ Like the where-eyes-were of a skull on the moor/ Staring across the peat". But there is another meaning: because death climbed in at the windows, he says, *Oherwydd dringodd Angau i'r ffenestri*.

The stress on the environment marks out the subject as the whole community in its connection with the land as the means of subsistence. It follows logically that we do not hear about any individuals. The speaker is not identified. Three of the stanzas are in quotation marks:

they are spoken by the dead in the cemetery, led in by the words "Nyni y meirwon", we the dead. They do not speak as individuals. They speak for others as well as themselves. We hear about people dying of TB. The last line in the poem is again *Because death climbed in at the windows.* We can think of a passage in a Lynette Roberts article about the lack of windows destroying rural health: the TB bacillus liked damp dark conditions and so sunlight was its enemy. The line may mean that the windows which *weren't* there let death by TB in. TB is a slow infection and so the illness is a product of intimacy: you infect the rest of your family. "They cannot live long/ When the living earth pushes itself/ Into the back of stye homes, and the tainted paw/ Of decline, slowly but surely dilapidates the flesh." (*Diclein*, English word, means "consumption". I think the houses were built into the side of the hill so that "living earth" means the soil itself shifting and coming in.) The compound phrases are not Welsh idiom and I think are there because he is thinking back to childhood and speaking like a child.

In the last part of the poem, we are led from the windows of the train going South and taking young people away, to the voices of the dead reproaching the young for leaving and letting the thistles grow rife, the fences collapse, and the stray sheep wander unheeded. "We can no longer look through the windows of the flesh", it says, turning on the Biblical phrase about the eyes as *windows* of the soul and on a different phrase about the "carnal eye" which sees material things, whereas the spiritual eye sees spiritual things. This suggests that the haunting phrase about Angau refers to a spiritual condition: death climbed in at the eyes, the young people lost sight of communal values, they went away, and the settlement died.

'The Sound of the Wind Blowing' (1951), a radio poem by James Kitchener Davies (1902–52), is a deathbed speech by a character who accuses himself of hypocrisy and selfishness but who seems more like a saint who is putting inhuman pressure on himself. He has been a street orator, labour leader and politician, of nationalist bent. We hear of him "thy dragon rampant hobnobbing with the hammer and sickle" evidently in the Thirties. The final tirade has him praying to God *not* to make him a saint but to allow him some margin for selfishness. The poem starts with hedges (called bushes) which his father plants to mark out two fields, of whitethorn and beech mixed. They are there to keep out the keen north wind from the fields. The hedge is a shelter which a human plants to defend his ego, and through which the wind whistles as a summons to action, generally ignored. The wind blows where it listeth and is the ruah, the voice of God summoning Man. We could think of this as an individualist poem. I do not buy this; the lead character does deliver a monologue, but that is because he is isolated by his imminent death. He focuses on his personal weaknesses as that is his Christian duty, because they obstruct his duties *towards other people*. The tension between social activity and mere inwardness is always interesting for a Christian poem. Davies' character says

> You were in your element in provoking the whirlwinds
> dangling deceitfully to amuse the open-mouthed rabble.
> Your raking with a sand-rake and a seaside bucket
> in the garden, with the neglected corner and its bindweed
> —the canker of Englishness is whirling through Wales—
> this was nothing at all but a chance to overhear through the fence
> and the untroubled passers-by so kind calling you simple;
> but you didn't hear their words after they turned away,
> —the Welshman is too gentlemanly to tell the truth to your face—
> "the daft fool, the lubber, the idiot" they say,
> "all he can manage is to keep one bed clean
> of the bindweed—his hearth will turn English in its turn
> like our hearths all of them when the children reach school age."

The fence is part of the hedge metaphor. Bindweed is a parasitical plant which twists round and round a rooted plant (the twist is like the whirling of the wind). Canker is also a plant parasite, an insect one this time, and might well be spread by the wind. The hero is isolated here but is speaking for a super-communalist vision where the people of Wales develop a coherence they don't have and protect their Welsh. The idea that defending Welsh is a Christian act is incomprehensible outside Wales.

In the nineteenth century, most European countries released a huge flood of migrants to the New World. The exception was Wales, where migrants from the whole country flooded to the booming industrial area in the south-east. Y Ffynhonnau (Latin *fontana*) means "the springs" and is the title of Rhydwen Williams' 1964 poem. The word is close to the English word "fountains" but it doesn't quite mean that. (It has double n in the singular but -nh- in the plural.) The poet (b. 1916) says he chose the word from a line in a poem by Waldo Williams *braw yn y ffynhonnau*, something like "pollution in the springs". The poem is a social history of the Rhondda valley and "springs" are the idea of the communal life of the valley as something which sustained life and could be polluted, but also the Rhondda itself, a river whose course through the coal measures left a trace on it:

> Listen.
> (Not tears is song, but steel.)
> The farm was sold for a price—
> And the dung from the stables thrown in, for luck!
> ("The manure of the stables was a great bargain").
> And from that moment, the epileptic depth vomited into the
>   waters,
> The confluences were polluted,
> The river lost its virginity,
> And the springs were ashamed beneath the stars.

The "epileptic" bit is the coal which brought so many people there. The *shame* bit means the water was too black to shine by starlight. However, there is a key use of the word *ffynnon* to describe the fluency of Welsh, the farmer who was there before the mines had a "ffynnon" of Welsh on his lips. (So unconsciously *English* is equated with *pollution*.) Williams presents the community through a school, Yr Ynys-wen, and three of its pupils: a miner poet, a shepherd who was also a preacher, and the third is James Kitchener Davies, credited as "teacher, politician, and writer". There is a passage: "The jubilation of the waters is in my ears tonight,/ Ynys-wen, Ynysfeio, Ynys-hir./All the way to Eglwysilan./ And the wild spring on Pen Rhys,/ As beautiful as a gem on two breasts,/ Is continuing to praise Mary,/ The springs are alive!" *Ynys-wen* could mean white island or in another sense blessed island. You can make big mistakes by treating place-names as ordinary nouns, but here for once I think we have a stratum of deeply archaic verbal and emotional material, and that goes with the odd line about Mary. We heard about virginity earlier on, *gwyryf(dod)*, which comes from Latin *virginem* and prepares us for the encounter with Mary. The link of springs to maidens is old. Alongside the concrete details about working-class life in the 1930s and 1940s we have this material from a thousand years earlier. If white=blessed then the black of the coal symbolises the secular.

The credit says it was written for the 1964 eisteddfod but the style is very spoken word and it sounds like a radio poem. Competition poetry can take lots of forms.

> He sat on a seat below Moel Cadwgan.
> Cap. Stick. Cigarette.
> Some half-memory of his face. This was left of him.
> Lleteca? They pulled the old place down.
> He was a poet.
> And the best collier from Pwllfa to Maerdy.
> A craftsman of the *englyn*.
> And master of them all in a hard heading.
>
> Drilling and barding. Chalking his *cynghanedd* on the face of
>   coal,
> He was the last writer of this mountain.

(Heading, *hedin*, is also called coal-face.) Like Davies, Williams is concerned with the decline of Welsh in this south-east corner, where the 19th-century population explosion could have led to a huge increase in speakers but in reality led to the adoption of English by everyone. In 1900 it looked as if the Welsh language was absorbing the immigrants and by 1931 it was no longer the predominant language in Wales. This was an astonishing and revolutionary change and was only possible because the Cambrian coal measures were at the heart of the world economy at that time and nailed to its astounding instabilities. It's impossible if humans live for 70 years for a language to die in 30 but social arrangements can change and *gwenhwyseg*, the dialect of Gwent in which a few lines of Williams' poem are written, was the victim. Both Williams and Kitchener Davies were deeply affected by this.

'Esgyrn Y Cynnen', a radio poem from 1951, by T.H. Parry-Williams (1887–1975, a prize winner at the Eisteddfods of 1912 and

1915), means "bones of contention", which in this case are the language, the nation, and the Land. *Cynnen* comes from Latin *contendere*. By having them as speaking subjects he exposes the artificiality of making them subjects at all. How can a language have agency? (It's interesting that three of the poems cited have Latin words in their titles; maybe the Latin stratum in Welsh tends to be more literary.) Parry-Williams pushes the whole clump of dark feelings about Roots into the light—within the poem, there is the possibility that they will be disproven, dissolved by light. But if you don't know what they are maybe your knowledge of them is in error? There is a sort of conspiracy to keep these ideas away from thought and yet let poetry suck nutrients out of them. If they are abstractions aren't they the product of thought, of linguistic fiction, in the first place? This combination of nimble argument and the presence of deep emotions is astonishing, something no one else could pull off. The other symbol of the collectivity was religion. It is omitted, clearly Parry-Williams was not willing to stage an argument for atheism even in order to disprove it.

One of the functions of this chapter is to identify ways in which Anglo-Welsh poetry is seen to resemble Welsh-language poetry and is distinct from English poetry. A number of solutions offer themselves. The identification and praise for three local characters in 'Y Ffynhonnau' is especially like English-language poetry in Wales. The modesty of the praise is noticeable. I want to suggest in fact that these impersonal verbal structures are so obvious to people in Wales that writers achieve significance by migrating out of them rather than by solemnly firing up the same symbolic machines to produce another warehouse stacked high with verbal products. The poems by J.K. Davies and R. Williams with their evocation of working-class life and direct reproduction of everyday speech with its dialectal detail are also very close to a thick line of Anglo-Welsh poetry. Emyr Humphreys' important long poem *Ancestor Worship* can be compared to 'Esgyrn Y Cynnen' as a debate on the collective values.

Gwyn Thomas wrote a radio poem for voices, *Blaenau* (included in the volume *Ysgyrion Gwaed* (1967), which conforms in several ways to the model of the radio poems we have just been discussing. It is not typical of his work. Reasons for bringing Thomas in are mainly that I like his work so much and I would now feel unhappy if I drew mine to a close and there was nothing about Gwyn Thomas. This is an important poet who has vanished over the edge of the project.

I want to draw on the depiction of these poems to suggest a qualification of the idea of the domination of the poetic world by the Movement. The key is the link between the Movement poets and the universities, with the obvious symbiosis with the New Criticism, close reading, and the experts who were going to write about the poetry. This link leads back to the USA. The vigorous wedge of American cultural intervention entered the university style face to face, as Donald Hall and Eric Homberger have documented, and was therefore not world spanning but intimate and also restrictive. It did not saturate all points in between. If we grasp the '50s academic thing as an organic unity then we can also grasp that it varied in intensity according to latitude, and that norms based on imitation after all rely on the presence of people to imitate, and so can sink to very low intensity where those people are thin on the ground. Alongside the high prestige contacts between cultural stars we have the spectre of a *geographical attenuation of radiant cultural pulses* such that the '50s academic norm despite its energies diffused at a finite rate and that the territory was large. Its degree of penetration depended also on the level of intensity of the local cultural investments. One of the investments or warlike installations that has to be borne in mind is recognition by intellectuals in places beyond the Trent-Severn-Exe line that the middle class in Southern England had hostile intent towards them and that resisting their cultural propositions was the key to survival. The basis in an Anglo-American academic industry is stronger in particular universities than in the whole of the island at large, and every region. Or even every university. The in-group which had such fascinating links to an in-group in the USA, which was going to scale the heights of influence, did not saturate the British Isles, and while many of those who were detached from this in-group were culturally inactive there were also those who neither assimilated to the southern elite nor recognised their own *unimproved* condition and speech as inferior. Thinness or thickness are the key concepts here. Nationalism is also thin or thick and is probably transmitted face to face. It is striking how English people who went to live in Wales ended up with the Anglo-Welsh poetic style and varying degrees of Welsh nationalism. When it looks you in the face you say "yes", at least after ten years or so.

189

We are aware of the Netherlands as an area where, in the 16th and 17th centuries, the nobility hardly mattered, although they did exist and shared in the wealth which more useful individuals created. However, this pattern of freedom and of the absence of a discrete group with paramount expertise in violence, the administering of law, and in land-ownership, can be traced back to a much earlier stage. H. Slicher van Bath points out that "Along the coast of the North Sea, between Vlie and Eider, there lay in the 13th and 14th centuries 23 small independent states." They were governed by assemblies meeting two or three times a year. "Here there were no counts, no holders of fiefdoms, no knights and no unfree." The area described is Frisia, with its own language of which the main records are law-codes, and was later under the sovereignty of different states—the Netherlands, Germany, and Denmark. This area had never been feudalised, having resisted the Frankish push from the south when the Frankish realm was succumbing to a feudal pattern of *curtes* or *hofs*, around the 9th century. His account suggests that the pattern of great estates with a corresponding servile estate was something which diffused from specific centres, carried by certain individuals, and which advanced virtually mile by mile. It had always a frontier and its expansion was impressive but took place against an external space where its patterns of power and law had not reached. It would follow, as van Bath does not say, that the existence of an aristocracy was geographically limited, that it was a niche which existed only in a certain geometry and this was limited in its ability to compete with other geometries. The region he describes is as follows "There were though exceptions, and specially Scandinavia, Switzerland, and the Netherlands, and for a while the old freedom of the people maintained itself also on the island of Britain. In Scandinavia the peasants, in contrast to Germany, retained the right to carry weapons, and the free folk community remained in existence as a result. Feudalism could not penetrate here[.] There was little difference between Scandinavia and the Anglo-Saxon kingdoms. But the conquest by the Normans in 1066 threatened to be catastrophic for the freedom of the people in England [.]" (*Herschreven Historie*, pp. 307–8). He points to a "North Sea culture unity" as a basis for this distribution, although we can also see this as the outside zone which Carolingian impulses expired before reaching. Van Bath, a Marxist, observes that the rise of feudalism, as a mode of landholding in the Frankish monarchy, was in part a reaction to a decline of commercial activity, a retraction of long-distance trade routes. As transactions based on buying and selling declined, static relations based on territorial hegemony and feudal obligations multiplied to replace them, almost as a traumatic response. He connects the different social system in Frisia and North Holland to the persistence of a money-based economy in these maritime areas with their skills in shipping and trade. The governmental form corresponding to those littoral commercial societies was the peasant republic, an original form of which the last example, in the Dithmarschen region, was swallowed up by the Danish monarchy in the sixteenth century, after a long struggle. Van Bath also compares the freedom of the Swiss, and says that the freedom is connected also to a pastoral economy, and to the need for collective endeavour. Perhaps in ancient times, he says, the mobility of nomadic bands gave them freedom and this arrangement persisted in pastoral regions.

The country free of nobility in the 17th century was the Netherlands, where however the great commercial cities were not in Frisia. It seems that freedom from landholding dynasties was total in Frisia but, on a gradient, was still vital in the region to its south, which was freer than the rest of Europe. The community of free peasants concerned with trade became the bourgeoisie and the Dutch bourgeoisie led all others in Europe.

This vision of a social system advancing only into adjacent cells, only by saturation through diffusion, in which face to face contact is crucial, is highly inspiring to us in thinking about the spread of the Movement style of poetry with its university base. As an expanding regime, it was always surrounded by alien spaces and was subject to attenuation as it flowed further away from its base, and to resistance from other patterns of cultural commitment which did not wish for their own replacement. The pattern implies the existence of frontiers of violent infringement where two systems of almost equal strength come into contact, and where processes can emerge into the written record as individuals become conscious of them and capture their momentary condition. Here also triumphal conquests and wounding losses of territory occur. Thinness or thickness are the key couple here. I find that class society itself has a geographical layout and has more assent from the population in certain areas and less in others. Some political parties are collectivist, others in favour of capitalism and disintegration. As voting patterns can then reveal, privatisation is a "diffusing wave" and so has a shape in space, splayed across the island geography. You can't possibly get the full picture of how things happen if you don't know that there is a principle of horizontal inclusiveness at work as well as one of vertical hatred and exclusiveness. There may also be horizontal exclusiveness, based on "in-group loyalty tests", but this is a secondary flow and only a minority of people try to impose that kind of reaction.

There were universities in many cities but the project of purging poetry of communalist sentiment and collective notions was much stronger where the middle class was numerically strong enough to feel itself autonomous and broke free from the communalist centre of attraction with its phenomenal warmth and richness of human meaning. While the educational aspirations of this class were focussed on the universities of Cambridge and Oxford, its political organ during the 1950s was the Conservative and Unionist Party, and the geographical layout of electoral resistance to this party, while it was winning elections on a national count, is a telltale of where dissent to its ideologies might be expected. I would like to point also to a Scottish mainstream which set norms on which Scottish poets converged, which were distinct from the norms of English magazines.

I am very content to use the examples of the Dutch Republic and of other parts of the Netherlands to illuminate the differences between England and Wales. This seems an appropriate way of emerging from the data and producing a notion of it which is based on sight or evidence rather than on unconscious, inner, identification. These terrains are after all adjacent cells in the great natural history project of cultural analysis. I have suggested elsewhere, following Beveridge and Turnbull, that the vogue of privatisation is much more vigorous in southern England, especially south-east England, than in many other parts of the United Kingdom. We can add to that now a suggestion that it spread by diffusion from centres or entry ports, and that the geographical pattern we see is the result of waves whose peak vigour is at their port of entry and which attenuate as they diffuse.

The geography affecting poetry is hard to show on maps because its spatial echeloning is not saturation of entire areas, but is traceable only on a much more delicate scale. One would not expect the industrial suburbs of Oxford to share the speech patterns or the poetological ideas of dwellers in the colleges. Conversely, poetic activities in Liverpool, let's say, might often have to do with reading books from Oxford and London, and with teachers or writers who had studied in Oxford and lived in London. Kenneth Allott, for example, was a lecturer at Liverpool University from 1947, but still made an anthology of British poetry in which 40% of the poets had studied at Oxford (and only 13% had links with the North of England). We are familiar—if we have lived in the relevant parts of England—with the double layering of speech, so that in Liverpool there would be people whose speech clearly belonged with the speech of the south of England, especially the south-east, whereas others could clearly be identified with the region they lived in. Similarly, I would suggest, there was a double layer of poetic sympathy, whereby one level of the poetically interested in a regional city would directly welcome the Oxford-London axis, while another level would perceive it as alien and undermining, and even if they did not have a portfolio of local poets or themes which they could loyally support, they had a set of ideals which could some day be realised by regional poets and in which indeed one element was regional loyalty. In this complex both Scotland and Wales stand out as *superregions* in which the polarity against southern England was at a splendid maximum and the actually existing *anti-centre* could cherish a tradition and offer an infrastructure to its writers.

We can see communalism also as possessing its high grounds of maximum intensity and its frontier provinces of attenuating thickness. It is a norm and ideal which can be understood relatively quickly and which can become frustrating if you dabble in cultural activity over years and decades after you have seized the repeating principles. It does not have an origin in any particular book or thinker but there are books in which you can saturate itself in its values and come to recognise its deeper and hidden levels of ideas. As discussed in *Centre and Periphery*, communalist ideas are set out in books by Alasdair MacIntyre and Craig Beveridge and Ronnie Turnbull. The latter two authors, collaborating, identify the origins of possessive individualism in 17th-century England, stressing that this came into conflict with the Scottish intellectual tradition, in law, theology, and philosophy.

They search out a citation from William Blackstone, author of the *Commentaries* (originally published 1765–69), the key summary text on English law: "we should want no other prompter to inquire after and pursue the right but only our own self-love, that universal principle of action […] [God] has not perplexed the law of nature with a multitude of abstracted laws and precepts […] but has graciously reduced the rule of obedience to this one paternal precept, 'that man should pursue his own true and substantial happiness'. This is the foundation of what we call ethics or natural law [.]" They identify a very clear statement of this new attitude in the writing of Thomas Hume, and this may be why empiricism is the keyword for Movement poets of the 1950s. Hume makes pride central to human aspirations, and observes that "the relation which is esteem'd the closest, and which of all others produces most commonly the passion of pride, is that of property." Our authors comment, "Hume took himself […] to be describing human nature as such, and human civilisation as such, but what he in fact offers is a description of the nature and civilisation of the eighteenth-century English propertied classes—and, we might add, their contemporary spiritual heirs." In Hume as elsewhere, empiricism was a precision tool for uncovering and destroying traditional associations and implicit loyalties. If pursuing self-interest is everything, then a faith in the right of the market to control society follows; if property is what every individual most wants, then the reduction of all other arrangements to types of property, to be owned and exchanged by individuals, follows too. Individuals assign their property, once freed from the claims of a community, to corporations, that is communities of interest; the corporation, something which barely existed in 1600 AD, extends rapidly to social dominance, and tends to dispossess other communities of their property. This train of events happened earlier and more thoroughly in England, and its offshoot the United States of America, than in other countries.

Regional differences in political enthusiasms in the middle and late 20th century are certainly due to a differential penetration by these ideals of possessive individualism. At a more parochial level, there is no doubt a connection between Practical Criticism and the project of empiricism in the 18th century. It is obvious that the idea of a society split into non-communicating segments was more attractive to those who could be seen as the apex than to others. The apex for literature was obviously university graduates, but within it those graduates of Oxford and Cambridge represented a super-apex. The reference group for contributors to projects like *New Lines* and *Critical Quarterly* regarded it as self-evident that the line of communalism, represented by T Glynne Davies or others, was archaic and that its location in the north and west of Britain was a feature of being distant from modernity and so belonging to the past, rather than of being a blossom of the superior vigour and intensity of social solidarity, in cells where there was a natural abundance of those ideals. People who cherished the idea that south-eastern England had a social order based on deficits of various desirable qualities usually also had the idea that the New Criticism and its attendant poetry were socially cut off and sterile.

Why do the academic poets feel so isolated? Presumably because in an exam you are isolated and win by demonstrating your superiority over other people and this stress situation was the source of their whole social identity and rank and they were clinging to it with fingers and toes. And their peers only respected academic achievements and if they dropped that cramped attitude for five minutes their peers would stop listening to them. So in fact the exam system was a bleak and accurate reproduction of the class society and actually concentrated its effects and made them more toxic. We are speaking of the toxin of the winner, to set beside the toxin of the loser.

Christian poetry in a secular era

We have just seen some communalist poets, for whom the parish of Christians was still the fundamental reality; although pessimism and nostalgia were a feature of quite a few of those poems. There was a crisis, starting perhaps even in the late 19th century, to do with the decline of the Anglican church and the sense that mythology was the natural home of poetry but was inaccessible to a modern person. Histories are often written as if the Anglican bloc dominated English culture until some point (1939? 1963?) and then abruptly ceased transmission. The truth is surely that the Anglican bloc was put under life-threatening pressure which caused mutation, radical in kind and multiple in outcome, and that the vital flow of Anglican poetry never stopped. In the 1950s, the strange diversity of Hill, Auden, Betjeman, Fry and Young is a sign of the mutative powers lurking within this ancient but protean organism. It would be possible to write a book simply about Christian poets, which would have compelling interpretations of Andrew Young, David Jones, Euros Bowen, Kathleen Raine, David Gascoyne, Lynette Roberts, Christopher Fry, George Barker, Dunstan Thompson, Emyr Humphreys, Philip Toynbee, George Mackay Brown, Waldo Williams, Anthony Thwaite, Peter Levi, Rosemary Tonks, Geoffrey Hill, John Riley, Isobel Thrilling, Pauline Stainer, Robert Crawford, Draycott & Saunders, and Sarah Law. The cultural creativity of the Christians is not less than it was in the earlier decades of the century; even the decline in their self-confidence has produced the adrenalin creativity of crisis, calling forth hidden structures as the splendid and sheltering buildings crash to the ground.

William Watson said, in the climactic poem of a sequence about the might of Britain while fighting, in defiance of world opinion, the Boer War,

> He throned her in the gateways of the world
> He 'stablished her on high before the peoples.
>
> He raised her as a watch-tower from the wave
> He built her as a lighthouse on the waters
> […]

He alone, who is first and last, shall judge her.
(from 'Alpha and Omega', published 1904)

This is evidently blasphemous, and almost unbearable to read. No one today thinks that God set Britain down across the main North Atlantic trade routes because it was part of His purpose that Britain should rise by trade and naval power to be the world's most powerful state. The conception of a God Whose purposes were of this kind is reprehensible, probably, to most Christians in Britain today. But in 1904 it was part of a vast nationalist fantasy, and the Church at least passively identified with the Empire because its project Number One was that of converting the world to Anglicanism, something a great deal easier when the law in a given colony was administered by officials reporting to an Anglican government. If something seems providential then you are vulnerable to forming dangerous illusions about what Providence wills. The link between Christianity and the component structures of the British Empire seems arbitrary and untenable, but the legal and institutional entanglement of the Established church with the State, and indeed with ministering to the armed forces, had let the Church swallow something which left a huge hole when it was torn out. The incredibly rapid development of the shared sentiments of the Anglican communion (a little less so, the Catholics and Nonconformists) may have been the pacemaker for literary change in general, over the decades we are interested in. Pop poetry may have arisen out of the Church of England's preoccupation, 50 years ago, with its lack of appeal to young people and to the inner cities, and its rejection of inherited fine language. Neither Geoffrey Hill nor Pauline Stainer marched with this column. Their ideas are marked by a deep continuity with the past, but their poems are a radical departure from the range of genres and scenes which were the voice of the Anglican communion and which had stored shared feeling so many times.

The great essay on the Anglican part in modern literature is Alan Sinfield's 'Varieties of Christian Experience', which recovers a great number of mid-century writers for whom Christianity was receding as a belief which once dominated the parish and could stand for civil society. The collective and ceremonial experience was mysteriously evaporating. The result was involuntary internalisation and privatisation.

He describes author after author looking for the Church service as the gathering of a group large enough to be the community, gathering also a wave of force large enough to sweep the writer off his feet and into a mighty current of collective feeling, intense enough to drown little private problems. The real experience defeated this expectation, and the subjects found themselves alone as spars from the wreckage of a great whole. The site of the supposed uplift became converted into an object of knowledge—scholarship and connoisseurship as consolations for failure. We can see history as a melancholic science in which the subject tries to find the story of failure and why he lives in an era where the true fruits are out of reach. In fact the sense of loss and isolation is the emotional centre of the poem, the shared feeling which brings all the readers together and so ends cultural isolation. Churches and the accoutrements of ceremonial are charged with a symbolism cheap to recover because they evoke so much loss, because the memory of wholeness is so easily present in any of the fragments. Conversely, the sense of not being part of an affective and speaking community any more is so deep for any self that almost any scene can bring on that sense of loss and silence. Indicative poets in 1950s England are Betjeman, with a pious but remorselessly undramatic and unexalted view of the religious experience, backed up by a loving but malicious view of church furnishings which shows class consciousness within the sacred place (he was the son of a furniture manufacturer). Auden, increasingly influenced by Betjeman, had an equal sense of disillusion with public activity, retreating into infantilism and love of domestic comfort, although recognising piety as more important than poetry. Christopher Fry had spent most of his career as a religious dramatist, but by about 1953 was writing sparkling comedies which with their endearing characters are visibly leading towards the situation comedy. Deflation and privatisation are to the fore in his work also. (Fry wrote most of the script for the remake of *Ben-Hur*, a Christian epic with remarkably few jokes.) Two of them (not Auden) reached huge commercial success; all three are making a break with what Christian poetry had previously been. All three are visibly *on the retreat*. Larkin's disillusion with everything, interrupted by visits to old churches which remind him of what someone else once really felt, could seem like poetry in this atmosphere.

This story agrees significantly with what Eric Homberger, writing about the same period in his classic *Art of the Real*, describes for poetry as a whole. It extends there to a sense of the failure of a whole cultured class to control society as it should be controlled, with a sense of the uneducated masses and their pop music and films as a threat to real culture and real goodness. Homberger, personally out of sympathy with this notion of bourgeois guardianship, evokes in great detail the era when English Literature teachers felt themselves as the natural owners and writers of poetry, when also their sense of caste largely blurred the difference between the academic and the Christian priest: they wrote as a mass of dominant lay worshippers, and their sense of unease was largely the same as the unease of the Anglicans.

> What man can celebrate,
>   can sing
> [...]
> when [...]
> Men disowning symbol
>   no longer
> own a sacred ground,
> but watch with literal eyes
> a literal world
>   (Peter Abbs, from 'Llanon Beach')

Sinfield's argument has an irresistible force. This is simply what happened, and this process also worked itself out in English poetry. He gives the dates of 1945–70, which of course were the limits of the volume he was editing on literature and society, but which will do very well to delimit a process whose limits are vague (and which may still be occurring). This sense of privatisation flourished in a time when the principle of collectivism was reaching an unheard-of extent, and when the mass media were bringing everyone into a shared public sphere.

We may feel surprised that university teachers did not express a surge of power and confidence at a time when the universities were expanding at an unbelievable rate and the government apparently thought they were the solution to all economic and social problems. It would seem that the Utopian left-wing poetry of the same period was more in tune with the "key growth sector" role of higher education. Conversely, it would seem that the sense of impending doom felt by the mournful academics who are Homberger's subjects was seized as a charter by the Underground poetry which replaced them, and that they were vacating a space which someone was bound to come and fill.

Meekness

The problem in the relationship between Anglicanism and poetry has mostly been meekness. Someone who follows the core teaching of the Church by avoiding conflict, avoiding to do that the false positions of pride which bring about quarrels with other people, may have trouble staging conflict in poems: everything is blurred and faded down, every colour made dingy and aged, while any self-assertion is undercut by inhibition and guilt. This is not a good formula for poetry.

This faintness of impulse is instantly recognizable to anyone who knows mainstream poetry as it presented itself in 1955 or 1965, but is not present in the most famous Anglican poets. Indeed, the Church was represented until quite recently by people who were powerful and who found it astonishing that other people, for example politicians or writers, should have any power at all, detracting from the authority of prelates. The parish clergy were, famously, drawn from the families of the land-owners and had solidarity with them at many levels. Tennyson had relations who were priests, some of his work is propaganda for the Protestant Settlement, but he did not for that reason lack cultural self-confidence or the willingness to create high drama, including scenes of violence, in his poems.

Meekness was more a quality of the parishioners than of the priesthood. It fitted in excessively well with the female personality, or, to be more exact, with one of the behaviour strategies which was compatible with social pressures on women in the 19th and 20th centuries. Gentility is described, quite often, as a trait of the English middle class, yet it is undeniable that this class is addicted to self-aggrandizement and that any assets which other classes get hold of are simply the ones which middle-class acquisitiveness missed for some reason. "Middle-class values" have to be broken down into separate roles which different people are supposed to adopt and which may involve quite opposite behavioural priorities. The rise of hedonism in the post-war period did not involve a decrease in the numbers of the middle class, but was actually linked to a rise in those numbers, and was a trait of affluence. So a more exact statement is that traditional moral planning involved a distribution of roles in which many people were not dominant, and *these* people were expected to admire self-denial and hard work, to have a distaste for possessions and assertive language, and to avoid making demands on the dominant or causing conflict. In fact, avoiding conflict was one of their assigned virtues. Bourdieu's description of the avant-garde artist as the dominated fraction of the dominant class is relevant here. Artistic creation could, in one way of playing the game, be a withdrawal into imaginary territory after evacuating the territory of real power: an elaborate strategy of the dominated for using up the spare time which was not required by high office. I looked at the works of Ruth Pitter, E.J. Scovell, and Elizabeth Jennings, and could find nothing to recommend. They fulfilled a behavioural ideal, at the cost of artistic impact, to its extreme point. The investment of English women poets, in the early and mid 20th century, in the role of the dominated, was key to their failure as poets. This was simultaneously a social and a theological strategy. If you expect to lose conflicts then minimizing conflicts is a rational strategy.

The collapse of the political role of the Church brought about a new situation in which old virtues had to be re-thought. Two shifts need to be identified here. First, women poets occupying a more optimistic role/strategy anytime after 1970 re-evaluated the past and were much concerned to attack, as failures, the values which earlier generations followed as their creative lights. Secondly, the structural mismatch between admiring peacefulness and being a citizen of an imperialist State was bound to become more acute as the State became more secular and the dominated role relaxed and came to involve more intellectual awareness and more vocal protest. The estrangement between Church and State could turn the true believers into dissidents. The most likely fault line to become active here was warfare, and, at the most intense, the question of nuclear arms and the intention to use them. This was where conservative Christians and new-style feminists could form an alliance. At moments, the State could provoke loyal Christians into archaic enactments of moral integrity—following Christ as dissident, fearless critic, and criminal, and the origin of Protestantism in courageous defiance of evil and corruption. We are going to look at a few poets of the period.

My sole companion in the forest:
Ancestor Worship, by Emyr Humphreys

There are 18 sections of the poem, first published in 1970. Humphreys, born 1919, is probably the major Welsh novelist of the 20th century, the other candidate being Islwyn Ffowc Elis. He refused to serve in the Second World War, as many young Welsh Christians did (not wishing to defend the Empire), but worked in welfare administration for refugees. Cheating slightly, I am going to evoke his novels by quoting from a review of *Outside the House of Baal* in a 1966 issue of *Anglo-Welsh Review*:

> The book is kaleidoscopic, a shifting series of pictures, a crowd of actors. One is reminded inexorably that Emyr Humphreys was a radio and TV producer. The cast changes, as does the scenery, most rapidly. The whole thing is a series of sketches and flashbacks; past and present are intermingled to give the feel of a moral and psychological history. [...] As a Welsh-speaking Welshman, I feel that this novel succeeds in conveying an awareness of a real atmosphere, but [...] no English novel can render the absolutely authentic quality of Welsh religious life. (L Alun Page)

As Page says, this is a novel about a good man, a minister of the Calvinistic Methodist Church. Its fragmented (or multiple?) style is a way of getting away from the Saint's Life, which of course is the burden all Protestant writers have to bear. Humphreys is much less interested by technical showing off than by goodness, itself. The first section of this multiple poem is "Ancestor Worship", which says the words of our ancestors remain; they laid out the fields and provided for us. We change the names and their will is broken up by drains and pylons. Our ancestors, who saw the first invaders (*scil.* the Saxons) beaching their boats, knew better, they carved metrical systems out of their flesh (to ensure remembrance?).

The title is sarcastic—the Welsh do not truly worship their ancestors, this phrase (which properly belongs with non-Christian groups somewhere far from Europe) is what might be used by a sneering English journalist to describe the attachment of the Welsh to their own ways and language, when they resist some intrusion by the world of corporate capitalism. The poet is standing in two places: in the melée, among struggling bodies, forcing back anglicisation; and high above the fight, mocking, besieged by memories. This twisted phrase is a clue to the tangled and genuinely fascinating relationship between the eighteen parts of what is, after all, a connected poem. At the outset, we know Humphreys to be a committed Welsh Nationalist and Christian. We could hypothesize, at the outset, that the scenes he shows are "reference sets" which embody in original and striking form the formative experiences on which he based his political attitudes. Indeed, their style seems to belong to his youth rather than to the 1960s. In VIII, 'At the Frontier', somewhere (in the fantasy of a nationalist?) six soldiers stop people at a barrier, who imagine them capable of unprovoked violence; and would be glad to see them killed. The soldiers get drunk, vomit, sleep, wake up again. The circuit the pictures could make is like this. *A small but good people is threatened by military invasion. Scenes from domestic life show the virtue of the citizens and attach our affections to them. They stay at home and do not commit acts of aggression. Acts of brutality by the soldiery arouse our indignation. We wish the small country to be free.* These images could be parts of many works of propaganda of the 1940s, urging us, for example, to sympathise with the Czechs against the German occupiers. Those works resembled saint's lives, incorporated them. The interest of the sequence is Humphreys' problem with the connective logic between the pictures. After all, one outcome of the 1940s for most Europeans was a suspicion of propaganda. Any European is bound to recognise these figures; but the argument seems to have broken, leaving the film footage behind, sharply defined and mysterious. The poems do not form a coherent statement, but define a potential space in which the reader feels inclined to construct new statements. I feel that the sequence goes beyond politics to ask questions about what politics are, and what drives our social imaginations to stage incidents, attributing a symbolic power to them. The pictures give us a task fitting for our intellects, helpful to an understanding of the world—but we have to work out what that understanding is.

Poem IV is 'An Apple Tree and a Pig'. There is an epigraph from a 13th C Welsh poem, addressed to a pig: *Oian a parchellan, Hail O little pig.* The topos is the madman who has fled society out of horror at bloodshed in battle; into a liminal state. We hear details of the deaths which drove him mad. He realises that in his own heart is the devil who tears the world apart. He lives alone, in total pessimism.

The repeated module of the sequence is a topos of Welsh poetry, too common not to be impersonal; summed up in the words *cof* or *cofiant*, or fond remembrance of someone newly dead. The memory is of what their life was like, so this theme is really completely open, or a blank. Humphreys' style is influenced by pre-modern Welsh poetry, with its lack of reasoning and bold use of gnomic statements; this dryness, and these odd jumps of theme, allow him to avoid commitment, building half-concealed themes behind a surface which is both emphatic and inexplicit. The poems are mainly about humble or psychologically marginal people: in line with the democratic urges of the mid-century, they are no longer about landowners and spiritual leaders, like virtually all older examples of the *cofiant*. V, 'Dialogue in a garden', is especially interesting in its refusal to say what it seems to be saying. Walking in a garden, it says, we are like subjects of a dream. He remembers being on a roof during the Blitz; it was like the Burning Fiery Furnace. He remembers digging for potatoes. He remembers being in an operating theatre, burying dead lambs, taking part in battle. I can't get from these memorable pictures to an argument. All the parts come from proving cases, or ideological fantasies, of nationalism; but they are not connected up in a circuit. Humphreys seems to be looking at the unrelatedness of the different scenes of a life and despairing of the much larger and more rigorous task of seeing a pattern in millions of lives, and forming new political principles, which rely on that pattern and necessarily fail if the exceptions to the pattern break loose.

Poem IX shows a second liminal hermit figure and is the most optimistic poem in the series. He lives in a hut, his feet wrapped in sacks (indicator of poverty) because of a failed marriage, where his wife bit his arm and spat in the blood. But he sees a message in everything. The doctrine of readability presumably reassures the believer that the Bible is still effective as revealing the code in which secular events are written. This is reasonably close to the problem of the nationalist wanting to see every Welsh family as essentially similar to each other one, and essentially dissimilar from the English; something which in the long run very few people believe. Poem XI, 'Uncle Thomas', similarly, shows a preacher who found symbols throughout Bible texts. Humphreys values the power to see analogies—and offers us a poem which obdurately resists coherence. He shows us the peculiarity of individuals—a trope frequently used (in the move we have called exceptionalism) to discredit the generalised sociology which the government in Westminster relies on. He realises that the same weapons which make a British discourse seem full of holes serve to blow holes in a Welsh-nationalist discourse.

I enjoyed noticing that the *Oian a barchellan* theme from *Darogan Myrddin* also appears in a John James poem ("o pigling you were my sole companion in the forest") but the small extent of Welsh literature, which makes it easy for the reader to share allusions, can lead to repetition. The comparison with *The Tribune's Visitation* helps our understanding of the issues which Humphreys needs to dramatise, but also points out the difficulties of linking nationalism with Christianity: the possible arguments here are so complex that they cannot be contained in a poem. David Jones magisterially draws nationalism into a directly Christian poem by having a Roman tribune worry about the destruction of regional Italian cultures, a figure easily understandable as a worry about the British Empire levelling Welsh culture to nothing.

When Humphreys writes about hermits, the mood is one of pessimism about the prospects for Welsh conservatism, and this secular despair brings him recognisably close to the theme, fashionable then, of *dropping out.* This is why a vessel from such a different literary generation can be blown up close to the underground poets. Humphreys was already saying NO in 1940. *Ancestor Worship* is a masterpiece through multiplicity and frustration.

From the classic lands of the Eastern Mediterranean: *Peter Levi, Collected Poems 1955–75*

I have chosen the whole *Collected* as this is the form in which the poems presented themselves to me, from the basement of Nottingham Central Library.

Levi (1931–2000) published a number of volumes after 1975 but there is no further *Collected*. He was a Jesuit, if we count the training years, from when he was 17 to when he was 44, at which point he left to get married. The *Collected Poems* come just before this point. We have to point out that the English and Dutch Jesuits are known as just about the most left-wing group in the Catholic Church. He was an orthodox thinker but the need to help the poor and the overweening arrogance and superfluity of the rich are part of the faith, as believed by everyone, from the start of the gospel. So in fact Levi was a socialist like most of the other good poets of this period.

His university subject was Modern Greek, rather than Ancient, so he was able to read modern Greek poetry with understanding and also to talk with Greek people. He translated a good deal of Greek poetry. He speaks from an east Mediterranean tendency—common to most English poets since the 18th century. In his case anglophilia has to be added. The family chose to come here. He said of the Greeks of Asia Minor, "I have a sympathy with them because my grandparents came from Istanbul." This is explaining his affinity with his friend George Seferis. His father was Turkish and Jewish, his mother Spanish and Catholic, he was English and Catholic. When someone loves English and Greek poetry so much, their tone of voice may be rather familiar to us. He was not a heretic—any more than other Jesuits, I suppose. If he sounds like some Greek poets, it is because each separate line is beautiful. Of course Levi's ability to do this all the way through a book is the significant thing, not the Greek touch.

Just after his first book, Kenneth Allott took Levi into his 1962 anthology of *Contemporary Verse*, allotting him a poem 99 words long groaning under a mincing and authoritarian put-down 368 words long, a shuddering introduction. Later anthologies omitted him. Allott wasn't going to let anyone get out of their *allotted* punishment cell. He uses the words "mannered" and "attitudinising"—a wrong choice but what my unpleasant colleague is referring to is the lines like these:

> The noose closes
> making the tragic
> young the pathetic
> in slum clearance houses

—(from 'The Gravel Ponds', title poem of his first book) At that point Levi was a fan of Gascoyne, as he told Allott, and the poem goes on "Never o never in the long distraction/ of the heart's inaction", which is an echo of Gascoyne, with the noble socialist aspirations for the relief of suffering and the fulfilment of hopes. Allott disapproved but I find this rather exciting. Gascoyne, author of 'The Gravel-Pit Field' (1941), to which the title of Levi's first book may refer, was too other-dependent and confused; Levi can write much better than him and had stabilised his theological state. 'Pancakes for the Queen of Babylon' (1968) is subtitled *Ten Poems for Nikos Gatsos* and is perplexing. A fascinating explanation in an interview discloses that the title is a phrase uttered by Ian Paisley in the Oxford Union while Levi was living in Oxford. It refers—for both men—to the Catholic Church. I believe the pancakes are the wafers of the Host. The transition from Paisley's mixture of invective and Revelations to surrealism is rather natural. Levi was playing a game with Gatsos in which lines are produced in isolation and then strung together to form surrealist poems. In them, context plays no role, it is only there by accident. 'Pancakes' is specifically an attempt to strip out of literature everything except the context, the implicit and tacit thing, to see if it can still work. 'Pancakes' is an extraordinary thing:

> I cannot keep my life out of my voice
>
> one came back from the Asiatic dead
> dragging a mass of Asian foliage:
> and those with white faces
> who rose early, who soberly rehearsed
> some few words that had broken greater sleep.

Storm-clouds were cannonading in mid-air.

horses through the mist
                              serpents in the dust
We have drunk dry the voices in the well.
wild fruit
        fresh water
                    those long-legged boys
the nightstick of the sun will batter down
shouting and swearing, stonily

But underfoot some kind of new grass with a dusky breath.
Moisture, whole threads of aubergines. Yellow and purple, ripe,
        ripening.

I don't find a unique selling point for Levi, whose poems are continuous with all kinds of writing and talking in England, but unusually graceful & exquisite in expression. He did write experimental poetry (as in 'Pancakes') and did write committed poetry (the sermons discussed below). He is unaggressive but hard to resist. What distinguishes him from almost all his contemporaries is an absence of thesis, which we can readily associate with the Jesuit role of defenders of orthodoxy. He is not arguing a thesis, either about his personality, or about poetics, or ideas, or theology. There is no drama of vindication going on, no fragmentation, no marginal and experimental state of mind. He lacks a territory but is able to contain larger spaces. We can say that orthodoxy defended Levi. At moments it seems that Protestantism produces not only insoluble inner doubts but also amateur theology. In this absence of terror and revolt he is oriented towards beauty, tranquillity, wisdom. If he has an abiding quality it is the evidence of his poetry:

The still rocks lay like a quiet husk
of the world burnt out and forgotten
before the first man's savage garden
drenching their hollow sides in windless dusk.

And then the level tops of rocks were skinned
and darkness peeled easily away

in a light like a remote mental day
and the full fury of the imperious wind.

There was a light so bare and equal
falling in that hard surface
it seemed some breathing element of the place
or infinite transparent fire let fall

from far above the white-eyed moon
        (from 'The Shearwaters', 1965)

At the moment he says anything it seems perfectly clear and natural. This invites thought, because obscurity must prevent poetry from being part of mainstream culture, while dumbing-down prevents poets from being part of poetry. Surely evidence and amplitude are common features of beauty. A manner in which lines endlessly succeed like the wind over a field of corn, never slowing down or falling to earth, is copied from Nikos Gatsos, but all the same is personal to Levi because the equanimity could only be available to someone who has no partiality and no traumatic blocks. I wanted to mention the specific quality of gracefulness which belongs to a cluster of Oxford poets, certainly including Levi and John Fuller. It has produced little good poetry but is a very distinct sound. Of course that lightness is compatible with detachment and also with choosing insignificant themes. The ability to eliminate everything which makes the flow of sense awkward takes a long time to acquire and is quite admirable.

    The quality which makes 'The Shearwaters', (a kind of bird), being an account of a holiday on Rhum in the Hebrides, so extraordinary is that it dissolves into a pure Now. His serenity shows a man who is not stooping down to collect stones to win an argument and clutching a collection of stones to their chest. His ability to dissolve into this Scottish and island landscape is the sign of someone who does not need to project their personality; the titles of his first two books, 'Gravel Ponds' and 'Water, Rock and Sand', also show this detachment—less of his personality but more of God's works and perhaps of His wishes. Incidentally, the physical scenery of this poem reminds us of some poems by Kathleen Raine, but that is not an artistic affinity. The receptiveness shown in this poem gives us the formula for his success: he could take in whatever he saw. He gave each new thing equitable attention because he moved on so cleanly from the previous thing, without retention or withdrawal.

The Left tendency is expressed in numbers 154 to 158 of this collection, the Sermons, which are produced in a spontaneous way in an archaic and even infantile language, developing an awesome momentum. They are simultaneously like a liturgy and like a block of things so horrible they are normally repressed ripping their bonds and gushing out and like a prophetic seizure, where ideas become pictures and sounds. This is probably the poetry Gascoyne dreamed of. Levi gains his political strength from saying yes to Christianity rather than to luxuriating in doubt as if theology did not already exist.

Number 159 is dedicated to the Stalinist John Berger. In terms of my group theory (is this serene orthodoxy or a new form of amateur theology and wilfulness) he must be associated with Hill, and Thwaite, the other Oxford poets of the 1950s (so utterly different from the Movement). But we can find Levi overlapping not only with these, and with Auden and Seferis and Gatsos, but also with Langley and Corcoran.

Peter Abbs' first full-length book was *For Man and Islands* (1978). I sought out books by Abbs (b. 1942), around 1997, because I found his poems in Welsh magazines of the 1970s and thought he was Anglo-Welsh, and I had to recover his work to complete my book *Centre and Periphery*. In fact he is from Norfolk, but while living in Wales he absorbed the local style of the "Second Flowering"; the hermit imagery matches poems by Emyr Humphreys. I suppose almost all the poets I like were happy about the crisis of capitalism in the '70s, the energies it released made them intoxicated. Secondly, there was a crisis. Abbs, conservative and gifted, wanted it all to stop: in the title poem 'For Man and Islands' he writes

> For the time's intolerant images
> Storm my mind.
>
> I find not waves but faces
> Marching to the Age:

Faces numb with the cold wash of phrases,
Faces frozen with slogans,
Eyes swollen to flashing discs,
Minds hardened by helmets.

This is his view of the demonstrations of the seventies. Was there anyone on those mass political manifestations more intolerant than Peter Abbs? He is against democracy; against popular sovereignty; against large gatherings of people; against debate and reform. No wonder the texture of his poems is so smooth and definitively sealed. The pressure of Left political activism in the seventies drove him to defend his position passionately, and, in this volume, he captures dramatic complexes in vivid and concrete images:

Morning's come
after night's spiked wind
bleeding wound and
sleep, dumb stone, in the turmoil.
Throw open the room's window! Rain
splintered glass
dazzles my matted eyes and
cool air eddies

in—then Trinity's holy bells!
       ('Resurrection')

Titles include 'The Sack of Learning' 'Into the Dark' 'After Bad Weather' 'Greeting the Ice-Cold Day' 'It Is Evening after the Maelstrom' 'I Would Sing of Life' 'Between Two Epochs'. The book offers a cycle of linked poems, dealing with a poet living in a farmhouse called Brechfa in a village on the Cardiganshire coast, and with his marriage and his feelings about how the world is going to nourish his family and their feelings. Some poems are dated in 1971 and 1973. Where the academic critical profession of the 1950s set poems as tests of the moral integrity of the poet, viewed in terms of Christianity and proper behaviour as a husband, and a wave of poets tried to pass those tests in short poems, it was obvious that life is led in long stretches of time. Showing someone's behaviour in a greater variety of situations, and in relation with the changes of other humans, was a better pass. This led to a whole genre of volume-length poem-groups about the poet's marriage and moral fitness, and *For Man And Islands* is one of those. The volume has only one voice, no dialogue, but rises to great peaks.

> Tonight, as we lie in bed, a battered moon drifts
> Through the sky—it seeks a glistening eye,
> It seeks a low-tide pool, a mountain lake,
> In which to dip its wounded face,
> Its scarred distended cheeks, its frozen mouth.
> Who will return its former life? its lost being?
> Its ancestral bearings? Who will lend the slack night
> The great curved mirrors of his mind
> To house this nomad face? We turn away.
> ('Estranged')

The poem quoted is about a moment of estrangement between man and wife, and the moon is a symbol of the ancient and yet unstable quality of love. There is a massive conflict between a story that changes every day and the pressure of certain knowledge, the Doctrine which dominates his thought and which cannot change because it goes back to the Church Fathers.

As he uses titles like 'Between Two Epochs' it is clear that he sees a whole age as running to an end, and the Spengler quote strengthens this. The date about 1971 makes it plausible that what he is imagining is the end of the Christian era and the start of a secular era, and so that the whole cycle is about the crisis of Christian domination from the standpoint of a believer. (The demo he describes could also be in Northern Ireland and so a religious confrontation, which would not fit into his scheme at all.) Rigid cultural positions make for hard symbols, and the cultural conflict of the time is dramatised, even if the other side are reduced to mere ciphers of chaos. This pessimism is that of a Catholic conservative faced with the permissive society. In the title poem, he moves on from the demonstration to use Dark Age apocalypse imagery as a vision of Western Culture being wiped out, but surviving in the monasteries along the Atlantic and North Sea: "I think of/ Skellig Michael. Iona. Lindisfarne. (…) And I pray that their black-cracked rocks/ be ready to hold the storm-borne/ Seeds again, to shield whatever/ Fragile spores of hope". The threat is of people acting spontaneously; the scenario is of de-urbanisation, removal of people. The death symbolism expresses a feeling of inner death, but also serves to make the landscape simple enough for Abbs' heroic gaze to see into the deep past, for his apodictic wisdom to meet all cases. Seeds, spores: it's remarkable that Abbs hands over reproduction to all-male communities. The whole script is Spenglerian, and indeed he quotes Spengler at the head of 'Winter in Wales'. That quote says that every culture is like an organism and has its natural cycle of growth and decay, and is placed alongside a piece of evidence to a Select Committee on the need to work Cardiganshire soils to prevent them from going back to the rushes, to unproductiveness. *Colo* gives both culture and agriculture: the message is that the West is rushing into decay for lack of hard work and discipline. 'Winter in Wales' goes on

> A world's undone. Flesh torn from the bone.
> After Alexander, Rome, the cold
> After London, Moscow, New York, the march
> Over which
> A blind wind moans.

"March" probably means "borderland", which in a particular view of human geography could be an area remote from the centre, where the benefits of culture do not reach, but also a land populated by professional warriors who when disaster comes are already adapted.

No evidence is given of things drawing to an end except that demonstration. The symbolic statement of chaos is the storms on the coast. The description of a whole coastline and the fragile human ordering of earth and plants destroyed by floods and gales has a strong sensuous impact. But storms have been happening for thousands of years. So he believes propaganda about society coming to an end but is astute enough not to weave it into poems. The symbols allude to a stratum of prose imagination which is not reproduced in the poems.

Much of the book is about gardening, physically labouring to make a patch of land flower. Islands appeal because they are out of contact, and so preserve the "right ideas" handed down in codified form from an imaginary era of privileged, divinely vouchsafed, insight into human nature. Sexuality is reduced to words (those "fragile spores") and preserved on isolated rocks. Its nature ceases to be change and mixture and becomes rigour; the unpredictable quality of behaviour is rejected, everything is crushed into black, neurotic, timeless slabs of knowledge, like the rocks. Surely Abbs' view is patriarchal; the threat to culture is invented to justify male strength defending it, and the need for arbitrary cultural rules is made up so that his knowledge becomes moral and necessary. He ignores debates about poetics because the authenticating gesture for him is to resemble patriarchal figures like R.S. Thomas. (Two of the poems I discussed in the communalist chapter are also, partly, about the toughness of soils in Cardiganshire; one of those coincidences that emerge whenever you probe works of art closely.)

Two traits complicate the picture. The first is his admiration for D.H. Lawrence, which intermittently animates his work a great deal; his views on the spiritual in art derive from Leavis, a follower of Lawrence. The second is a curious half-belief in flux. The transient, irrational, present moment was the content of Lawrence's poetry; Abbs believes that he believes this: *A poet should be out/ In this, his mind coinciding/ With all that flows and// Undergoes metamorphosis*, (from 'As Descartes') but he scrunches every moment down into hard, massive, petrified lumps of moralised knowledge. We need a new vocabulary to distinguish aged-objects from novel-objects within a poem. Abbs' exit into skellig-geology shows a transition from refusal of change to denial of other people's wishes. The rocks threaten whatever they reject with crushing or drowning; they are authenticity and selfsameness; they are simply the patriarchal power.

The paternal power—of the Roman priesthood or of the grim sage of Carmarthenshire—was tight-lipped and undemonstrative. Its utterances ended thought. If he isn't into this, why has he picked up all the stylistic attributes of an older generation? What is the motive? So the trajectory is determined from the first by the quality of the initial intellectual influences. The poet has no belief in originality, being preoccupied with any failure to reproduce an inherited set of commands.

Note that there was an intellectual vanguard in the 1960s; if we leave out science, technology, and business methods, as simply being too important for poets to understand, there were in the unimportant humanities things like structuralism, semiotics, feminism, new variants of Marxism, the rise of sociology, the spread of anthropological ideas, the expansion of history. What do we find of this in Abbs? Nothing at all. There are no embedded versions of decolonisation, of the new history displacing kings and queens. His vision of demos is his reception of the New Left. Abbs believes in a single perfect pattern surrounded by variants which are useless deviations, whereas other poets active in the 70s believe in an endless variety of valid patterns, and in surfing that variety without seeking to impose rules. This is made apparent at line level in the opposition between free verse and repetitive regularity. Universal liberation grants people the right to be rigid and fussy, all the same Abbs' no-saying does give us a hint of the lack of logic-information flow in his poems. Abbs has made a brilliant poetic complex out of the ideas of Spengler and Christopher Dawson, cadaver-ideas as they seem to me; gloom, fear, and discipline tend to drain the mind of activity.

He has unresolved radical conflicts which sap the work from within even if they offer a way out. What is happening then in 'Man and Islands' is a struggle between awareness of change and defence of the certainty of Doctrine. His later career resolved this by an exit from the personal into the Sublime, museum-poems explaining what Really Matters in history. The sea-rocks became marble statues making frozen gestures. Free verse was replaced by restorative classical versification.

Abbs released a volume of *Selected Poems* in 1991 which, very confusingly, detaches numerous poems from the *Islands* cycle and integrates them into a different cycle, about Abbs' father. This seems to change the meaning, although I have been unable to get with that, because the structure of *Islands* is so tight and the poems fit so deeply into it.

§

There are few common points between these three poets. The lesson is that Christian poetry is remarkably diverse even if the central doctrines are shared. Indeed, if we floated up another twenty books of Christian poetry we would find even more diversity.

Whereas meekness posited a lack of power, and even a lack of theological authority, as a virtue of good Christians, Abbs and Humphreys prominently draw power from their belief, and are willing to exercise ethical and intellectual authority. Their poems are claims to the truth. Both of them have written large bodies of prose which may give in voluminous form what the poems give in intense and compact form.

A Turning Point in the 1980s?

My standpoint, my trajectory, my cherry-tree:
New British Poetry, edited by Don Paterson and Charles Simic
(Graywolf Press, 2004, 184pp.)

The main issue here is with the introduction, not with the poetry. Paterson describes his chosen team negatively, as the opposite of what he calls the Postmoderns: "this essay is concerned with the Postmoderns and their general ubiquity", whose work (he says) cannot be understood even by its fans ("Mostly though their work is incomprehensible") and is prevented by its use of a system for composition ("No, they have a system") from expressing anything. No poet is named, and no single poem quoted, in support of this alarming claim. When Paterson cites *Poets on Writing*, a selection of prose accounts edited by Denise Riley, as proof of his thesis, we are inclined to fall down before the evidence. If he's willing to name names, we feel in our marrow, he is telling the truth. However, I reviewed that book, back in 1992 or 3. Out of eighteen poets who write in it, I am afraid that the count of those who use "aesthetic systems" which prevent comprehension, self-expression, humanity, etc, is zero. Had Paterson even read it? I think Riley would be more likely to stick the heads of incomprehensible poets on poles than to publish their self-justifications. I suspect that by "Postmodern" he means the poets represented in *Conductors of Chaos*, in the Mottram and Edwards sections of *the new british poetry*, and *A Various Art*. He is avoiding clearer terms like *small press, underground, innovative, Indy*, and *avant-garde*.

This is a good anthology which systematically excludes the British Poetry Revival and its successors. It is blazoned as "the only definitive anthology of new British poetry", whereas examination shows that it should have been titled "new poetry by conventional and middle-aged poets". This aroused some dissent—as did Don Paterson's paranoid and wildly misleading remarks in the Introduction. It was hardly graceful to attack every poet not included in his anthology. All the contributors were aged between 40 and 60 in 2004. Their key developmental stage was presumably in the 1980s.

It would be simple to write Paterson off as false and malicious and aiming at an audience which knows no better. This diagnosis is not wrong, but we must dwell a little longer in his cell of confinement.

The usual account of what Postmodern is would include a number of the poets here. Most treatments of Glyn Maxwell use the term "postmodernist". His work makes a point of being spun out of momentarily invented possibilities, being too light to be bound to fact or logic. This is a loose term, but it often means a drift away from the authenticity (peaking in the '50s and linked to Existentialism and moral guardianship) which was the virtue of choice of British poetry at a certain period. It is not clear to me that most of the poets in *Conductors/ A Various Art* are postmodern in any of the common senses. Paterson's usage could be seriously misleading here. If we consider that the freedom from literal truth, free play of signifiers, inventiveness, magical reversal and distortion of terms, of marketing-speak are the basis for postmodernism, we may have found the heart of Paterson's discourse: this is a fantastic jacket blurb swollen to the length of an essay. He is no more dishonest than someone selling soap powder.

Most problematic is the idea that all the poets he dislikes are wholly incomprehensible, and that they are completely different from the poets he includes, and calls Mainstream. The idea of a huge empty space with no transitional forms in it is surely a sign of violent stabilisation of an image by managerial intervention. The cultural field allows of clusters of stupidly besotted imitations, but not of depopulated gulfs. Truly, meaning is built of oppositions and culture is continuous; this does not mean that cultural leaders arise by creating violations of continuity.

My guess is that Paterson is motivated by a wish to grasp the cultural field, which fails because he interjects an image vitiated by simplicity and by another, baser, wish, for his clients to win. This is nothing new, but it may be a stimulus to visualising the cultural field with its real, serene, features.

Perhaps this field resists knowledge because it has too many moving points and our curiosity gets fatigued. Another key factor is surely the prevalence of bad information. This may be another reason for studying bad information—as passed by Paterson. If we can seize the nature of the deceiver, we may become enlightened.

That word "ubiquity" suggests hundreds of poets, thousands of books. But Paterson says this work is incomprehensible. How many books has he actually read without understanding them? 200? Or, maybe, one and a half. I have a problem with Paterson saying that he can't understand something and then acting like an expert on it, knowing why it was written, knowing where it comes from, what it's trying to do, that it's similar to hundreds of other works he doesn't understand. I don't believe any of these claims. I think he's lying. I think, simply, that he really doesn't understand what he claims not to understand.

Paterson tries to brazen his way out of trouble by extolling how risky it is to be conventional. This, he says, is true risk, whereas being innovative and discarding conventions is not. The risk of being found trite and conservative is not the same as taking the risk of being too original and too complex. Any really bad pop group is taking a risk by going on stage before an audience. Paterson is being deliberately stupid here, and his misunderstanding sheds no light. He has a conservative taste, and it is the innovators whom he loathes and distrusts.

The many Paterson poems which show self-disgust may be linked to the disgust with Paterson which his prose is bound to inspire. Perhaps he is inclined towards situations where numerous people hate and despise him, because he is used to them, and has weak strategies for avoiding them. This personal problem may point us towards the dark side of aesthetics, the fact that revulsion is as deep as aesthetic delight, and deeply intertwined with it.

Take these examples of the kind of poetry Paterson favours.

> Let there be braziers, holophotal lenses,
> Polished golden flags, champagne and candles,
>
> Let rays shine through the rose window of Chartres,
> Let there be cowslips, myriad splats of rain,
> Trilobites, new parliaments, red neon,
> Let there be twin-stone rings and mirrorglass
>
> Skyscrapers, glinting jumbos, Rannoch lochans
> In which huge skies can touch down in the sun.
>
> Let there be Muckle Flugga's phallic pharos [.]
>   (Robert Crawford, from 'Fiat Lux')

The enormous mentality
of the south bank abutment's
embedded concrete block
is not impassive
though it copes with the westering sun
as remorselessly as any god with petitions
        (Peter Didsbury, from 'Part of the Bridge')

The Long Man
of Wilmington winces with the dawn; he has just
endured yet another mythical, pointless, starry
vigil. His ankles ache, and the weather looks
irksome and moody; the early traffic whizzes by
regardless, but the news and emblems borne
by each car permeate the soil that sustains
the straggling furze, various grasses, and the odd
towering oak. Across the damp fields a distant
siren pleads for attention; he cannot
move, nor, like a martyr, disprove the lie of the land.
        (Mark Ford, from 'The Long Man')

There is no revolution of the word here, but these poems are pleasurable. The new parliament is probably the devolved parliament in Edinburgh. 'Holophotal' is a reflector which throws back all the light from one source with no perceptible loss.

It is difficult to see poets such as Peter Didsbury, Robert Crawford, Ian Duhig, John Ash, or W.N. Herbert as belonging to the mainstream as opposed to personal poetic worlds. Insofar as they have found a way of writing in a personal way without becoming "difficult" and unpalatable, they are worth studying. Reaching a wide audience is one of the goals of poetry. But this is not strictly a question of matters within the poem; I suspect that all good poets become palatable once you grasp what goes on in their world, and it is by chance that Paterson is familiar with these poets (and able to admire them) but not familiar with a hundred others (who thoroughly earn admiration). However, if these poets are acceptable to the gatekeepers, there has been a fundamental change to the landscape. A famous poison has lost its virulence, and stocks of it may be ineffective. The split in English, or British, poetry was mainly due to the rejection habits of the gatekeepers. If these habits have been improved, then the whole cultural map is now different. We will return to this.

It seems fruitless to attack Paterson's choice of poets when the American consumer probably has no use for 36 British poets and can so easily spare a 37th or 38th. There are far too many good poets on the scene for the audience to take in clearly. The audience is so small that new poetry is commercially marginal. This brings the poet, in a fairy-tale way, to a fatal crossroads: if you try to write like everyone else you will be indistinguishable from dozens of other poets, and you will be invisible and not get the gigs. If you write in an original way, you will be unfamiliar to the public, and will dip below the margins of commerciality; you will not be published and so will be invisible. Additionally, you may incur the wrath of managers who want homogeneity. The landscape shows too many living poets of talent. If reality is so kind to us, why plunge into falsehood? We're winning. The hills are alive, the braes are alive, the bloody bus-stops are alive, with it. Something does not need fixing, even if it turns sibling rivalry up to the volume of the Castle Donington heavy-metal festival.

The whole quality of being comprehensible is not a physical thing. I read Geoffrey Hill's first two volumes in 1975 (was it?) and didn't understand what they meant. I read them again in 1993 (roughly) and I understood everything. I had picked up a lot of culture in the interim. You can't base an elaborate theory on facts that change and vanish. Clearly, understanding is something happening in the reader's brain, and depends both on the abidingly stored knowledge there but also on the temporary state, the mood (time pressures? levels of excitation or saturation? level of alcohol) of that brain. The experience of incomprehension may tell us more about the attitude of that particular reader than about the poet. It doesn't tell you anything about *King Log* that I flunked it in 1975 (or *The White Stones* a couple of years later). Paterson's wholesale rejection of poetic alternatives suggests that he is very short of sympathy—indeed blinding territorial rage seems to be the reaction on show. I don't see why poetry should be obscure. But you can't make cultural maps if you have no ability to enjoy what is different from what you would write yourself.

Let's just float the possibility that the change to a society dominated by leisure, and the operation of pre-existing individualism and self-determination, and the advent of mass higher education, have produced a literary scene which is so complex as to be beyond the grasp of one intellect. If the whole is incomprehensible in this sense, perhaps parts of it are too. What happens when you try to sum the whole landscape up, for example for a short essay aimed at American readers who haven't got a clue about the scene you are evoking? Perhaps you struggle for a while with lack of facts and problems of pattern fitting—and then drop out, into rage, projection, denial.

Things take place as if the audience recognise certain cultural assets of the poets, and as if they themselves own these assets, and value them for that reason. One of the factors in any of the social atmospheres evoked by any of the anthologies I examined would be neutralisation, writing-down, of certain assets; ethnic solidarity is unimpressed by intelligence (and vice versa). This may apply also to poetry collections in general. The experience of pure freedom is perhaps restrained by cultural anxiety (and by revulsion?).

My understanding of the Underground is that its poets pursue individuality and expressivity, searching for the authentic even at the cost of being unfamiliar to the reader. The mainstream, conversely, avoids difficulty at every step, producing something which is colourless when looked at closely, although it is possible to combine fixed elements to form large units which are unexpected. The key phrase may be *offsets defined as peaks*. The Underground poet regards distance from a statistical centre, in terms of language and experience, as a height. Bardon Hill, in Leicestershire, is described as "90 feet short of a mountain": to be 950 feet away from the centre is felt as height and dominance, more desirable than a site 850 feet away from the centre. Thus, offsets are defined as peaks. Once you share this metaphor, a great deal follows to affect how a poem is constructed.

This is a very good anthology. It is an ideal way of reaching the poets included (36 talents aged roughly between 40 and 55). It puts a sheen on things which may make them look better than they are—which is what everyone wants from anthologies, isn't it? Poems by Selima Hill, John Ash, Peter Didsbury, Robert Crawford, or Ian Duhig make it all worthwhile. There is no need for excessive loyalty in this area. How many more people would have read *Conductors* if it hadn't started, in alphabetical democracy, with Bergvall and cheek—stretches of self-struck vacuity wide enough to drown the average poetry lover? Let me point out, ducking behind the parapet, that *Conductors* included all the bad stuff submitted and *NBP* rigorously rejects it. Take Glyn Maxwell's poem 'Helen and Heloise', 90 lines long and the longest in the book. It concerns two sisters, "breathtakers" in looks, expats, affluent and sheltered, in a private swimming pool in some arid, sandy, oil-rich country. The style is suave and not at all obscure:

> [...]
> What they can buy in the town, or the only quarters
> Blondes can be seen alighting in, and only
> As guided shaded daughters
> Into an acre of golden shop. "Lonely"?
> Who told me this had told me: "They have no lives.
> They will be children. Then they will be wives."

The plainness is blurred by shifts of modality: a reference to a girl's face arriving "near where I'd pictured it" is followed by the qualifier "it's not a guess", preceding the whole stanza just quoted. The shifts do not seem to change very much. The poem seems about to become a narrative, like some film, but deceives this expectation, at least in that the sense of the story, some scheme in which the scenes would add up to a cogent whole, never arrives. Nothing here is more cogent than the demands of the ABABCC rhyme scheme. In the world of film, the ability to show two pretty girls in their swimming costumes would be motive enough, with a story hastily added as a cover. Maxwell's poem gives a sense of affluence because of its lack of purpose. The scenes of two young girls almost reach aestheticisation, because no purpose is deployed. They do not get there because the poet is not sufficiently interested by the details of the scenes. This combination of affluence, the enigmatic, and the straightforward, is present in many of the poems in this book.

Perhaps conscious understanding, overall pattern, are being avoided because they would demand a language which would be intense and new and so breach the rule of being straightforward all the time. Maxwell's poem is like some film in a foreign language: we are caught up in visual and formal details because we do not understand the dialogue (in which everything not obvious is being said). In Underground poems, you can hear the dialogue (and nothing it says is obvious).

The ambience reminds me of the legend about the tenor-sax player Lucky Thompson. He played, in the '40s and early '50s, with Miles Davis, in the modern style. Times were hard. He moved to France and found a durable living. In those clubs, people would be happy just because he was black and played sax. They didn't really understand jazz. Also, there was the problem of collaborators. So he shifted to playing the standards (American classics, actually), with a beautiful tone but without playing jazz any more. This was within the comfort zone of his audiences (and European rhythm sections). He never went back to America. His late recordings have a peculiarly serene quality, with a wonderfully burnished tone. He is not taking those autumnal tunes by storm, nor imposing his personality on them; familiar melodies in an egoless state. This is the atmosphere of this anthology. It recovers feelings from the past. Because of the simple handling, elements of originality stick out with pinpoint clarity. These are poets taken late in their career, and it shows; I did read early Jo Shapcott and I thought it was junk, but the poems shown here are really a great improvement. Words like *evergreen* and *middle-aged* suit these poems. Insofar as this anthology represents a pop playfulness which has mixed with the conservative academic current (at one stage so violently opposed to the disposable quality of Pop), we can see it as the Mainstream, intimately mingling the two major currents of the 1960s (as upheld by Brian Patten and *Critical Quarterly*, respectively). This is what Paterson says, and he is probably right. Of course, these are high quality poems, and one could be Mainstream without being that.

Clearly there has been a huge improvement in this whole sector since the hated Motion/Morrison anthology and the laughable *Poetry with an Edge*, or again since the *New British Poetry* edited by Hulse, Kennedy, and Morley. This change over time suggests that the historical continuity with the mainstream of English poetry (or, with everything good since time began) is illusory. This something had an origin in time, and would come into much clearer focus if an editor confessed that it was a definite something, and that it had a shape—an aesthetic.

It seems to me that any artistic standpoint is just a point on a spectrum, with no reason not to drift in either direction, but for Paterson it's a *locus standi,* a yard to be defended at all costs. In this way he constructs the landscape as a visual cone, seen from a fixed standpoint. Such cones can contribute to true knowledge if there are enough of them. But in the introduction he is telling the most shameless lies about, apparently, hundreds of people—for when he says "ubiquitous" we can hardly suppose he means three half-crazed pamphleteers at the dodgy end of Mill Road. Such lies must lead to terrible hatred and even violence. This is not conducive to the serenity and fraternity which I like best in our scene. Many of the people on the scene would be unhappy to see the truth told about themselves. Very few can be indifferent to these malicious and partisan lies.

I would sum up the problem here as (a) people should not tell abusive and obvious lies about their peers, (b) attacking the poetry you have left out may not help the sales of your anthology in a direct way, (c) it would be terribly wrong to associate the chosen poets with Paterson's monkeyshines (and define them all as "the enemy").

He is missing what separates this new complex from The Movement, dominant force from the '50s to the '70s or even the '80s. (Although *The Mersey Sound* sold a quarter of a million copies, of course.) Most published references to the Mainstream certainly refer to The Movement and its second generation of imitators. There was an Event where this sense of things broke up—more probably, many similar events in the artistic lives of thousands of people, echeloned out over decades. Poets, willingly or unwillingly, gave up the priestly office of moral instruction and tried to write in an aesthetically attractive way. They began to use figures or figments rather than direct I-speaking (and the figures they used were not just Christian parables). Discarding moral duty implied the autonomy of the text from sociological realism. The change had quite probably a lot to do with the acceptance of mass media, i.e. rock music, film and television (principally), which had no moral load and were forced to appeal, directly and simply. The new poetry was not realism, but it included lots of detail—freed by the camera, or shown up by the camera. Poetry became less selective, and stylisation became a key problem.

The collapse of Movement hegemony had a structural cause, and this was quite probably a titration within the universities: the gradual *outnumbering* by secular, hedonistic, pluralistic feeling people, of Christian, moralising, people who see the same patterns everywhere. This is not a point that yields vital results, or is wholly clear, but it does yield something: the "underground" poetry of the '60s and '70s was rejected by the mainstream publishers mainly because it was secular, hedonistic, pluralist, etc. The zone of contention, separating mainstream and Underground, is not in contention any more. The titration had a lot to do with the arrival each year of people who had been children soaked in TV and pop music.

The image Paterson presents is of Theory producing a set of rigid responses, repeating each other without confirming each other, preventing conscious direction of the text, and shut in the precincts of the original assumptions. However, the Underground would claim that all these features apply in poems based on reproducing the poet's character. Unexamined intuition is caught in a circle. In fact, the thing which repeats may not even be character, but a set of beliefs about how a poem should go (or how a scene between two people should go).

On both sides, people agree that conscious direction of the text is best. But how can you *think* if you're forbidden to *theorise*?

What *is* a compositional system? Take *Dart*, the book-length poem by Alice Oswald, a poet included here. It is not free fantasy or autobiography; it is governed by the course of the river, something outside the poet's wishes, and much older than the poet as an organism enjoying life and consciousness. It is an arbitrary set of real, connected, data, which the poet both adheres to and expressively varies as parts of the creative process. This is what Paterson means by a system. This is just such a set of rules and set of external data as the intellectual (or conceptual) poets submit themselves to, in order to find a supply of the unknown and the knowable sufficient to feed their next book. I don't understand why there is so much mystification about this. Poets rely on the world of information almost as much as a photographer. You would not forbid a photographer to leave his own house, or to photograph anything he had not made. The mind (you may think) does not function much unless it encounters the unknown, and turns on its admirable faculties for understanding and arranging the unknown.

Finding a dataset which is sufficiently unknown and complex is no simple matter. Conceptual poets do this in an orderly way, and the positive results argue strongly in favour of this method. It does not prohibit self-expression any more than the use of a camera does. Is it really true that following the course of the Dart, towards the sea, is an intolerable limit on the freedom of the poet? We cannot merely share knowledge, we must also share something we both do not yet know. This is how the poem which is a transmission of data can transmit its data. Oswald's poem reminds me strongly of '40s documentary (specifically, of the poet W.J. Turner's book *Exmoor Village*, for Mass Observation, and the film *River of Time*, with words by the poet Paul Dehn). It is obviously quite simple and old-fashioned, as a project, compared to the poetry I am used to reading. Yet, documentary led to conceptual art. Oswald uses different procedures in different parts of the poem. If we imagine the poem as consisting of data plus procedures, we can readily say that the procedures can be varied by arbitrary rules in a similar way to the data. Where they are both varying together, we have a new world of possible poems, letting us travel far away from the gravitational drag of repeating 19th-century poetry, or 17th-century poetry, at the level of structure.

Max Bense describes his compositional procedures in these terms: "It belongs to a series of linguistic experiments whose goal was to select and compose from a preset quantity of words or texts, linear quantities and words, in such a way that a "verbal product" came about, which could still be perceived as an assimilable, i.e. identifiable, text, text fragment, or text-ruin. The repertoire for selection, which was carried out stochastically, i.e. by use of random numbers as far as nouns and adjectives were concerned, consisted of roughly 1,200 words from the literature section of a medium-circulation daily paper." (*Doppelinterpretationen*, ed. Hilda Domin, 1969, p.247) The text in question begins "My standpoint and the cherry tree or the trajectory and the overview" and is from a 1961 volume. This is what a German professor of the theory of science (and former research physicist) was into in the high period of the 1950s, with cybernetics and information theory as apparently new wonder sciences. His poems really were without personal expression. This is a "system". But what the bloody hell has this got to do with modern British underground poetry?

No one does this kind of thing. Sampling and random methods are everywhere, (arguably they are biologically given behaviours of the brain), but the output is always subject to selection, criticism, and humanistic intervention. Bense didn't even see himself as a poet. The accusation Paterson is making is wildly untrue. It has plausibility only for someone with access to no other sources of information.

(The stuff about Lucky Thompson may be just a legend. I got hold of a CD of Thompson recorded playing standards in France in 1956 and 1960, and it's uninteresting. If this is post-jazz, give me Art Blakey.)

The Beautiful Inventions
Postmodernism and the recovery of the m-stream

If in 2004 we have a revitalised mainstream in which a proportion of good poets can thrive without intervention by authority, and in 1977 we have the crisis of the British Poetry Revival and its demise as a cultural force in the wider world, we are left with the question: when did the mainstream recover?

We set out from astonishment at the way centralist perimeter guard Don Paterson was using the term postmodernist, as a shorthand for everything he hates, in a 2004 introduction. If Paterson's poets are all over 40 in 2004, they were at least in their 20s in 1984, and we should look as far back as the 80s to find where the good poetry comes from. Light can be shed on this area by the work of Ian Gregson, *Contemporary Poetry and Postmodernism* (1996). Gregson claims that much of the English poetry scene is under the influence of the PM thing and that many of the poets anthologised by Paterson are, in sober fact, postmodernist. This is a fault line which may either lead us to a deeper level of reality or lead to the building collapsing around us, but which anyway seizes our attention.

I should emphasize that the question here is not of one individual reaching a style, but of the rules changing for a large group of poets; not of poetry changing but of the rules of the permissible changing, so that official, High Street, publications start to feature styles once available (perhaps for decades) in the fertile wilderness of the Underground. Its thesis is quite similar to that of Alan Robinson in *Instabilities in Contemporary British Poetry* (1988), which is a valuable reinforcement of Gregson's propositions. Gregson's subtitle uses the words dialogue and estrangement. He later defines postmodernism as something which involves dialogue, a multiplicity of voices, and dissonance. The poets he discusses are principally Craig Raine, Paul Muldoon, James Fenton, Fleur Adcock, Carol Ann Duffy, Edwin Morgan, Christopher Middleton, Roy Fisher, Veronica Forrest-Thomson, Denise Riley, John Ash, Ian Macmillan, Andrew Motion, George Szirtes, Matthew Sweeney, Simon Armitage, Glyn Maxwell, Paul Durcan, Jo Shapcott. Fairly obviously a number of these have little to do with postmodernism and little to do with each other. It is fair to say that his major concern is to place all these poets on one stylistic map, which no one has ever done before, and so establish a universe of discourse from which the semantic toxins of the balkanised state have been drained. It is also fair to say that most of these poets have very slight artistic achievements to their names. Gregson is not searching for the best poets but trying to write something wider and less intense.

Gregson's qualification of the usefulness of the term postmodernism, which he took at the outset from the introduction to a 1982 Penguin anthology, is at pp.249–50. He says he identifies a group of *mainstream postmodernists*: "What marks them as mainstream is their greater adherence to metrical norms and sometimes conventional forms [...] Nonetheless, their poems are sceptical about language, self-reflexive, playful, self-consciously fictive, and deconstruct themselves. [...] The crucial point, though, is the way that postmodernist elements are combined with real ones." He does not find excellent poetry in this style (viz. mainstream poems with a small dose of modernity) but offers it (p.11) as a design which someone in future might be able to use in a brilliant way. Gregson is sympathetic towards the underground scene and makes a very important point on the kind of innovation which has penetrated the m-stream: "British poetry does seem to have an astonishing ability to domesticate such influences and accept them only in an altered form, and it is the hesitations between radically contradictory modes which make contemporary poetry what it is."

Overall the salience of postmodernism in explaining the poetic achievements, and changes in shared style, which he is discussing, is low. The trouble with proposing dialogue as a key element of style is that the dominant condition of poetry in the 20th century was obviously to be a monologue, and it draws most of its strengths from that. Poetic drama was one of the most popular genres of the 19th century, involved many voices all the time, and has almost vanished from 20th century poetry, all over Europe. Dialogue is a feature of everyday speech in its entirety; small doses emerging in poetry do not enable poetry to compete with, for example, television or newspapers in polyphony. In this list, the excellent poets are Morgan, Ash, Middleton, Fisher and Riley. No one would describe the last three as postmodernist. The merit of the group he is mainly interested in, emerging roughly 1978 to 1990 then, was grievously limited up till 1996. Morgan is a major poet but he was already writing wonderfully ludic poetry in the 1950s. Gregson does not offer us any statement by one of the poets he foregrounds to the effect that postmodernism is what they are doing. The path is open for us to find a developmental route which was less theoretical, more based in concrete examples of older poetry, more English, more tied to social assets and to admired speech patterns of English.

Gregson does not give us a proposal about the chronology of style changes, but it seems reasonable to pick out of the wealth of data he has collected a story in which, from a 1978 volume by Craig Raine onward, a series of books sharing qualities of the ludic, the sub-modernist, doubt, indeterminacy, secularism, were published, widely read, and accepted by the gatekeepers (so that they flowed into High Street shops and borough libraries). They would include books by James Fenton, Christopher Reid, an anthology edited by Motion and Morrison, others by Andrew Motion, Jo Shapcott, Glyn Maxwell. The cumulative impact on poets looking at the scene around 1992 was a sense of being free—and even that writing realistically about moral obligations and politics was old-fashioned.

If we want a synthesizing description of the new English poetry of the 1980s and 1990s we would like to choose a term which has a definite meaning. The social historian Patrick Joyce has evoked the term, in a heated polemic defending it: "The major advance of "postmodernism" needs to be registered by historians: namely that the events, structures and processes of the past are indistinguishable from the forms of documentary representation, the conceptual and political appropriations, and the historical discourses that construct them. [...] A recognition of the irreducibly discursive character of the social undermines the idea of social totality. There is no overarching coherence evident in either the polity, the economy or the social system. [...] Thus with the notion of social totality goes the notion of social determination, so central to "social history". [...] Gone too are the grand narratives that historicised the notion of social totality." Leaving aside the question of whether any such change in the reading of history has actually occurred, it is not obvious that there is any connection at all between this version of postmodernism and any aspect of the poetry in question. The correlation of the poetic changes with anything so philosophical and high-flown as what Joyce says is utterly unlikely. The poems in question are not philosophical. Gregson offers no statements by poets which could be tied to this line of theory. If postmodernism is such a weak term, used in hundreds of different ways by thousands of different people, it cannot run the race: we would surely do better to coin a new term, or several.

The conclusion we can draw from Gregson's valuable work is that

- British poetry migrated away from the moralistic and sceptical inhibitions of the old mainstream, and a new standard was developed;
- this was ratified by the "official" editors and publishers shifting the limits of what they would accept or "take seriously" so that a very large number of people were affected;
- the discussion around postmodernism played a vital role in this redefinition of the acceptable;
- this process was happening rapidly in the 1980s but had already begun in 1978 with the flap around "Martian" poetry;
- the result is a much more benevolent and less closed landscape.

Post-modern means, we understand, the situation of an intellectual who no longer believes in the "grand narratives" such as Marxism, other historicisms, Christianity, expansive nationalism, etc. This post status might show up simply as an absence. The problem with applying this to poetry is that the absence of overarching ideas may not be diagnostic of any particular intellectual state, might actually be an indicator of leisure poetry, what you call salon poetry or light verse. If someone is not an intellectual, the absence of grand narratives from what they say is not remarkable. In a secular society, the absence of dominantly Christian themes from poetry does not even show that the poet is not Christian, as they may be simply writing a casual poetry in which their deeper beliefs do not peep out. Even a priest can take a day off. So a classification based on an absence of diagnostic traits is vulnerable to a grand error, and we might well wish to find a classification which would have the *presence* of named traits as diagnostic test, thus giving more reliable results. A variant of this is the idea that absence of modernist traits is a sign of having gone *beyond* modernism and so become postmodernist.

The same absence can as plausibly be read as conservatism and banality. All in all we are entitled to look for another way of integrating the primary material, in its variety, into a classification or explanation. More than that, it is desirable to devise several different classifications, to uncover the arbitrary aspects of classification. They should compete so that the weaknesses of each one are exposed. If we go back to the raw material, a book of poetry with its typical 80 pages and 1400 lines obviously shows a large number of features, and any classification of the type "postmodernist" "modernist" "*vers libre*" "Oxford" "mainstream" etc. is going to miss the majority of these features. The labelling is only plausible if we do it gently and if richer information is available to eke it out.

Resettling Status

If we look at the '50s and the '80s side by side we find that both had very conservative governments in power in both the UK and the USA, that they were periods of intense anti-Marxist propaganda, that they were times of deregulation for business and business domination of government policy, finally that the 80s saw up to 1986 or so a return to the Cold War. Reagan and Thatcher were keen to roll back everything "radical" which had happened since the fateful first year of the 1960s. In poetry we may be seeing less "the long 1950s" than a return of the 1950s. In *Some Contemporary Poets of Britain and Ireland* (1983), Michael Schmidt chooses 18 poets, who were mainly born in the 1940s. This was the decade when the majority of the radical figures of the British Poetry Revival were born, but none of them features here. The editor does not even bother to revile them in the introduction. The package looks like an attempt to roll back to the state of 1959 but the editor is unable to make this explicit—an inhibition on central issues which pervades the poetry. The missing title would be "anthology of neoconservative verse". Schmidt's self-identification, a few years earlier, was as "Left neo-conservative".

I should say at once how much I like the work of Wainwright, Kuppner, Brackenbury, and Ash, as displayed here, and how much weaker all the other poets are. Wainwright is straightforwardly a socialist writer, inspired by the past of political protest by the poorest against the social order, and the other poems in the book dilute his message where they do not blank it out from view. Derek Mahon is an admirable poet but outside my subject because of his nationality.

I spend my career finding typical texts that show the Shining Path of the whole big thing. With Schmidt's anthology I reluctantly conclude that it is simply a representation of the deeply aberrant and eccentric views of one individual and typicality is not a feature it genuinely possesses. When I read in the introduction that the nineteenth century is shining out through the poets of his choice the conclusion, that Michael Schmidt has rejected every new thing since 1895 and has rejected every poet who has accepted any one of those things, must be obvious to everyone but him. So the 1970s were dominated by a return to late 19th century poetics and attitudes? I don't think so. Did anyone else think this? So what was happening in 1973–83 is probably not being displayed for us like a room in some brilliantly organised museum.

Does one decade stop when another starts? Another view would be that the conservative sentiment with all its ideological and cultural arsenal was there all the way through but that its ability to dominate the public arena oscillated up and down quite sharply. This is clearer in some ways, for example no one is claiming that the conservatives of 1950s poetry suddenly became hippies in 1965 or that the conservatives of Schmidt's anthology had been writing Marxist concrete poetry in 1974. By my count, seven of the poets here are formalists, reminding us of Homberger's comment that this style seemed archaic by 1961. Some poems rhyme, others use unusual variants such as assonance.

One of the noticeable features of many of the poets included is the pointless nature of their work. Elsewhere, many poems have an artistic climax and resolution, they expound a situation and then take us somewhere astounding and conclusive, and we see a reason why we had to learn about the situation. But the poets Schmidt likes seem to follow a different formula. Their works describe a situation and then peter out. Silence falls and we wonder why we ever began. Defining the artistic purpose of the whole is therefore a challenge. The meekness and tastefulness on show are such that we suspect the 19th century quality is simply a coincidence, the poets are so besotted with qualities that are aged and undisturbing and faded that their poems resemble things left over from the 19th century simply by being subdued.

The data look remarkably consistent with the theory that this 1983 anthology reflects Donald Davie's strategy for the marketing of English poetry. The rumour in the usual bars was that Davie was the *éminence grise* behind Carcanet's bad decisions. Insofar as the meekness and passivity showcased in this anthology have continued over the 26 years intervening (written 2009), they represent a continuity of the 1950s, and the cultural plan which devised *New Lines* is still at work in 1983. This is the long 1950s in action.

What was the context in 1983? From the point of view of a bourgeois literary scholar, there had been a tidal wave of Left-influenced speech over the previous 15 years. The poetry of that era gave up the ancestral task of announcing status, in order to question everyone's status. The use of a projected future as the setting of poetry had a fatal flaw. If people disliked that future, they disliked the poetry. This disabled men reading feminist writing—and other forms of equality were equally threatening. It was like a cell made of words inside which they were to be confined and humiliated. They felt like slugs tossed into a bowl of salt. You would not expect them also to vote for it. The new thing apparently attacked their right to have subjective feelings. It invalidated by a stroke of the pen the consecrated knowledge which they had spent so many years acquiring and which they earned their living by. It forbade them to speak by virtue of being white (to be thorough, of being white, male, heterosexual, highly educated, middle class). It replaced the pleasure principle within literature by an array of rules to do with distributive justice and status-creating rhetoric. Here, mocking the secular religion of culture was not only permitted but was apparently to be the daily activity of the new generation of academics. The backlash against the new dissident poetry was like a middle-class tax revolt—defending system-validated knowledge in order to be validated by owning it.

A large interest emerged, a stratum of sensibility which represented a market in latent form but which was too disconnected to be called a group. Their wish was to find a refuge area in which the thorough exclusion of these radical penetrations was the precondition of aesthetic experience. Consider now what this might mean in the literary sub-realm of poetry, usually considered as a *refugium* from a harsh world. Poetry had been massively involved in the left-wing culture which reached incandescence in 1968. This latent market could be summoned into being by an impresario, a publishing concern, an anthology perhaps, which promised them poetry in which everything modern and anxiety-making was not even a possibility. Such an anthology would be staffed by poets who had noted all the innovations of the era since 1960, and systematically rejected them. At this point we can drop the mask and return to look at Schmidt's anthology and say that it is an attempt to console the conservative literato for their refugee status. The strategy is something like ejecting all the phases of experience which are mixed with the hostile principle and cutting back to the last untainted extent of sensibility and awareness, even if that means going back to an unimaginably dim and indistinct grey clay, something which has no present time left in it. At this point we can think again about Schmidt's insistent recollection of Victorian poets and realise why a minority of poets writing in the 1970s should have purged away anything that was post-Victorian in origin and aspirations.

These poems are very different from the sententious manner. They do not offer finished views of situations. They are meek rather than tough, vague and withdrawn rather than authoritative. These qualities may represent an ideology as set forth by Andrew Motion, not very explicitly, roughly that Edward Thomas represents Englishness by the very lack of distinction of his poems about peasants, widely admitted to be great. Their plainness of language, their subtlety, preference for tawny and subdued colours, for lack of climaxes, interest in rural implements, are egalitarian and speak for a sensitive and quiet people. As egalitarian values and the Welfare State advanced this meekness came to the centre of politics. It is the democratic voice. The abandonment of artistic means was a feature of the Movement and especially of its greatest figure, Philip Larkin, even if he was right-wing and anti-egalitarian. Thus Motion, in writing books about Edward Thomas (1980) and Larkin (1982), was constructing a highway that *leads towards his own work*, confessedly dull as ditchwater and supposedly democratic in its lack of high points. John Lucas has also written from this point of view, defining this small scale and timid quality as Englishness. This ideology is not necessarily shared by other poets in this anthology, such as Robert Wells or Dick Davis, but their work resembles Motion's in a way which is not wholly in their favour.

It has a peculiar and pervasive flavour for me which must have been with me since I read a related work by Schmidt (*Eleven British Poets*) in around 1983. The style is like an entire landscape viewed by candlelight, a dying-away dimness in which colour is not visible and the whole world seems to be made of a great number of moths' wings, receding in a million tones of grey. Here the centre is also a penumbra and nothing is vivid. This tone has pungent associations of compromise, of cultural restoration after the excitement of revolution has died down, of elder figures singling out notably feeble young men because their negativity is unthreatening. I find it hard to admire the quality of their inhibitions on request.

We have to ask how close all this poetry is to the poetry of the 1950s. I think the answer is that it resembles subdued poetry of the 1950s. The *absence* of all the innovations which rushed onto the scene after 1960 is a negative quality, it is not a salient resemblance to particular '50s poems or to their dominant aesthetic purposes. Within *New Lines,* Elizabeth Jennings and John Holloway are the most plausible ancestors. This whole anthology fits inside Holloway's *Wood and Windfall,* and is notably closer to that than to, say, *High Windows* or *A Walk Round the Estate.* Some of the poets use rhyme and monotonous line lengths.

However, there is another element here, which is that three of the poets are examples of the ludic quality which was beginning to be called post-modern. They are Fenton, John Ash, and Frank Kuppner. Their work is also of a higher quality than those around them. If postmodernism was a thin stream in 1983, we can at least locate its emergence as a mighty current to between 1983 and 1995. Better evidence may yet emerge.

Schmidt's anthology documents a particular feeling present in the 1980s. Very obviously this feeling was only one cultural sentiment among many, even if it did speak for a group which had this sentiment persistently and wanted to read poems about it. My thesis that the 1980s saw a radical break with prevailing poetic models is thus flawed—the heirloom phobias continued to generate poems, if only as one instrument in the orchestra. This is an illustration of how diverse the mainstream is. I describe minor currents within it but most of the objects remain undescribed. I wonder if there is a line of dim and inconspicuous poetry which has continued the 1950s up to the present day, unilluminated by fashions and ideas or theories. I have not tracked this one, but perhaps it is there all the same, too faint to see.

The Oxford line wins the line-out

I said that postmodernism had a low salience as a descriptive classification of the cluster of features Gregson is describing. His primary description is perfectly satisfactory, but there remains the possibility of finding another overall classification which is a better match for the same primary features and trumps the low salience problem.

A notable fact about the Martian thing was that the poets using the style and the managers promoting it and talking it up all had close associations with Oxford University. Gregson produces a vital quote which shows the word "ludic" being used in 1978 in a review by John Osborne in the Hull magazine *Bête Noire*. He says exactly "the ludic, fabulary style" (of Craig Raine). The ludic strain, though, was most obviously present, in British poetry of that time, in the work of Edwin Morgan and George MacBeth. MacBeth responded to *Crow* in 1970 with an epic poem about a cat named Orlando who starred in a recurring myth travelling across different times and cultures. MacBeth, a producer of programmes for BBC radio, was a classic rider of the Oxford-London axis, travelling down from Oxford in 1957 to take a series of literary jobs and to supervise other people's careers. Ludic certainly wasn't new in the 1980s—it was just that antiviral defences had been eroded.

One of the prominent mainstream postmodernist works produced in the 1980s was *The Illusionists* (1980) by John Fuller (1937–). Fuller had been at Oxford since the 1950s and was one of the influential figures on the university poetry scene. He didn't have to move very far to become a "mainstream postmodernist". He was an influence on a large number of poets, too many to count, but notably Glyn Maxwell, accepted as one of the new stars of the 1980s mainstream thing. As was widely pointed out, Maxwell was influenced by Auden; but the mediator was John Fuller, and that odd streak of rather dandyish poetry was a living thing because Fuller was a scene-maker and made it so. Around audenite student poets were audenite student readers and fans to make the sound credible and fashionable. One angle on the new tonality is that it is "Oxford revisited". A quick check shows that Raine, Reid, Fenton, Maxwell and Shapcott shared the same Oxford background.

The Illusionists had (in its original form) a jacket showing a painting by Hogarth in which perspective geometry is exploited to show impossible spatial relationships, and the eye forever cheats the brain. This was a whole book of trick perspectives, with a theme of art forgery—again, a scenario favoured by post-modern theorists, with endless forensic detail being implanted to create an inauthentic and untrustworthy experience. However, the Hogarth painting suggests what reading the text confirms, that nothing specifically 20th century is going on here:

> It's true. He did. The chap could dabble
> In any period of paint.
> His fakes were indistinguishable
> From genuine: he'd do a saint
> In gold leaf or a whore in charcoal,
> Sketches of pest or patriarchal
> Desert temptations, Dutch still-lives
> Or portraits of the artist's wives
> (Or of the artist's aunts or nieces),
> Murals of mayors in roomy furs,
> Elizabethan miniatures,
> Fairy dells or altarpieces.
> Give him a bottle or two of Scotch,
> He'd even tackle the *Night Watch*.
>   (*Illusionists*, 5:7)

This is reminiscent of Browning and of W. S. Gilbert, not of Ashbery or Lyotard. The fake painting on which the plot turns is in fact a Hogarth. An acrostic in chapter five shows a dedication to the 18th century light poet Matthew Prior. The trickiness in the plot of this bafflingly minor tale in verse is directly related to the enigmatic quality which Auden's verse possessed from *New Signatures* up to the 1940s: a central void in the semantic structure of the poem which although empty of information can have by reflection a colour, suggesting either idleness, the secret and looming conspiracy of fascism, the unknown which surrounds the "data space" of one individual, or even the Future.

One of the features of imaginative freedom is that it lets anyone choose the most privileged social slots, ones available to a minority in real life. The Left was preoccupied with keeping art from simply offering upward mobility through fantasy. The eclipse of the Left revealed a simpler landscape in which art gave you the things you want—the Oxford manner, for example. A key feature of the favoured art of the '80s is smoothness and high finish of surface, and a key feature of the '80s politically was the rise of the middle class, with the eclipse of its traditional enemies. The working class was in decline, either rising into a new middle class or under pressure of unemployment, with union busting the flavour of the day. I think it is difficult to separate these two processes. The rise during that time of prestige of the middle class in the West was deeply related to a new (or merely updated?) artistic style which signalled affluence and leisure. Popular music was largely depoliticised and it came to seem anomalous that it had been so very politicised during the second half of the '70s. In this context it comes to seem more than a coincidence that the cultural style associated with the old middle class came to dominate the public face of English poetry. This would lead us to suspect that the label *post-modern* is just a brand and that the real process is a return to dominance of the Oxford style, with its alluring promise of access to the cultural privileges of a less democratic age. It would seem odd if during the phase of triumph of conservatism the most culturally legitimate style of the previous generation would not soar to new eminence.

I should make clear at this point that the poets concerned were not consciously of the New Right or even affluent. The equation with the New Right is misleading, much as the link to postmodernism is, because poetry is a world of its own and even if it is largely made up of reflections of the outside world those optical panes are dissected and diffracted on their route. I don't think anybody experienced Craig Raine, Maxwell, Armitage etc. as a new cultural experience, a new thrill. The question of how they came to be promoted as such has to do with the history of publicity rather than with artistic thought.

The appeal of the ludic was also a rejection of Nonconformist attitudes to pleasure, in favour of frivolous attitudes incarnated not least by aesthetes and dandies. A new reform of verse brought smoothness and sweetness, departing radically from the reality principle of politically committed poetry. It is quite possible that the decline of the Left gave a respite for art, allowing it to recover elements of play and fantasy. What is hard to believe is that those elements were genuinely new rather than archaic. I don't know if other people have observed that what was supposed to be a big new sound in the 1980s actually felt very familiar and predictable. The reason, perhaps, why its surprise value was so low was that it was a momentarily obscured facet of the Oxford thing emerging into the full rays of the sun, and the Oxford line was the dominant streak in English literary culture. The most successful TV series in the 1980s was the 1981 adaptation of *Brideshead Revisited*, a primal example of the cult of 1920s Oxford with a theme of the virtuous middle class falling prey to the siren song of the decadent aristocracy. It was a blueprint for falling prey to the wiles of bourgeois culture. The elements of pose, fantasy, decadence and irony bear a telling resemblance to the new poetry of the 1980s—closer I fear than the hoped-for resemblance to post-structuralism and the New York School. In poetry, Auden and Betjeman covered a large part of the visible landscape—and they were genuine parts of 1920s Oxford.

In sum, rather than see the new tone as "postmodernism lite" we can grasp more of it by pulling it into a new perspective where the need for moral drama has been absolved and historically abiding features like fantasy, the game, dialogue, hedonism, casualness come to the fore again. We can label the new manner as having Pater at one end and affluence at the other.

This in no way devalues the link to postmodernism bound in a cluster of values to do with secularism, scepticism, detachment from moral dramas or historicist grand narratives, love of surface values, interest in doubt and in the fake, playfulness, etc.

I do not find much of interest in the poets whom the media were promoting. There is an element of self-deception and mistaking wish for reality in the reception of the poets who got patronage. However, if we search through the impressively large number of books being published, we find a row of artistically successful poets who were developing out into this new world of the playful, non-political, bright, and sophisticated. Eminent in this delightful and fresh group were Frank Kuppner, *A Bad Day for the Sung Dynasty* (1984), John Ash, *The Branching Stairs* (1985) and *Disbelief* (1987), Edwin Morgan,

Themes on a Variation (1988), Jeremy Reed with *Bleecker Street* (1980), by John Hartley Williams *Hidden Identities* (1982) and *Bright River Yonder* (1987) and by Robert Crawford and WN Herbert *Sharawaggi* (1990). The new atmosphere was sympathetic towards these writers, and as they broke through prejudicial resistance to work not based on documentary, moral critique, and political commitment weakened.

Everyone agrees that the mainstream of English poetry went through a bad time in the mid-century. The end of this condition is certainly associated with the cultural barrage of postmodernism during the 1980s. This was preoccupied with pleasure, prestige, dizzying variety, the availability of the most exotic and diverse textures, at the expense of authenticity and moral commitment. The most elemental assumption of this current was that the bourgeoisie was on the increase, and that to assimilate to it was the logical outcome of all endeavours. The effect of this was to release certain problems which had for a long time handicapped British poetry. I think the effect of this is visible less in any strikingly successful poetry, which I am not able to produce, but in a large-scale shift of attitude. Poets who could not do something exciting and showy were simply afraid of being overlooked by the market, which was so easily bored and so easily distracted by a huge offer of cultural pleasures. The historical effect of identifying with an Empire which was simply running down and breaking up was restricted to a certain generation—it was bound to be a vanishing factor for people born after about 1948, and with the passage of time this group came to dominate the literary scene. The "overseas frontiers" stabilised at some point in the 1960s, and effects on the delicate balance of the ego have presumably been slight since then.

The least awkward solution would be that the lurch Right in the 1980s cut the ground away from under the critical and collectivist poetry of the 1970s, and so an empty space emerged for a new poetry which was ludic, full of fantasy, full of sensuous data and exotic scenes, and quite free of political or also Christian and moral interests. Admitting the existence of market forces at least distracted people from a built-in preference for austerity, greyness, and moral instruction. This is a seductive proposal, but it is possible that this is an explanation for something which did not happen. The problem with searching for evidence is partly my own withdrawal from the official scene during the '80s (I just thought it was a world of lies and rubbish) and partly the lack of credible critics interested in the field. If there were ludic and fantastic poets active, they were Edwin Morgan and George MacBeth, successful poets but evidently hangovers from the 1960s. An alternative proposal is that the Eighties were simply a very bad time for art, with the vast majority of people who had the means of producing it being so committed to the progressive, collective, and pro-working class slate of the Seventies that they were unable to relate to the new affluence and the New Right. The New Right were running the country but had a deep problem in relating to the culture-creating tier. It was unrealistic to think that the people interested in writing poetry were going to identify with the new political order within a short time, or that they were eager to do so. The momentum of the Seventies, with its incredible upsurge of Marxism and feminism, continued to be a vital factor in the Eighties, unaffected by relatively small shifts in voting patterns. Indeed, the creative class was still acutely attuned to disputes between faithful Labour voters and the "outside left", whether anarchist or Marxist. I think everyone remembers the Eighties as being a miserable time when the voice of the most hateful person in the whole world was on the radio every day telling us what to do. To sum up, I don't think the revival of the mainstream happened during the Eighties. It is easier to find evidence in the Nineties. In fact, it seems as if the revival of the Underground happened at the same time as the revival of the Mainstream. The national nervous breakdown came to an end.

The new mainstream had to have, constitutively:
• distaste for the methods of the Underground;
• distaste for the Christian framework;
• indifference to the standard inhibitions of EngLit academics of the '50s and '60s;
• detachment from the left-wing view of history and art;
• optimism about poetry and about the poet's own talent;
• detachment from Pop poetry, imitations of pop music, or dumbing down.

Perhaps the number of people within the realm defined by these limits was in the 1980s very very small. Perhaps the collapse of the

Movement was more significant than the sidelining of the "BPR" in the development of a new and relaxed centralist poetry.

This was a shared moment of cultural existence, or at least I have memories of the same cluster of ideas occurring many times, and a feeling that everyone else was reacting to them, one way or another. This is, though, the point at which I lose any sense of shared experiences—an absence which postmodernism offers an explanation for. The same absence makes it difficult for any poet to attain the role of voice of a generation, which had seemed quite natural not so many years before. The concept of great poet implies a role which a reorganisation of culture could simply rub off the map.

As a result, I think the problems of mainstream poets in 2008 are completely different from the problems which we observed—too often and too close up—in the 1970s. Naturally, if you are a conventional poet, the collapse of availability of an artistically polished convention brings specific problems. I don't want to exaggerate the vitality of the official poetry world as disclosed by samples taken around 2005. The outcome seems to be that about 1% of the poets in the terrain are artistically effective. This however leaves a couple of dozen who need to be reckoned with—more precisely, discovered, admired and cherished.

Self-insertion

Mary-Sue wanted to write something which wouldn't divide the audience and wouldn't be just another foot of ground for opposing sides to fight on. She created something which was autonomous and where every episode had to be uncovered for itself, rather than being recognised as steps in an argument which everyone had worked through thousands of times even if fruitlessly. It had an information complexity which derived from the recursive operation of pattern generating algorithms rather than from documentary capture by cameras or witnesses. It threw people out of the social roles they had grown tired of or rotted into and faced them with a pristine array of data: with the fluency of a dream and the endlessness of a bolt of textile. **Mary-Sue** says I devised a game in which people have perfectly clear roles that have no relation to real life. Because there was no didactic thread the separate features were all like ornaments and because I was studying Baroque textile and print designs the ornament was ornate and splendid and scrolled in endless variations. Because I wanted the separate poems to be objects of desire in themselves I spent a lot of time in the Victoria and Albert and Heal's and the Design Museum looking at the beautiful objects there and how they were strange and yet integrated at the same time. I wanted to make something for people on the dole, that unfolded endlessly to give them beautiful time and which didn't face them back with the economic impasse all the time. I designed it to have the time of textiles so that every part you looked at pointed to the other parts and yet nothing led to the end. I wasn't interested in the faculty of moral judgement, but I focussed on sensory discriminations that generated endless series and could go in endless curves without going anywhere, giving me the autonomous and acephalous lines I wanted. Because the variations weren't dictated by a pre-existing story I could focus on making them arrive at exactly the perfect pace so that every step was clear and every feature varied in turn. I looked at books of unbuilt architecture so as to think about constructing imaginary space because I wanted to get people away from imagining damaged cities and political struggle.

A New Freedom?

Jo Shapcott, *My Life Asleep* (1998)
Jamie McKendrick, *Sky Nails* (2000)
Alice Oswald, *Dart* (2002)
John Stammers, *Panoramic Lounge-bar* (2000)
Robert Saxton, *Manganese* (2003)

We set out, a while ago, from the 2004 anthology which made us ask whether there was a whole world of fascinating m-stream poets. Because the poets in that anthology were of a certain age, it looked as if their formative moment had been in the 1980s, and we went back to the 1980s to discover the change of artistic atmosphere which could have enabled that group to exist. We were stimulated by Peter Barry's claim that the set of innovations described by Mottram, round about 1971 to 1977, had been profitably absorbed by the m-stream and no longer represented a distinctive selling point for the u-stream. Now it is time to discover whole books by individual poets to see what the anthology, as a sampler, leads us to.

Jo Shapcott's poems in the Tuma anthology are about a mad cow. These were of a sexual and surreal nature, expressions of love in oblique and mythologized terms which recovered mystery from underneath deposits of convention. Shapcott's poems invent a whole persona: departing from the political and medical scandal of Mad Cow Disease (BSE), which in its irreversible course caused cows to act in a striking and irrational way. This is merged with the poet's I-figure to invent a whole area of play, of unreason, of unpredictable and complex behaviour aberrations:

I like to dance. Bang. I love to dance. Push.

It makes me savage and brilliant. Stomp. To
my own rhythm, rhythm. I lead or I don't

have a partner. No market for partners,
just this wide floor for the dance.
I think I was born here. Swoop. I don't care.

Even if I'd been born in the back of a car

the chassis and each blessed spring
would have jumped as I leapt out

of my mum. Up. Down to the ocean, perhaps
the beach? Hah. Stone steps and stone walls,
the pebbled strand, try to stall my special

high-kicks for the sea.
('Mad Cow Dance')

The phrase daft cow is contributing without being named. This poem is shocking because the affected cows made movements that looked like dancing once neurological damage had erased their ability to walk straight or to any purpose. The poems are scattered over the books *Phrase Book* and *My Life Asleep*, which may suggest that they began around 1991. They come as if from a simple, very female, capricious, creature who gives way to impulse all the time. Several thousand years of functional repression are being shed, and the speaker is more like a goddess than like a modern professional. These are delightful poems, and Shapcott's vein is an accurately blurred waking dream experience in which the poet is taken over by fantasy and a series of inexplicable and delightful events take place in a late 20th century urban landscape in which certain features have stealthily mutated. A connection with surrealism is likely, but the ego is becoming stronger rather than weaker; the indulgence of wishes, trivial or major, is important, and an attack on the cult of the army, the French Empire, etc., as favoured by the surrealists, is not part of the story. In 'Brando on Commuting' the sight during a journey on London's underground railway of a poster with an erotically suggestive image ("nurse lies on a bed/ strewn with important documents/ her white uniform bunched/ round her waist") leads to a whole dreamlike exit from daily consciousness. An everyday setting mutates into the scenery of a fantasy, inhibitions are released:

In the heat of the underground
among the rainbow lines

the trains nuzzle the platforms
like fish. They are deaf
and their lives are quiet
and glorious [...]
photography can't snap them in the tunnels
as they crisscross and interweave,
playing like marine mammals.
I think they do the works
down here, present themselves
in courtship colours, each
segment gleaming like ice.

As in advertisements, ordinary people are drawn into extraordinary events, desire takes over control from prudence, striking and inexplicable visual effects make us wonder, etc. This is really the formula for a Shapcott poem, and the symbolic impact of the strewn papers is that we always have the chance of putting aside business and responsibility for self-indulgence and the imagination. The question whether Shapcott's poems are really more brilliant than the ads with their visual and digital resources is superfluous, those ads are wonderful aesthetic creations and in my opinion they would be completely pleasurable if not for the sharpness of the manipulative intent. The commercials aim to liberate the unconscious by switching off functionality, but since they have a functional and businesslike aim of making you spend money they essentially fail. When I came to read a whole book of Shapcott, I was disappointed, because the original plan is carried out too many times. While I admire the efficiency of the method, the suavity of the results, and indeed the boldness of the basic design, the book does not go deeper than the individual poems. We are brought up against the rationality of Shapcott's irrationality; she opens the curtains on the fascinating scene but also closes them again, after a measured time, and returns us to everyday life. The claim on the cover (of *Her Book*) that "her concern remains for the chaotically unaccountable in humanity" needs qualifying to say that her rendering of the chaotic is neat and predictable. Hundreds of poets have tried to write about chaos but few have been so well organised and unambiguous in their language. The smoothness of technique is after all the great virtue of m-stream poetry;

the timing is very precise, the effectiveness of the individual poems is nowhere compromised. We are not asked to believe whole theories of why society is alienated; when we enjoy entering a waking dream there is always the implication that entering a working office is something we enjoy a great deal less, but we are not made to feel guilty about leading a rational life. The atmosphere of these poems is something like a Hitchcock film: if you imagine *The Lady Vanishes* before the emergence of the anxiety symbols, espionage, etc., when it is simply a series of disconcerted, eccentric, comic, and erotic scenes, that might be the world from which Shapcott's poems are single but complete moments. This world is capacious and stable; the poems keep going back there and it keeps acquiring consistency. In *Phrase Book* we first of all get a poem about Tom, as in Tom and Jerry. You can't attack surrealism without attacking Tom and Jerry, Betty Boop, Mickey Mouse, and so on. Then we get 'Goat': "Dusk, deserted road, and suddenly/ I was a goat." The goat has an interest in texture far beyond the spectrum that we could accept—the ultimate consumer, perhaps, willing to nibble away entire forests. This one eats hedges including the "intoxicating tang of the odd ring-pull/ or rubbers to spice the mixture". We are used to gourmets praising snails' eggs, tender young nettles, etc. but the used rubbers blow us right off the neurosensory map. Wow. Finally we get the Mad Cow poems, which obviously follow on from the nutty animals, the cat and the goat.

Two poems which deal either with the speaker being a lettuce which is eaten by her lover or a speck of dust which flies into his ear are based on Donne's poem, 'The Flea', in which the lover describes becoming a flea on the loved one's skin. The shifts of perspective are based on the Metaphysicals. The transformation into a goat is based on a novel of the 2nd century AD by Apuleius called *The Golden Ass*, in which the hero is turned into a donkey.

At some point in this research Shapcott acquired stature in my eyes because I realised that without Shapcott there could be no Moniza Alvi; Alvi's poems obviously have the extra layer, that the disconcertment has to do with the contrast of two cultures, but the influence is clear.

The work chosen by McKendrick is actually a selected poems (1979–97) rather than an individual volume from one space of time. I am sorry, but this is what was available in Nottingham Central

Library. The term "sky nail" (also occurring as skyhook) is a fictitious implement, useful for sending callow youths to the Stores so that they display their ignorance and give everyone else a laugh. (A similar one is *elbow grease.*) The selling feature of these poems is an atmosphere of wit and sophistication which is *quite delightful.* I am averse to discussing this in a way which is slow and thorough and so considerably less sophisticated and delightful. McKendrick has recognised his great virtue and has devised ways of making it available in quantities and as the principal content of these poems. Anyone can be witty and sophisticated for one line, while for the rest of the time they try to thrust their tedious philosophical ideas and unsaleable personal experiences at us. To work on something which relies on the appearance of ease and unconsciousness, and which depends often on surprise, calls for a steel which few modern poets can lay claim to. This determination to entertain us and to make us contented and amused is not the most common thing in the literary world. Since one of the features of the u-stream is to load the text with information, indicating perhaps a frustration with the limits of everyday speech exchange, it is plausible that these debonair qualities which wholly rely on knowing when to stop and not stressing anything belong in the m-stream and are native to it. The charm has often to do with rueful self-exposure. Nostalgia plays a role, as in this poem which seems to be about the poet's father as a manager at Martins Bank, perhaps 40 years ago:

> I was however once invited to
> the Liverpool Head Office, a temple
> of trading ringed by gilded iron spikes
> and the finial crockets of acanthus.
> The manager led us down into the vault
> where gold bars from Johannesburg were wheeled
> about on trolleys, then up through a skylight
> to the parapet above the dome. From there
> the kingdoms of the city spread beneath us
> rickety with fire escapes and aerials,
> all blackened bricks and base metals:
> bombsites, dockyards, the Mersey's pimpled zinc.
> Between us and nothing the lowest of handrails.

The bank's emblem was a grasshopper
with back legs triggered to unleash the bulk
of its blunt brow and plated thorax.
        (from 'Inheritance')

Martins Bank has long since disappeared. The number of precise details in this description is very striking. A number of McKendrick's poems also exploit the combination of grandeur, neglect and decay in Italy, where he lived for a long time. Somewhere behind McKendrick is the picturesque, an aesthetic quality of objects which are neither inherently beautiful nor on a grand scale, as much explored during the 18th century. This was much derived from Italian paintings by Salvator Rosa and Alessandro Magnasco. The firmness of his poems is due to a highly developed visual sensibility; there is an unvanquished Mediterranean beauty about the scenes in which he presents himself. Although the elements of decay, damage, and dust always qualify the experience, these yield beauty in the 18th century style, and the rendering is wonderfully firm and clear. He is good company. Evidently the qualities of poetry come principally from the vast and unseizable territory of speech, and people are being witty and dégagé in speech in all kinds of places, too many to permit drawing a map. The phrase "sky nail" can be leaned on to suggest that language is made of thin air, that atmosphere is made of sky, and that if you hang a nail on thin air it can still produce all kinds of good atmosphere and this is what we breathe in.

It's still sky nails I need today
with their faint threads
and unbreakable heads

that will nail anything
to nothing
and make it stay.

Both Shapcott and McKendrick have solved the problem of socialising irrationality. Anyone can produce irrational behaviour, and most people get into poetry because they want to do that. Less so, people wishing to be matter of fact and plain. But irrational behaviour can be unattractive—like the mad cows, someone staggering around and gibbering may initially seem ill, not high. There is a vein of "radical subjectivity" in which people recover from super-academicism by acting irrationally in art, but mostly this is embarrassing and unnatural and quite often it is alienating. Why are you acting like that? what's wrong with you? So the problem is in the social semantics around the irrationality. The poems just discussed have wonderful qualities of clarity, smoothness, consistency, and suavity. They feel safe and so allow other people to enter into their atmosphere of fun and even debauchery.

Alice Oswald's poem *Dart* (2002) is a book-length documentary on the whole course of the river Dart, in Devon, and the human activities on its banks. It starts on Dartmoor and ends in Dartmouth. Two things arise at once. First, the depth of the experience offered by a poem of such amplitude. Few of us would not welcome the opportunity to indulge in something so expansive and yet so focussed. Secondly, the reputation of rural poetry. Some cognoscenti would speak mockingly of a poem which so thoroughly stays with a river and its rural surroundings. I except myself from this—I spent holidays not far from that part of Devon as a child and I have no doubts about spending a day simply immersed in a south-western landscape. The headline for *Dart* is its highly finished quality—every page is perfect and there are no visible weaknesses. I have already mentioned that the plan reminds me of a film (made for the Festival of Britain) called *River of Time*, with a script by poet Paul Dehn, which follows the Thames from the estuary to Teddington, in Middlesex, where the flow ceases to be tidal. I am very fond of this film. The match of words and images is very satisfying. At that point it seemed as if poetry was about to enter a marriage with film —that poets should regularly be given film crews to work with and that indeed this was about to happen. Documentary relied on detailed field research and Oswald has evidently done a great deal of this. We hear monologues from, in order, a walker, chambermaid, naturalists, eel watcher, fisherman and (river) bailiff, tinners, forester, water nymph, canoeist, etc. At moments in *Dart* language gives way to subjectivity and is taken over by more elemental practices.

> will you rustle quietly and listen to what I have to say now
> describing the wetbacks of stones golden-mouthed and
> making no headway, will you unsilt

how water orders itself like a pack of geese goes up
first in tatters then in shreds then in threads
and shucking its pools crawls into this slate and thin limestone phase

three hayfields above Buckfast where annual meadow grasshoppers
flower and fly to the tune of ribbed stalks rubbed.
will you swim down and attend to this foundry for sounds

this jabber of pidgin-river
drilling these rhythmic cells and trails of scales,
will you translate for me blunt blink glint.
                    (p.15)

The subjectivity is very discreet, as the last three words go off into sound effects at the expense of literal meaning. This could be compared to the avant-garde but is too restrained and small. The section about the sewage treatment works is exceptional in modern poetry—Oswald uses language to the natural extent of prose, using it to render whatever the mind can grasp. The "vérité" dialogue is naturally in prose. The simple documentary narrative about daily work reminds me of Aelfric's *Colloquies* (circa 1000 AD), where people speak about the jobs they do. There is something a bit spooky about the way she does not use any verbal devices which were not available in 1951. This is as if a virtuous restraint—as if any use of linguistic creativity were a retreat into subjectivity and an avoidance of proper hard work in facing the subject matter. Oswald seems very knowledgeable about Latin poetry. The river's name means oak, she tells us. I checked this and the standard work confirms that it comes from a British word meaning "river among oaks". Older forms are *Dert* etc. so the vowel change is like clerk to (as pronounced) clark. There is a Welsh word *derwydd* "oak" which may have had an earlier form "*deredd*" or similar. Oswald uses this (p.13) as an excuse for an invocation, in the pagan Latin style, to the river as an oak, starting *O Rex nemorensis*. It addresses the river as "flumen dialis"("river of Jove"), punning on the *flamen dialis*, priest of Jove.

The cover of *Panoramic Lounge-bar* has a picture by Patrick Caulfield, whose style is familiar from the covers of books by David Chaloner and Andrew Crozier. Stammers does offer some points of similarity to McKendrick. You could claim that someone who enjoyed McKendrick would enjoy Stammers. What I feel as the original virtue of this book is that it is a fresh start, from someone who apparently doesn't have any connection with past literary feuds and also doesn't have the legacy qualities of a literato such as being introverted, sensitive, wan, etc. The title refers to a kind of room where poets spend much of their lives but which doesn't feature in poems all that often. I am not sure about panoramic—the word means literally "all sight" or "view of everything" but whether this means a bar with a long curving window or simply a bar without internal partitions and with the wide proportions of a cinema shot also called panoramic I am unsure. There was a pub in Nottingham called the Belle Vue (beautiful view) which had a splendid view out over the Vale of Trent. The cover picture is called 'Foyer', which is probably a theatre foyer, as it has what looks like a bar at the back, with Caulfield's depiction of bottles set out on a shelf, all rendered with a flat colour, which makes them look like terra cotta jars. The poems are simultaneously uncommitted and full of excitement—they typically show the poet in the act of consuming culture, something he enjoys but can detach from. Fictions are cocooned within fictions: 'The Wolf Man' is narrated by a figure from one of Freud's case histories, a Russian who had a dream about white wolves which Freud interpreted as a primal scene, the sight of coitus. Freud may have been wrong. The Wolf Man was in analysis again later and said that Freud had done nothing to cure him. Stammers has the Russian in monologue, it is after the Revolution, the family estates have been lost and he has to work. This is in a sort of prose versets, like a translation of the psalms:

> The royal road to the unconscious, he liked to say. But to me
> it was such as you might see as a small boy in a fairground booth,
> your head beneath a black sheet, peering at a magic-lantern
> spectacle of horlas and ghouls, too afraid to move,
> too entranced to shut your eyes.

(Horla is a monster from a short story by Guy de Maupassant.)

Rather than being in the grip of a neurosis (the reason for seeking treatment), the speaker is urbane and genial. The poem does not validate the truth of what it reports and remains detached from it. The typical poem here shows the speaker in the early stages of a love affair where the landscape is effectively a decor for the emotions of the lead figures and the attempt to seize power by too much intentionality would bring a speedy end to aspirations (which power is too purposeful about fulfilling). He says "we were only twenty-four minutes from Tulse Hill/ when you swept me, sweet you, just precisely off my trolley" ('Torch') which is a joke—based on Gene Pitney's 1966 hit '24 hours from Tulsa', which also, admittedly, features someone falling in love in the middle of a journey. The passage before this runs:

> It is a written fact that the courtiers of the Emperor Ho
> would burn feathers of the egret
> to ward off demons, traitors and demonstrators
> of halon fire extinguishers
> (which they, of course, invented
> many declensions before the rest of us
> along with the retractable hoe,
> *Ovaltine*, made with real ovals, and *very old* gingham)
> and is where the myth of the fire-breathing dragon
> is said to come from, if you follow van Rympt.
> Or they would, once a life, light chaffinch down
> to mark the stolen, or half-inched, as they almost felt it, love
> they had taken from the world as if from the air.

This owes something to Ian Duhig and something too to W.S. Gilbert. (Half-inch is rhyming slang for pinch.) The figure connects to the burning of the torch in the title, which is also "my torch is burning for you" as in torch song.

This poem is a little confused but the confusion is also a sign of falling in love and razing psychic defences. Stammers is different from Caulfield in using these feathering and expanding associations or mis-hearings to fill the poem as if with a spiral. Caulfield is minimal and disciplined, always trying to use the smallest possible number of formal elements. He makes paintings which look like block-prints because the tones are so simple and flat. An example of the mis-hearing is 'Aspects of Kees'. Weldon Kees was an American poet who, in the 1950s, left his car on a bridge in San Francisco and disappeared. He wrote definitively melancholic poetry, perfect, terse, unanswerable. The poems are black and this allows Stammers to link him to a film noir, *Double Indemnity*— where the lead character also fails to complete his journey—the film is a flashback as he, on a train, narrates it to Edgar G. Robinson; as Robinson (called "Keyes") works out before the end that he is the killer, he jumps off the train. Stammers links to "Kees posturing like Robinson at the Keys", meaning his character in a film called *Key Largo* set on the Florida Keys. We see "Kees slamming the typewriter keys./ Kees x-ing out words, cursing at his absurd,/ purposeless verbs; zips out the dead sheet/ from the roller. Kees mumbling, blocked[.]" Finally, we get to the bridgend—Kees leaving his car keys in the ignition on that last, abbreviated, ride. This wordplay reminds me of David Thomson's book on Welles where he talks about canes which Welles had to use once he was forty and infeasibly bulky, and how many of his characters used canes and how this could connect to his most famous role, Citizen Kane—a name invented by Herman Mankiewicz, in fact. "Kees" is a pet name for "Cornelis".

Robert Saxton is impossible to summarise as his poetry is so various. Generically it seems to have sophistication, a polished sense of form, detachment, smoothness, and a fascination for bizarre and esoteric scenes and details. The level of inventiveness is astounding. 'The Heart of the Ocean', the last poem in *Manganese,* is built on the formal principle of a villanelle, where the final words of the lines in the first stanza recur in each successive stanza, starting thus:

> In Skibo Castle, a film-maker, Guy Ritchie,
> and an actress/rock star,
> Madonna, married yesterday in a whirl
> of Scotch mist. The press
> were expertly shut out, despite
> the enormous budget for dirty tricks
> the tabloids commanded. The day before
> was the baptism of their son
> Rocco. Two men with a camcorder squatted
> for more than sixty hours
> in the organ of Dornoch Cathedral
> with bin liners to piss and crap

—the end words of lines 2, 4, 6, 8, 10 and 12 recur in six stanzas. The final stanza is six lines long and uses all the compulsory words. The stanza quoted is of no interest whatsoever to the poet—he is only interested in the formal scheme, and almost certainly the whole poem is just full of things that were in the newspapers or in the poet's domestic life that day. No point looking for repeating personal themes if the poet's urge is to be completely free and susceptible. Perhaps the key to the 85 poems in *Manganese* is that they are all the product of chance, improvisation, and the wish to avoid repetition—driven into final form by a powerful wish for order. If the poet gets his adrenalin going by being thrown into a game where the poems must be written by fast reactions in response to new and arbitrary local rules, that would remind us of Edwin Morgan. The fetish word *ludic* must come to mind here. Saxton uses careful rhythmic regularity and many of his poems rhyme—features which belong with the "rules of the game". The effect is a poetry which does not express a personality:

> His vowels bent eastwards, care-worn, buffed in mink,
> a honeybags befriends the frugal whelk,
> the bardic he-bear, watering England's milk.
>
> Singers of fifty smokes in a hundred hands,
> blunt fingers plough the thickest, foxiest blends
> of tea, at dawn, cologning England's hounds.
>
> Far from the census thundering on its drum
> he sleeps in leaf-mould watered by the stream,
> snug, uncounted, snoring through England's dream.
> ('The Watershed')

This reminds me of linguist Gotthard Lerchner's lists of words which show the distinctions between different dialects of North West Germanic, mostly obscure items relating to rural life. Specifically, whelk (*weoloc*) is one of his words, one common to English, Frisian and Dutch but not to any other dialect of Germanic around the North Sea: *busy, blossom, brine, dag, cleanse, cotset, croft, mirth, nag, sprit, film, whelk.* What I think this points to is that Saxton is choosing words in a divergent way—accessing a range of vocabulary many times wider than personalised poets, touring through semantic complexes which are numerous, peculiar, specific, and unexpected. Saxton is picking up a much wider range of objects than most poets bother with. (His vocabulary is relatively poor in abstract terms—he prefers the one- and two-syllable tickets.) What is this poem about? Of course, the core is the game rules (to do with rhyme, line length, the repetition of the word "England's"), but further it may be about a poet who is also a dairy farmer (like Ted Hughes?), a fictional character whose mythic feats may include loving honey (like a bear, and even a *teddy* bear) and even watering the beer (there is an old music-hall song about the man who waters the beer). The watershed is one which divides rain flowing out into Welsh rivers from water which flows outwards into English ones—somewhere in Shropshire or Herefordshire, then, and would account for the refrain-word *England's*. He would be a friend of whelks because they might be able to *live* in milk if it is watery enough. The mink points to a dead mink, which may relate to a later mention of water-voles, facing extinction because wild mink eat them; the poet has perhaps shot a mink. The bit about "vowels bent eastwards" may refer to a dialect boundary—a sharp division between Welsh accents and West Midlands ones.

The rigorous pursuit of rules which mandate divergent results steadily generates unique clusters of sounds and meanings. The work of retrieval and distinction to decode so many rapidly following, acute, and distinctive words/sensations is a restorative one. The poetry is not high in affect because the principle of selection underlying it is not the reproduction of monotonous and egocentric infantile states of mind. The cover of the book shows a Japanese embroidery of cranes (from a book of 1882), and the book has many words for animals (and so many animals). However, if you look at the English language as one very long list of words, a high proportion of the words name different kinds of animals, and poetry which migrates randomly through that list would touch many species-names. Further, the cranes picture is very specific, very colourful, and very striking—qualities which are arguably more found in birds than in other objects. It is likely that these qualities are the sought ones, and there is no archaic-symbolic burden of the type "cranes—migration—far countries—yearning" and no interest, either, in anatomy or aerodynamics. The metal which provides the title for the volume appears once, in a poem 'Glass' which includes window-cleaning, mould on old glazing-bars, a storm, sopranos, ladders, and passionate love. The poem says "iron in the sand that stains old glazing green", and a quick glance at the internet suggests that manganese was used either to make glass clear (by removing iron impurities in the sand) or to give it "pink, purple or black tints". It is also used to colour earthenware.

Saxton comes from Nottingham, where I live, and 'Lud's Church' may actually be about east Midlands politics, something unaccountably under-represented in poetry. It is about Ned Lud, founder and chief theorist of Luddism, a movement which throve around 1820 in weaving towns like Nottingham and Loughborough. My father used to make speeches claiming Ludd as a local boy. Illegal meetings were held in the woods, hence 'Lud's church' is ironic—"A chasm roofed with ferns was our assembly room".

> Damp leaked into our lungs, like the soft wedge
> of autumn in the trees. Long-suffering, we sifted
> sense from sound, and only then spoke out,
> clothing new sense as best we could
> around a skeleton of borrowed eloquence,
> to drill another soldier for the cause:

> *As our lives were treated, so we would treat their laws.*

The delegates "knew the niches where our lamps would stand": this sounds slightly as if they were quarrymen rather than weavers, but chasms are not exactly hard to find in that part of the Midlands.

Conclusion

There are probably dozens of valid generalisations that could be made about the last 20 years (*written 2009*), but I don't have the knowledge to make them. We got into this terrain because we looked at an anthology of excellent conventional poetry and there was an evident need to find out how the new poetry of the Eighties had moved on. After a search, these books were chosen because they illustrated that excellence. No doubt there are other m-stream works which lack that quality. The m-stream offers especial problems to anyone trying to cover the field. The new wave swept up too many people not to create an off-brand range of indulgence or poor design. Readers looking for more m-stream strength should certainly look at Robert Crawford, John Hartley Williams, Frank Kuppner, Pauline Stainer. I want to avoid a claim that these poets form a group. They appear here partly because they show things changing in the official poetry world. The point I am trying to make is that the era when artistic conformism made the entire m-stream grey and uninteresting has now closed. The charm of these books is I hope not affected by the argument of local interest I have been making about literary politics.

You may well ask how this new wave relates to the other wave of poetry known as the Underground or the poetry revival, which was hitting problems at the end of the Seventies. I think they are just two channels of a big delta. They are validly separated by the visible issues of who publishes them and who they appear with in magazines—which may also record who reads them. Jumping from that to valid tests of stylistic links and boundaries is a jump too many for me.

It would be easy to write a history of the Eighties in which Christianity, the Left, radical lifestyles, the Underground, communal feeling, moral commitment, vanished from the scene. But none of these great British institutions disappeared. They got weaker, but only by a few notches on a scale miles long.

Gold Audible in Death : notes on Jeremy Reed

If you search on Reed's name in the linked set of second-hand book dealers' lists, you come up with a thousand books. Reed, more than any other poet from his generation, ventured into the world of popular culture, made himself available for consumption as a myth, poured everything into the poem, and so reached a large audience. Reed's poems do not need rewriting to sound like a Mary Sue story. They are already written like that. The clogging elements of realism and moral imperative have already been evaporated. They are pure enactment. This achievement has not so far translated into attention from critics, and in fact the little world of High Street poetry is inhibited by its obsession with fashion from recognising Reed's greatness: he is just "someone who was popular in the 1980s". The key thing abut Reed was the dropping of resistance: he has so few problems capturing experiences in poems, and he has so much belief in people's personal mythologies, the easiest things to refute. So his book about Elvis Presley, as a burnt-out rock martyr, *Heartbreak Hotel* (2002) has 200 poems. In future, maybe everyone will have to write 200 poems about Elvis to get a union card as a poet. When I bought *Elvis: the Sun sessions*, in 1976, I had a friend who had a valve amplifier to play '50s rock'n'roll on. In those days, transistor amps were for *hippies*. Teds were paying £120 for copies of 'One Hand Loose' on 78. As a rockabilly fan, then, I have to admire Reed's unlikely attempt to build a whole chapel of pinup vitrines, or soda straws through which the Power jumps to touch us. He really is more interested by the subject than by himself, he does come up with new research. His engagement and formal creativity are stunning throughout. *Heartbreak Hotel* could be better at one fifth the length: Reed is unable to get close to Presley, his polar opposite. Reed is not a redneck's redneck; some way short of a shit-kicker. Bowie got closer to Vince Taylor, lost English rocker, acid victim, (and author of 'Brand New Cadillac'), the model for "Ziggy Stardust". The poem about Presley's car having a moody "on the road between Hope and Texarkana" around 1956 is brilliant—

<blockquote>
black smoke
volcanoing upfront, the car on fire,
</blockquote>

> their quick hands jettisoning instruments,
> ejecting cases, as they run for clear
> and watch the limo crumple into flames,
> a blue and orange surfing roar
> sheeting the bodywork
> ('Burning a Pink Cadillac')

Reed has a doctorate from the Courtauld in reading fan magazines—and he can name every fabric and shade, as he writes a thirty-line poem about neckties, but the fiddly, erudite, dinky instrumental touches on '60s records like 'Wooden Heart' are acknowledged to be the worst thing about Presley, and Reed's fidgety brilliance sounds like them. Look, Elvis' minority ethic was rockabilly—where *Baby don't bug me with that North Forty talk. A lot of lip-flipping makes my bad blood boil.* When Reed adapts his house theme of metabolic displacement to Elvis' gluttony we get extraordinary poems:

> The man's a cheeseburger mausoleum,
> an appetent contortionist
> snake-bloated on cholesterol junk,
>
> intestinal-roomy as a silo
> housing a grain harvest: he'll eat his way
> through bear-sized stacks of burgers and French fries,
>
> a deconstructing monument
> of sinuous eddies in fat(.)
> ('Junk-food Junkie')

The poem goes on to describe "a colonic labyrinth to a tomb/ of decomposing treasure". Even more terrifying is "Juicy Lucy cannibalises Elvis", a base somatisation of living for ever, darkened with religious references.

Due to disaffection among songwriters, mostly, there was a gay subtext to Elvis (cf. 'Jailhouse Rock': *You're the cutest jailbird I ever did see*, well, we've all got *your* number, Convict 99), but Elvis didn't know it was there. Reed's vision (pp.164–7) of fat as feminising Elvis, just as his taste in clothes and jewellery did, is new and deeply satisfying. Like so many sixties housewives, Elvis was preoccupied with fat, food, barbiturates, and shopping. John Cale, who played organ on 'Sister Ray', said "I thought Elvis died when he heard my version of *Heartbreak Hotel*": Reed fits the King into a myth (from the uncanonical *Gospel of St Thomas*, originally, via Moorcock's *The Final Programme*) whereby the future will belong to androgynes. Life will go on through asexual means like viruses, cloning, digital transcription, and cryogenic immortality. Maybe a subculture which reproduces itself through photographs is like a crystal which grows in solution. Maybe the crystals in Ballard's subjective landscapes are like the barbiturate downers which dominate the book—and Presley's life. Not a high, but a kind of apathy in which dreams were possible. A TV of the soul.

A previous owner of my copy of *Red-haired Android* counted all the colour adjectives and came up with an average of 4.4 per poem over 280 pages. This is a trademark but not necessarily a lapse of taste:

> Gunpowder smudges of black seed
> line a down-curled scarlet petal.
> They seem to drink their colours from water
> with amethyst cocktail straws.
> I look around them. I am seer seen.
>   ('Anemones')

Consideration of Elvis' song 'Baby Let's Play House' suggests that a pink Cadillac is indeed qualitatively different from every other kind. I have in my collection of rockabilly at least two other songs about pink Cadillacs. (Isn't this an anti-gay thing? If someone talks about colours for ten minutes, don't you assume they're gay?) Reed's interest in clothes, hair and the weather recommends the attention paid to colours; being besotted with decoration is an artistic investment like another. The language has to be light enough to register these floating fragments of subjectivity. The cover shows a photograph of the poet —tinted red. The title poem describes an android who comes from another planet and becomes a rock star, attended by a clone looking just like him who never speaks but watches his every move and copies them. The android is a science fiction convention:

"Is that what you are? An android?"
"You could find out if you made love to me."
Faustaff smiled and shook his head. "Sweetheart, you're just not my type."
"I thought any young woman was your type, professor."
"So did I till I met you."
Her face remained expressionless.
  (from 'The Wrecks of Time', episode 3, by James Colvin, *New Worlds in SF*, issue 157, 1965)

James Colvin was a pseudonym for Moorcock and wrote a novel called *The Deep Fix* in which the hero was an addict in a cosmos threatened by the rippling anti-causal effects of time travel who stabilised everything by taking fixes of his chosen drug. Moorcock later recorded with a band called The Deep Fix. The novel is very weak even by Moorcock's standards, but it does provide a key to the later Jerry Cornelius quartet and to certain Reed poems. Red hair was a feature of Bowie's stage appearance around the *Ziggy Stardust / Diamond Dogs* period, when he wrote a song called 'Drive-in Saturday' which is key to Reed and so may also have produced the red hair of the android. Bowie played an alien in the film *The Man Who Fell to Earth*. The epigraph for the whole volume is a set of four lines from Bowie's 'Ashes to Ashes', a 1981 song recycling Major Tom, hero of Bowie's 1969 song (and first hit), 'A Space Oddity'. In the 1981 version, astronaut Tom slips helplessly away from Earth but is fed an addictive, sustaining drug by space itself; he is accepted and nurtured by Space much as the hero of Ballard's *The Drowned World*, regressing to reptile level, is accepted by the warm ocean of a neo-tropical earth. At the end of the poem 'Red-haired Android' we find that the two aliens (one rock star, one golem copying his behaviour) will procreate in such a way as to bring their species to the Earth; recalling the end of the 1973 film *The Final Programme* (based on a Moorcock novel), where Cornelius and Miss Brunner fuse into an androgyne, a new creature. The appearances of Ballard allow us to speculate on *The Crystal World* as the origin of Reed's myth of metabolic displacement: a novel where whole regions freeze as crystal, exanimate; gaudy. Moorcock also wrote a type of novel based on fictionalised autobiography and with frequent appearances by real people, a genre invented by Jack Trevor Story and taken to the heights by Iain Sinclair, who as editor was responsible for *Red-haired Android*, in which Ballard makes a personal appearance (at p.156, 'The Novelist' "he is lost/ to big money, the gold-fin striking high/ against an incandescent azure sky"), as again in *Duck and Sally*. A character named "James Colvin" appears, dead, in Sinclair's novel *Dining on Stones*. We can recognise this as self-insertion, the new grammar of popular culture.

Part of feeding the High Street is keeping the product coming. The published poems may reach a thousand but there are many more unpublished ones. Perhaps it was the sound of being told so many times that he was heading for decadence, alienation, and waste which gave him such a work ethic. This has made for a distinctive design of volumes, where the same theme is dealt with many times.

Reed, like some other people, belonged in a nether world, rejected by mainstream and official Underground from the start. So his attainment of mainstream success from 1981 or so was a breakout, a self-insertion into High Street glitz. Reed made his poetry much more accessible, less extreme, less pessimistic, more affluent. Carcanet, Cape and Penguin took it and published it. Reed's new poetry, preoccupied with textures and hedonistic acts of consumption, is presumably the most persuasive version of postmodernism in English poetry—a complete jettison of the religious mode, as we are invited to float through warm waters, tinted by sunlight, for ever. He is the poet of the beach, of endless leisure, display, rites of attraction and association. Decoration and de-repression. His new style for the early '80s (captured in books like *Dicing for Pearls, By the Fisheries, Nero*) sums up the artistic atmosphere of the times more than any other work, and is my personal *lieu de mémoire* for the new luxury. I actually prefer *Bleecker Street*, the last book of the preceding period. He abandoned a distinctive and highly wrought (overwrought?) style in favour of transparency allowing new strengths in action and character. It may be that he abandoned his proprietary style in order to allow readers more access to the poem. Because he had something they wanted, he was willing to give it to them. I don't think there is any overview of Reed's career. It may be helpful to list some of his full-length volumes: *Target, The Isthmus of Samuel Greenberg, Night Attack, Saints and Psychotics, Bleecker Street, Walk On Through, A Man Afraid, A Long Shot to Heaven, By the Fisheries, Nero, Engaging Form, Nineties, Dicing for Pearls, Red-Haired Android, Kicks, Patron Saint of Eye-liner,*

Heartbreak Hotel, Duck and Sally Inside, This Is How You Disappear: A Book of Elegies, Bona Drag.

Reed was in a strong position to hit a wide market in the '80s because he was astonishingly productive in the 1970s. A string of books emerged into a landscape torn by glam-rock and punk rock, each revealing a singular facet: *Target, Night Attack, Saints and Psychotics, Walk On Through, Long Shot to Heaven, Bleecker Street, A Man Afraid.* Weak flesh mutated under the commands of superhuman emotions, language was redesigned by forces determined not to compromise. Reed's masterpiece was written back in 1978 and promptly disappeared for thirty years. Waterloo Press publisher, Simon Jenner, and I worked on Reed for a number of years to get him to release some of his fabulous store of unpublished poems from the 1970s. Eventually, a huge bundle of typescripts emerged and I was given the task of selecting some of them for a book. There was a poem in there called 'Junkie Tango Outside Boot's Piccadilly', which was renamed shortly afterwards to 'Stratton Elegy'. After twenty-five years of reading Reed, with greater or lesser amazement, I realised on reading these recovered typescripts that here was his masterpiece:

> 4
> Known to me, your ineluctable all
> against. That restless urgency which remains
> inexpendible: the dampness of walls
> blooding your despondency at Kilburn
> exacerbating the asthma that threw you into
> the sub-dark of our kitchen,
> unable to endure, yet not renounce
> the strangers who stared back in bed at you,

> 5
> and were always premonitory, their veins
> loaded mauve with subliminal narcotics;
> come in from the aorta of London
> for refuge, and to steady a needle's
> incision without bandages. Inhered
> for days, white in their combustion. A room

in which dictates had no volitional
credence; and you turned crying to the wall,

6
imploring that your nerves would find balance,
a moment's magnetization from death's
ouroborous: some black tread to a tyre
gone on burning though quite motionless.
You never could. Ariolatio
on Piccadilly concrete; then ennui.
Someone always had to find a chemist.
Death's a superfetation of who push.

Such a sense of purpose and such delicacy in revealing a world of feeling
were never before combined. This work has been hidden from its origin
in 1978 until now. The history of this occlusion is impossible to know,
hidden beneath the incessant intrigues, passions, chills, flurries, losses,
austerities, excesses and compromises of the poetry world. Hidden too
behind a score of other projects. The first word of the poem is Necro-
aleph: death as the first letter of the message. *gold audible in death.*

Shortly before this moment, Reed was working on the revival of
Samuel Greenberg, a poet never published in his lifetime, a poor Jewish
immigrant who died at the age of thirty-three, with a weak command
of English, who nevertheless wrote a few jewels (*The Isthmus of Samuel
Greenberg*, 1976). Reed preferred the biographies of victims because
there was more pressure, more revelation of the true depth of character
in endlessly repeating situations of strain, ambiguity, exclusion, and
abuse. The martial hue of struggle was overlaid on the secret anatomy
of unusual natures. The final legitimation by grace was reached in the
face of walls of pressure, pride and joy in the margins allowed by the
laws of sex and power. The absence of a social position allowed free rein
for self-communication, the return of expressivity in a society dedicated
to business.

Reed was besotted with the works of Scott Walker, Lou Reed, and
David Bowie, oratorical masterpieces where the angelic reached into
the everyday and degradation merged with transcendence. In the 86
stanzas of the dizzying 'Stratton Elegy', a spiral into depression, drug

abuse, and death is turned into a modern saint's life. The descent of something inhuman and hungry onto a human prey becomes transformation. Reed takes a junky, one of the civil dead, and adds a last document to close their medical file, a high pomp and obsequy in the Egyptian manner. Like the Pyramid texts, it records a ritual journey. The obsessive naming of streets and underground stations locks the action into physical reality and pursues the late-'60s lyrics of Scott Walker, in songs like 'Montague Terrace in Blue' and 'Copenhagen'. An immediate verbal equivalent is George Barker's *In memoriam David Archer* (1973), equally graced by an invisible death's head, a poem sucked down into the cold torrents of a London of decades before, cataracts ebbing through the channels of a dying consciousness. The responsibility of acting as a herald for someone dead drew in a splendid and sombre array of descriptions of funeral rites of remote tribes, and the recollection of the Egyptian lore of the realm of the dead, of Reqaqna, the ka, of Kher Heb. Like them, Reed offers a compendious account of the darkness, or turns the afterworld into syllabic form. The cortège advances to his recitative, written in gold leaf on papyrus. Ariolatio is soothsaying, goetia is witchcraft; the Hotel Wentley, a San Francisco flophouse where transvestite poet John Wieners pursued the new drugs lifestyle in combination with a Symboliste aesthetic, also floats across screen:

> A cithern in a metabolic
> flue; we never temper its note. Meet you
> at Green Park subway; at Piccadilly.
> You're light for any black peacock counting
> out silver confetti on a coffin-lid:
> apocalyptic pyrites on Blake's skull
> lifting with vision. The *Hotel Wentley*
> jacket design, inside, around my head.

The credulity of Wieners is turned to gather the floating fantasies of the lost, to give a respectful account of the weak. *Unlidding of etheric eyes*: the frequent reference to etheric creatures shows us a realm of thought forms, the spiritualist belief in an *aether*, as a metaphor for the private worlds of emotional rebels against the dictates of a cruel and insensitive society obsessed with power. *Yarrow petalled into a Taoist's head:* moments of behavioural beauty are handled as reverently as jewels. *Superfetation of who push* means something like "the pushers make the victim pregnant with the trip and then simultaneously with their death", or possibly "first the pusher and then death pushes into your womb and drains out your resources and hope". I don't find a tango in the rhythm (maybe Brel's *Tango funèbre?*) but what is present is a group of people engaged in stylised motion, in stylised clothes, according to a compelling rhythm. Other creatures attend this dance:

> Everything spins away,
>
> 66
> a damaged mind rolled on a black marble
> into an incandescent yellow flue:
> the burn-back registers on my ticket
> to the escalator, to fuming gaps
> between the circuit of blood-stained mummies,
> crooking like geese in pursuit, and the dolls,
> (their features twisted), who pursued you through
> the subways, wound up with aggressive teeth
>
> 67
> pincering your ankles. They have returned
> to feed other psychoses, to spit white lead
> into the pineal. There is no space
> living or dead we can retreat into
> or realize with impunity
> [...]
> Homunculi
> Floating above the Circus, no torsos,
> but frog-like flippers attached to a skull
> too magnified for microcosmic space
> A ka -prism through violet through orange,
> and when recognized in the temporal,
> it was something husking its wings at Kew,
> an insect flisking on a leaf of eyes.
> (from st. 65–70)

White lead is ceruse, a kind of cosmetic lending an artificial pallor. It emerges into the temporal, the sphere which is subject to Time, because up till then it had its being in the eternal, outside Time. The part about husking is the emergence from out of an old body, which insects do: shedding wing-casings, most probably. The husking is actually emerging from invisibility into visibility. The *ka* in Egyptian religion is a kind of soul, the one which is reunited with the body before its rebirth. The entity may have no body but manifests as colour. We will return to this because colour is of abiding importance to the poet. "an insect flisking on a leaf of eyes": as the insect might live on the leaf this agency lives on eyes. So it may be pure colour. As a ka-prism its nature is to shift light. Looking at the nearby text, we find a reference to "edged back invidiously into light/ by informers", so the drug users are seeking darkness but forced back into visibility; then "photospheric isolation": emergence from darkness into the sphere of light, unwillingly, and in the light they are *cut off*. The strip of bodiless colour is like an aura, something which specially sensitive people see.

These poems (due to be published as *Black Russian at the Airmen's Club,* although the book seems to have been delayed somewhat) have rested unseen for twenty-eight years. The earth has grown sicker and hotter and their time has come.

I was shocked at the realisation that Reed's great artistic effort was for a woman. I was suffering from a simple view of what it means to be gay. What I wasn't allowing for was the depth of someone's emotional investment in a woman even where that investment didn't also mean a sexual alliance, the idea of marriage, of children, of spending your lives together. I hadn't anticipated that his relationship with this young woman, Paula Stratton, was so deep as to inspire this truly momentous poem of regret. The story is simply about junkies hanging out outside the celebrated all-night pharmacist in Piccadilly, getting closer to each other, and one of them dying. But nothing is that simple. One angle is that Reed's choice of themes was not simply an artistic calculation, a free act in a weightless zone of boundless possibilities, but something dictated by the life experiences of the people to whom he had become attached, in an earlier set of choices. That is, it was realism driven by character. The use of words like *ariolatio* and *superfetation* was at the core of Reed's early style, the one he abandoned and which was so full of caprice, piercing incommunicability, and Gothic dread. His role of lending solemnity and dignity to figures buried by misfortune, moral transgression, and inability to compromise has been carried out with gallantry and fidelity. He has used fine language to ennoble the lives of those whose journeys led them repetitively between the pharmacy and specialist clubs. The model is the empathic intimacy of the singer-songwriter record. Another poem about Stratton reads:

> All of those Paula
> impossible fixtures
> lived on at Strawberry Hill
> Richmond all anterior
> intimacies; the uncaged crow
> room-hopping for rings, the
> gypsy scarves from Notting Hill,
> Kaftans and frangipane incense
> and parables we exchanged
> over red silk conjury
>   ('Devotions')

The poems capture the rich and fantastic world of the bedroom, "red silk conjury" to externalise shy meanings. The crow's eye for trinkets is a metaphor for the decorative drives of the room's owner; buying trinkets or writing poems, both ways of acquiring personal objects, are definitive actions, slight barriers against the impersonal. This is the box of beautiful things; Reed takes the new youth culture, the new culture of the bedroom, its music, mirrors, and dreams, and adds it to literary culture. If you look at books like *Red-Haired Android* (1992), *Heartbreak Hotel* (2002), and *Duck and Sally Inside* (2004), they are full of good poems and blossoming with the genuine Reed pollen. He did not lose his mojo and it would be possible to learn what Reed is all about just by reading these books, without reference to his back catalogue. Like a bat to its cave, Reed recurs to the glam-rock era of 1971–3 or 4 and especially to a record by Bowie called 'Rock and roll suicide', which is about a burnt-out rock star. Reed found fulfilment through glam-rock because it was close to what he had already become: he was there *before* the bedizened epicene sexualised birdlike creatures of the era. What helped Reed to become what he was not yet was much earlier, and is, so far as we know, condensed in Scott Walker, someone having achieved greatness when Reed was still a teenager. Walker has had a very complex career, but at a minimum we can say that he had huge success with (mainly female) teenagers, devised his own sound, and moved from the pop world to the avant-garde. He was Phil Spector's bassist, wore dark glasses, had bigger hair than Dusty Springfield, watched Continental films, said he had come to Europe (in 1965) to be closer to Jean-Paul Sartre. He fled from the pressures of fame to be closer to the truth, was found cowering in a monastery. Even on stage, he extended invisibility and tension to the maximum, endlessly withdrawing himself up till a few moments in the spotlight. "This is how you disappear" is a line in a song from his 1983 album *Climate of Hunter* and the title of a recent Reed book. After leaving The Walker Brothers, he made solo albums of an unbearably glamorous intellectuality and advanced quality. Mark Almond, of Sheffield hi-NRG group Soft Cell, edited the Walker retrospective which includes 'Big Louise'; another selection (edited by Julian Cope) is named after a line from it, "Fire escape in the sky". Enthusiastic quotes by Almond adorn the jackets of late Reed books and a poem to Almond appears in *Red-Haired Android* (p.97).

It is so easy to imagine Reed *circa* 1966 watching Scott Walker on TV and being rapt out of everyday suburban reality, into a fantasy which was alien and yet completely organic to the society in which every child was entranced by TV. The poems in *Red-Haired Android* have the thinness and openness of those old black and white TV shows. In 'A New Order', a whole community forgets how to live:

> And there were models seated in the empty rooms,
> silicone structures with empty faces.
> In time we gave them individualized features,
> cosmetic masks, and spoke to them.
> We'd come here as a small community
> and failed to multiply.
> (…)
> We didn't dare to penetrate
> the forest density. We faced the other way,
> confident the models would come alive,

and govern us, impart a new order
to we, who'd already learnt to survive.

This is evidently a re-run of Bowie's futuristic 'Drive-in Saturday', where couples, bored by sex, copy courting behaviour from ancient films. It is also a commentary on how television works. Each of the poems in RHA offers a scenario—a view into a fantasy scene—whose availability depends on its lack of personalisation. They are as thin as glamour photographs—limitless and inconclusive. They offer a therapeutically perverse environment. 'State Burial' is evidently set on another planet, where twenty flamingos sit around a missing zoo (it has perhaps disappeared into another dimension? is a dream that has slid off into someone's reality?). The President's girlfriend engages in ritualistic and display dressing for a funeral. The details are set out as if for a photo display in a glitzy magazine, detailing the clothes and the President's pets. The planet changes its sun as an expression of mood. The leitmotif of metabolism here is signalled by the switch of planets—"He switches on the sun,/ the artificial one in their own planetary/ system, and then the daylight stars/ which flicker brightly above the city" —and by the two pythons, sliding into apathy—"torpidly/ withdrawn into a blank". So much depends on being warm-blooded. Many Reed poems involve this complete change of sun—a pilot crashes but has a photo which shows an alien sun. His journey has inexplicably taken him to another planet, an alien sky. The basic image is that creatures on the Earth are in harmony with the sun, obey its edicts to procreate and so on, but the Stranger is the stepchild of the yellow sun and needs to find another planet for his metabolism to work properly—biological imperatives arriving as a flood on the rays of the sun. Here again colour is a key. The influence of the planets is also an obvious metaphor for time, and the attuning of inner-body clock processes to the external time of celestial bodies is a variant on the abiding poem about the seasons. Snakes are peculiarly dependent on ambient levels of heat and light, broadcasts from the celestial. It is as if the TV is using the snake as part of its reproductive cycle.

The president looks out from his balcony where he can no longer see a view which used to be there "before the interzoning changed". "Interzoning" refers to the "international zone" around Tangier, home of William Burroughs in the 1950s and 1960s and so of the "cutup" style which radically shifts the narrative outside the grip of Time and was used by Bowie to generate song lyrics. Tangier was the home, for decades, of rich European homosexuals who had trouble with the law in their own countries but found a welcome in the Zone with its lack of police and extradition treaties. Recreational drug use was another custom of the place. *Red-Haired Android* is glamorous but low-affect: each poem is light enough to dissolve and give way to the next one, each one offers a glimpse of a louche but affluent life where moral and economic restraint never intrudes. Meanwhile the imagery around the black sun may have started as a lament or curse, but has evolved with time into a way of switching mood at will: stylisation allows a way out of character and unhappiness and the rearrangement of props that influence mood supplies freedom. Reed's poems are primary material, like fantasies and dreams, and not formally connected. All the same there is an underlying mythology; if you grew up with Ballard and glam rock it is rather easier to connect with the poems. *Red-Haired Android* has almost 200 poems, each one acting out a scenario soaked in fantasy, the exotic, rich objects that sustain inner journeys. *New Worlds in SF*, back in 1963, featured an essay by Ballard on Burroughs: the cutup method is basic to Reed but also plugs into the main line of British SF. That wasn't quite a fan magazine, but brings us to the point of saying that Reed has accepted that all art has to be like a magazine for fans, a litany for acts of erotic worship. John Wieners made a whole book out of cut-ups from adoring film magazines (*Behind the State Capitol*). I know Jeremy will be disappointed that this essay is not like a glamour magazine.

The point about photographs is to trap the invisible, not the visible. The cover of *Duck and Sally Inside*, (for *Salvatore* I guess), shows a piece of kitsch-masochism by a Munich photographer, called 'Homage to B Soubirous'—the civil name of Saint Bernadette of Lourdes, played by Jennifer Jones in *The Song of Bernadette*, itself the subject of an adulatory book, written from film magazines, by John Wieners. Duck and Sally are two characters from a Velvet Underground song named 'Sister Ray' on which the guitarist deliberately played loud to obscure the lyrics, so I can't tell you their story. 'The Song of Bernadette' is about Jennifer Jones being bullied by Vincent Price ("I am the Imperial Prosecutor.

Do you know what that means?") but sticking to her story about seeing the Blessed Virgin in a grotto—the gem Reed took away was of piercing loyalty to a story. Reed, like Ballard, and Sinclair, took popular culture as his starting-point; to get away from the didactic staple of English poetry, the porridge of authenticity. Defying this bureaucracy which deals with selves, he scatters blessings on Outsiders loyal to weird scenes—Ray and Sylvia went to photograph sites where radioactive creep is taking over and "discovered soldiers cleaning up on minority ethics". (Or, "ethnics"? no.) Jack and Jacky offer bespoke funerals for the inauthentic—"One was to be buried in a pink fridge". The stories are modern and perverse and inspire a certain apathy. The singularity of gesture could be like modernism in language. The poems have a lack of constraint—disengagement as a form of psychic protection. The poet finds a protected zone where narcissism is possible because normative reality does not obtrude. The poems deliberately offer only roles, a journey back to a moment of pure flexibility and so pure choice. The level of investment is very low and so correspondingly is the level of loss. We can also see the poems as being completely made of ornament, with no central scene at all; an endless shimmer which never carries a burden of information. This lack of engagement can itself be seen as a symptom of depression.

Reed became a poetic myth, a star crystal, and so outside cellular time: after writing 2000 poems, where can you go? Vincent told me that, for Reed, these are the Vegas years; benign, indulgent, glamorous, sophisticated idling while we recall the great days of *Bleecker Street, The Isthmus of Samuel Greenberg, Saints and Psychotics, Stratton Elegy*, when he was fired by more violent anxieties, going through more carnal transformations.

Any batch of poetry by unknowns will include a share of poems based on Stars, with the intimacy and yet distance which we find in glamour magazines. If I make no historical comments on this it's because these poets don't make it into print. Reed is a gleaming exception. I have a dim memory of translating (under the supervision of Dr van den Beukel) a Flemish poem by Paul van Ostaijen, of circa 1915, about Asta Nielsen. I realise that isn't a history but it was a wonderful poem. *Asta! Asta! Asta!*

Indigo and Arctic fox: on Pauline Stainer's *Selected Poems*,
with some reflections on modern Christian poetry

Stainer seldom deviates from the miraculous. A simple example is a
short poem about the discovery of Stone Age footsteps preserved in an
underwater cave reached by divers. It is dark and they are relying on
touch. They are underwater so sound is muffled. Suddenly they hear
the footsteps—of the feet which left the prints, of course. This idea of
an event being trapped in rock is a ghost story, a hallucination, close
to hysteria—but also an imaginative leap and finally a miracle. Her
work is typically an arrangement of spiritual ideas, then a collection of
objects as their analogy, then an ordering of words to trap the objects.
The object choice is deep enough for its motives to be uncertain. Take
this image, for example:

> You would think her
> cool as a flute
> from the long-bone of a swan,
> her flesh the lit wax
> for all suppressed pallors
>   ('Girl on Silbury Hill')

—strikingly repeated a few pages later as

> After nine thousand years
> a Chinese flute
> made from the wingbone
> of a red-crowned crane
> is blown again
>   ('The knowledge of water')

Both follow Sacheverell Sitwell's line about the flute made from an
eagle's wing. Do the wingbones signify lacerating pain and death, or
the eerie prowess of the hunter, or the survival of the soul, as a sharp
breath, after death? I find this so fascinating that it lures my soul out of
my body—what would I say, after 9000 years of burial. These *mirabilia*,
marvels, are the substance of the book. Rigorously uninterested in

reason, realism, or preaching, it always delivers its spooky charge.

Religions like *relics*, often bones, often worn and ancient, and like the *relic words*, perhaps of the bones' owners, also fixed in binding patterns by writing and reciting. An exhibition on in London while I was writing the first version of this piece showed 15th century Rhenish manuscript painting, where the small size of the objects is connected with a larger number of people buying paintings, with lay literacy, and with privatisation. The church becomes portable and is no longer an assembly. As lay literacy really gets out of hand, you get Protestantism and printing. The bourgeois household is the new authority, it wants relics small enough for portable devotions, and no priestly tutelage. Eventually, you get a privatised faith; poetry is then the Offices of a private mythology. Stainer is gathering objects of veneration, and forms of words to hymn them, in one. The sacred objects thus gathered are losing none of their almighty efficacy: they are nothing less than windows on a universe of miracles. They are present less to attach human memories to than to act as lenses for forces far more powerful than those of the visible universe with its domesticated frequencies. Lay literacy takes undivided power away from the priests: however powerful the array of traditional and inherited Christian literary forms, 20th century poets wanted to create new forms of Christian poetry, and they did not want a sense of guilt about pride in this personal creation. Stainer is making a very radical break from Christian poetry as it might be found in the Anglican hymnal or the Psalms. She draws very extensively on non-Christian sacred imagery or legends. At the same time she is not a heretic, a pagan, or an occultist.

I failed to understand 'The Ice-Pilot Speaks', Stainer's great poem published in the 1993 volume of the same name, when I first read it, and, since its design may be puzzling for other people as well, I will try to clarify that design.

> *St Brendan's monks*
> *sail through the eye*
> *of the iceberg.*
>
> At first, they ran
> with the shadow of the land
> through light bluish fog

later, by moonlight,
the ship caulked
with tallow, shamans

clashing over the Pole
as if to earth
any dead in the rigging,

and at dawn,
floes gliding by,
chesspieces in Lenten veils

the sea a silver-stained
histology slide,
the O of the iceberg

whistling like Chinese birds
with porcelain whistles
on their feet.

Even in prayer
they could never replay it—
the purity of that zero

Varèse, playing
the density of his flute's
own platinum

the intervening angel
bearing a consignment
of freshwater.

This is section 7 of the thirteen sections of 'The Ice-Pilot speaks'. Before
going into the images in some detail, I want to point out that they are
balanced in a strange way: it is not that a series of examples illustrates
a primary concept, but that each image is a primary focus and they all
support each other. There *is* a key statement: the monks of St Brendan,

sailing around the North Atlantic in perhaps 500 AD, find an arch of ice thawed in a O shape and sail through it. Other icebergs, melting in southerly waters, have eroded into shapes like chess-pieces, their colour like old ivory. The shamans are associated with the deep north, for example in Siberia and in Eskimo territories. They clash over the Pole, presumably in duels to see who has the greater magical power; the vital feature for them is the Pole Star, rather than the late invention of a "pole" on the earth; the loser falls out of the sky and is snarled in the rigging of Brendan's ship. The iceberg whistles, as is reported of river-ice thawing, and then we move on to two wonderful images which illustrate the purity of that sound. They are the "porcelain whistles" tied to birds, to pipe as they fly; and a composition for flute by Edgard Varèse, called 'Density 21.5', referring to the platinum of which the flute was made. The angel brought fresh water to Brendan's monks (which presumably has the purity of Varèse's music). The images form a series running out into space without curving back. Many of them relate to a voyage, but actually to many different voyages, even in roughly the same waters— the far North Atlantic.

John Layard's 1944 book, *The Lady of the Hare,* consists of two parts. The first is an account of Layard's patient, of her dreams, and of her family. These sessions yielded a dream about a hare whom she sacrifices, which as a willing victim is also Christ, and linked with Easter. He says that the hare stands for the moon, and is therefore a symbol of intuition, because the moon lights up darkness and is a guide for the perplexed. When the vegetation is on fire, the hare will not run away until the last moment, but waits until it has itself caught fire: he says this is a symbol of instinct being turned into spirit, as fire transforms what is base. The second is a catalogue of legends or symbolic scenes involving hares all over the world. These are (a) the story that hares sacrifice themselves, taken from John Aubrey (b) a legend of the Buddha (c) the hare in the moon as symbol of Intuition (d) a hare which leaps into the fire as a symbol of the transfer of instinct into spirit (e) folktales showing the cunning of the hare, justifying the claimed role of "Intuition" (f) African elephants worshipping the moon in the Roman writer Pliny (g) a modern child's dream. We have not got beyond the first few pages here. He accumulates dozens of stories. As Layard points out "this inquiry covers four continents and includes mythological belief current in India, China, Ancient Egypt, and in the classical periods of Greece and Rome […] and in North America where beliefs strikingly similar in essentials were held until the advent of the white man by the Algonkin and by the Aztecs of Mexico, as well as modern folk-tales from many parts of Africa and a mass of mediaeval and modern folk-lore from Europe […]". He draws material from the four continents. The details of the different scenes are not important. What is important is the serial principle: the idea of constructing a book out of images $n1 + n2 + n3 + n4…$, and the egoless action whereby the actor in each successive scene is not the same person but yet they are obeying the same impulse and are kin. We could almost say that actor C is carrying out the wishes of actors A and B, is the free version of what they are not free to do, is evidence for what is really happening inside them. It would follow that the reader is also one of this series of people, and that this state of freedom which is also testimony shows how the reader is meant to feel about the text.

I believe that there has been a reversal of field whereby the mainstream of Anglican culture has moved away from an exclusive orthodoxy towards an encompassing view of divinity, which can take on spirituality from all over the world. This liberation follows on from the realisation that the English way is not superior to all others, so that going over the boundaries is not the path to disaster. This correlates with other changes in the status of Anglicanism, and of the British State, but comparative folklore, and its extreme form, diffusionism, played a role in this shift. If the dream of Layard's patient contained traces of mythology from all around the world, it is logical to think that an English poet could use themes of mythology from all around the world. To put it another way, if you free all myths from the taint of being "heretical", you also free all the poems someone might write from the same taint.

Layard's *Hare* consists of a series of thoroughly disparate images connected by a theme which he says appears in the world of dreams but comes from a deeper reality. If we turn back now to 'The Ice-Pilot Speaks', it seems that the poem is very much composed on this design, and that we can understand its thirteen sections with their wonderfully energetic piling of image upon image if we grasp the syntax for composing books which Layard is an example of. This solves the puzzle. Or, it simplifies the puzzle to a task of recognition, as we think about the images of the poem one by one and by recognising them see also how they link to the overall theme. Pauline Stainer has clarified (personal communication) that the title of her new and selected poems, *The Lady and the Hare*, is *not* a reference to Layard. It is named for a poem within the book, which obliquely narrates the legend of St Melangell and a visit to her shrine in Pennant, Powys (formerly Montgomeryshire). Its website is at www.st-melangell.org.uk. Melangell was an anchorite. One day, the prince Brochwel Yscythrog ("of the tusks") was hunting a hare, which took shelter in Melangell's skirts. Brochwel was so impressed by her that he first made an offer of marriage and then granted her the whole valley.

Graveyards. This is not a line. *Graveyards/ shutting up the sea/ with doors.* Nor is this a stanza. I have serious reservations about the metrics, which seem fixed and arrested. The definition of these fragments of spoken word groups by wilful line-breaks achieves control at the cost of hobbling verse movement. There is a lack of momentum. The flavour is elusive—could we speak of a liturgical solemnity and stiff-leggedness?

The lack of interest in the organisation of sound goes along with a consuming interest in objects. It would in fact be effective to approach Stainer's poems as primarily a collection of objects and to treat the verbal organisation as secondary. To put this another way: where some poets are collectors of rare rhythmic and verbal moments which they carefully generate, Stainer is a collector of rare objects and scenes.

In the poem 'Frequencies' (from the volume *The Ice-Pilot Speaks*) five parts are somewhat connected by a theme, which yet dissolves into illustrations of beauty and fragility. The (apparently) most basic level is a cello recital, at a gallery and arts centre in Cambridge, by a musician who died young of a wasting disease. The first part gives us the courtier death taking the cellist, then a scene of a willow which was also cut down in its prime. Part 2 is more difficult as we are shown effects of vibration: a burning-glass shaken by vibrato, and a scene (a real event?) in which musicians gather in a dry valley to find the frequency at which various stones resonate. Then a depiction of a geode: "Geodes are essentially rock cavities or vugs with internal crystal formations or concentric banding." (Wikipedia) "A geode is a simple term for a rock with a hollow in it[.]" (Wikipedia) The hollow allows crystals to form if the right drip comes along. The poem speaks of "answering intensities", which must correspond to the resonance of the first few lines, and says that we do not know if these intensities are wounds or wide roses. This is difficult, but perhaps the idea is of invisible forces with which sensitive souls resonate, and which at high intensity cause damage. This may connect with the transformation of the ammonite, a shelled cephalopod, "the ammonite/ coldest of grave-jewels,/ clear quartz where its body was", as it fossilises, into something precious and exotic. Lines 7 to 9 are the most mysterious, as "below foxholes/ the great frieze floats/ across the calcite crystal". The "calcite crystal" is a gemstone, although I can't identify this one with the buried frieze. The bit about "below the foxhole" is odd but has a literal and real solution in the shape of a Greek temple (possibly, Egyptian) buried by time (much as the ammonite is transformed by much deep time), so that it is under a thick layer of soil in which a fox has dug a hole a few feet deep. But why in this poem? there is a sort of unconscious fantasy going on in which the buried temple resonates to the tone of some instrument played above ground. This may be a pointer to something really mysterious, "the implosion of the geode". Why should the geode implode? In context we would have to look to sound as the agent: the stone has a hollow interior containing (probably) air, which could be made to resonate. Instruments too have hollows in which excited air moves. The implosion sounds like damage and so could be connected to the theme of death which permeates the poem. Geodes are made of crystal, often, often of quartz, and one could very well look like the ammonite fossil—a visual rhyme. In some implicit way, the force focussed through the burning glass in line 1 builds up to destroy the geode (which is also made of crystal) in line 15. Part 3 is fairly simple, involving a comparison of music with a painting of musicians; called 'Mirror canon', it copies this musical form by reversing itself, so that line 1 is identical with line 15, line 2 with line 14, and so on. Part 5 is easy to assimilate, describing the "Aoroi" (Greek for "untimely"), those who died before their natural span was up. Part 4 is more difficult; the core idea seems to be a focussing of white light as an act of mourning. This departs from a prism in a pure white room, kindling on an entombed Pharaoh, then a crystal used to shed light to make a face look lighter (an ear-ring?). Stanza 4 evokes the thigh-bone (tibia) of an arctic fox, marked with nicks to act as a lunar calendar—this comes from the results of Alexander Marshack, working on Palaeolithic relics. The brightness of the moon is the charge. Later we get a steppe fox, struck by a blunt arrow which kills without impairing its perfect white fell. Then, the ancient snow from the coldest parts of the earth, drilled out for study by climate scientists, and quinces hanging heavy and golden in a frost. Turner's all-white paintings crop up. A prism splits light into component wavelengths, producing signals of greater unity and intensity—this part of the poem is a prismatic concentration of whiteness. Wavelength varies in direct ratio to frequency.

When I walk along a beach, I find bottleglass, bladderwrack, the plastic nooses which restrain six-packs. But Stainer's sea is much pickier—

> Such argosy—
> the sunk merchantman
> with cabins of sandalwood
> in the brushed cobalt;
> saltpetre and squirrel-pelt,
> ivory gull and porcelain crab
> on cannon under the kelp.
>
> The sound is watered silk,
> the sea foiled
> by white sand
> to simulate emerald;
> that spume on the causeway
> scrimshaw and crucible,
> muslin from Bengal.
> (from 'Salt over Skara Brae')

—it is besotted with accessorizing and has a credit card with No Limit. (Foil is the back of a mirror. The sound is a body of water; the spume is compared to a smelting cauldron which spurts with heat, to ivory carved by sailors with many perforations, and to a diaphanous textile.) The 'Ice-Pilot' poem is also set in a remote part of the planet, where the entire geography is exotic. Pondering on the hidden principles of these poems, I conclude that there is an unconscious fantasy at work, in which the strange substances were mutated during exhaustingly long journeys, and conversely the long journeys are undertaken, in sailing-ships, for the sake of rich and alien substances. Perhaps this is only my fantasy. Perhaps in some way the miraculous substances are the product of geologically long journeys in which their quotidian nature is slowly eroded and their strange identity embodies perfected transformations. All the furniture of the book seems to have emerged from a grave along with an Egyptian who, as the Egyptian book promises, has come forth by day and survived the ages of death. To put it another way: Stainer still knows where the box of beautiful things is.

On the jacket of *The Lady and the Hare*, poets gush about scientific knowledge, but to say "The swan/ entering Leda/ like a laser/ through alabaster" does not argue a learned study of optics (or of poultry-breeding). Stainer's world-view is completely pre-scientific, a hoard of marvels and exotica sorted by analogy. I noted "indigo, cinnabar, ice, water, arctic fox" as recurring images; a mixture, I think, of pigments and surfaces of high reflexivity. These optically saturated patches are either slits where the invisible shows through—or dazzles which confuse our sensory organs and expectations. In 'Thomas Vaughan experiments with mercury', we hear the sound, of retort glass falling off the backs of birds after his mercury exploded, but not about what he was trying to find out. Indeed, Vaughan was an alchemist and Neoplatonist, a pupil of Robert Fludd—he had little enough to do with science (and was probably trying to turn the mercury into gold). The whole world which, along with Fludd, Frances Yates described in *The Rosicrucian Enlightenment* is close to the one Stainer records: magical analogies, the virtues of precious stones, Protestant mysticism. Stainer recalls the red ochre with which Palaeolithic Man marked burials, a symbol of blood and life—like the cinnabar which, in its guise as mercury oxide, blew up Vaughan ("heavy shining oxides/ of yellow and red"). She likes burials and their assemblages of symbolic objects, and the parallel fixed riches of photographs. She mentions albumen prints. Fox Talbot, inventor of the albumen process in printing, was recently outed as a Neoplatonist, who spent his time photographing scenes reproducing the hieroglyphs of Horapollo, locking knowledge in Hermetic visibility. English photographers were not interested in amorphous reality, but in making icons of the English mythology.

I have had great difficulty getting anyone in the "underground" world to accept Stainer's work. I suppose it follows that she is a mainstream poet. If that is true, most of the objections to mainstream poetry collapse. Her books (the first one published in 1989) are hardly hampered by convention, yet show nothing in common with the writers linked to the Underground of the Seventies, who seem in this perspective to cluster together—however much rebellion was their founding charter. The hindrance was presumably her dedication to a certain range of inherited English enchantments and keepsakes. She shows no worries at all about visiting East Anglian churches or going to cello recitals at Kettle's Yard Museum in Cambridge. I can't quite define what the worry might be, but it is probably an adolescent trauma of the nervous teenager on the path to becoming a modernist, subject to *moral collapses* on being caught by other aggressive adolescents in a lapse from pure Marxism into bourgeois pleasures or a lapse from pure geometric form into loving things that have genuine links to religion, to the Middle Ages, to the national past. These unconscious blocks confidently resist being dredged up and made articulate, but anyway Stainer's world of objects and scenes is alien to the Underground tradition, with the single exception of shamanism. Stainer once lived in Saffron Walden, and the sequence of poems about paintings by Eric Ravilious (in the collection of Saffron Walden Museum, close to where Ravilious lived) is especially unlikely to thrill a modernist snob. Ravilious designed china for the 1937 Coronation—rather good designs. The poems are quite brilliant.

If the Anglican massif is no longer a monolithic bloc, but has abandoned orthodoxy and has diverged into individualism, international mythology, and personal originality, the problem yet again may be distinguishing the orthodox from the radical. In fact, it looks more as if there was a flood wave picking up all English poetry and moving it into a new terrain of obligatory originality. The history of the mainstream must be written to include the structural changes within the Anglican world, or within the Protestant realm as a whole.

Is it true that in the new dispensation all poets are original? No. There is a new unoriginality which is partly based on lack of talent and partly on the pressure to dumb down and write poems which are simple and inevitably resemble other simple poems. Original poets are always rare. Perhaps 1% of the poets now practising can manage something original. It is worth going to Saffron Walden to find them.

Muzzleflash Two:
what happened after the 1950s

Having got as far as the Nineties, we can return to Keith Tuma's great anthology and sketch some draft conclusions about the shape of the period since 1950. The establishment bristled at the publication of Tuma's anthology because it based the list of poets on merit and so included roughly 50% Underground and avant-garde poets for the post-1960 period and thus admitted that this sector existed. This led to some astonishing non-cooperation from the English offices of the publisher and from conservative reviewers. In fact, I was hired to write a second review of it for one magazine because the first one was seen as so biased that it had to be obliterated. I took the money.

We set out with an appalling list of anxieties affecting poets, but also with a promise to write about genres—which can be seen as safety zones, tender green spots where the poet takes refuge from the anxieties. It may be that genres are connected in a "field effect" where the retreat of one means the expansion of another. Further, that genres are like forms—they can rise or fall in value and go out of business.

There is a line of Underground poetry. However, the precept of this book is to leave out the Underground, and it is a world which barely overlaps with mainstream poetry, so we are passing it by. At the end of the '70s, the small press sector split between pop and "experimental" poetry, a strict division of assets. Only then did the avant-garde emerge from behind the swinging world of Pop poetry as a separate entity, defended by walls of formal rigour which gave a secure identity. To quote Bourdieu, the audience for the poet consisted entirely of rivals. Thus what had originally been one sector or genre split into two and forgot that they had ever been one. Tuma's anthology has wide coverage of the whole century but falls apart rather after 1980. Things have gone seriously wrong for this sector, but we will move serenely on.

The composition of the cohort of poets by gender changed quite rapidly from some point in the 1990s. The new wave of women poets fitted snugly into the existing preferences for the domestic, the intimate, for colloquial language, and for mild alienation from the power structures. The nucleus of feminism had been definitely Marxist, but only the depoliticised came to be widely read. There was a transition from Left to consumerist. The social message favoured common sense over originality, and the new accession strengthened the mainstream against experiment.

The "grand titration" (as the share of women in new poets rises to 50%) was presumably coupled to the composition of students entering higher education, as the "feedstock" of poetry. We do not know if this titration will stabilise at, say 60% or 65%. The issue of why it did not happen in the 1970s is still perplexing. The mid-century situation was evidently a state of oppression, and this colours all historical memory of the era.

The change weakened critics—if every other faction disagrees with you, and feminism undermines the basis for artistic judgement (free from menial ego-investments), your authority no longer authorises very much. Critics could only exert power if they agreed with each other. This loss of prestige was probably helpful to working poets. The social shifts in the role of women must have given rise to arguments, but it is hard to find these specifically in the realm of poetry.

English song improved immeasurably in the early Sixties, and constantly renewed itself throughout the period. The scene is drowned in music. The balance between poetry and song—words with and without music, actually—changed irrevocably as popular music disenfranchised itself from paralysing inhibitions. While poets personally found inspiration in listening to music and found their styles inside various forms of music, poetry set to music conquered 99% or 99.9% of the contemporary market. A credible solution would be for poetry to have renounced the area where it was competing with pop music and to develop massively into the unoccupied area of intelligence and critique. This however did not happen. Poetry typically was deeply influenced by pop lyrics and had considerable problems with moving away from that numbing sociality into the area of autonomy and possible isolation. All poets I interviewed listened to music a lot but it makes a big difference whether you listen to the Spontaneous Music Ensemble or Elton John.

The most startling feature of the age is linguistic bareness. This has multiple sources but it leaves blank a surface which could have been very attractive to people outside the poetry world. The feature which really differentiates poetry from song lyrics has been squeezed out, or compressed to a thin dime.

We could see poetry as being threatened, from the other side, by the world of academic prose. Individuals who could have written poetry wrote essays, then theses, then learned articles, instead. For this there were status rewards which writing poems notably did not bring. Yet this was a counter-balance to the destructive influence of pop music. Intelligent poets could draw on the strengths of both these thriving cultural zones.

Existentialism gave rise to hedonism and made the Sixties atmosphere possible. The repeated command to be authentic put pressure on writers to purge, and the final step after purging inherited structures condemned by their age was to break out into improvisation—and hedonism and games. The Existentialist stress on the present moment and nonconformity mutated into a blissful indifference to consequences.

Everything cultural has to reflect capitalism as the dominant form of social organisation. This takes the psychological form of possessive individualism. It is arguable that the whole period saw a movement away from the pole of community and towards the pole of individualism. It is also arguable that the combination of individuality and instability characterises English society and is much older than capitalism, which is a consequence rather than an alien or autonomous thing. The preoccupation with talent (as opposed to other considerations) would thus be a realisation of a rule that favours secession, separation, competition, objective evaluation and testing, above solidarity—the nuclear family.

To begin with being slighted and ignored; to fail to inherit the central place; to be exiled and move into a wilderness where you discover freedom; to move from the periphery to the centre of the world; to out-compete everyone else; to prove everyone else wrong; to dream of new ideals. This is simply the myth of succession in a nuclear family model and is the projection of that one-level structure. For the ideals stage to go beyond the simple wish to set up a new household under one's own authority—i.e. self-idealisation—is rare but also the key factor for such poetry achieving significance. The subdivision of styles in the innovative wing was mandated by the need for unallotted assets: colonisation by dissimilation. Writing history in such a regime is truly recording a pauper estate—what nobody owns. The attempts of poets to reach the liminal, and *communitas*, under such a regime, are crippled by the poet's conscious intent.

A predominant feature of the period was the great expansion of possibilities. The key fact here is the statistical one—as Wolfgang Görtschacher has reported, "In the 1960s, there were 2,000 poetry magazines". If you think there is a dominant line in '60s poetry, you're not looking at the evidence. More cogently, we can divide people on the basis of where they date this expansion, which presumably happened once only—generally experts try to claim that they were responsible for it, and date it accordingly to the time when they were influential.

The growth of the available styles is not identical with the moment where an individual sheds social and stylistic blinkers and comes to realise that they can enjoy a huge range of styles. Of course, it is quite possible for the country to contain twenty different styles and a swarm of individuals who each only like one style and are willing to close down every other kind of poet.

Perhaps we can describe the supermarket as the new central place, with an abundance of goods, variety, lack of constraint, mass togetherness, symbolic exchange, acquisition of status objects, acquisition of knowledge, feats using acquired knowledge, etc. We would seize on the bookshop as such a site—the site where, crucially, people mostly don't buy poetry. The new abundance of data brought an eclectic style which was called Postmodernism but which was obviously heir to the panorama style of the late 19th century. The interaction between imperialism, tourism, travel writing, and a New Age grasping of images from Third World religion helped to set the scene. The new virtuality, with new media, aided a drift away from ethical, political, and social reality. Disengagement and exoticism could feel like deep indifference.

The panoply of inconsistent patterns makes it impossible to give a unifying account—which at least gives me a let-out for not doing so. And instead spooling off all kinds of disparate rags and tags. Maybe it's all true.

There is a lack of temporal depth to traditions due to the nuclear family regime, in which the household destroys itself in every generation, and always has to be set up from zero. Possible exceptions would be the Anglican Church, or the academic EngLit tradition, with its "institutional immortality" and stable syllabus. The discourse about "the death of tradition" never points out that the nuclear family makes this a structurally inevitable event. Always starting from scratch meant that proving yourself was a compulsion, and this competition led to a fascination with sport, numbers, and status objects. The idea of tradition has very little to say about the history of modern English poetry. I have an uneasy feeling that the elders have almost total indifference to young poets, and very slight expectations of them. The absence of disciple relationships, as other cultures have them, leads to a thinness of technique which makes innovation problematic and so can be mis-recognised as "traditionalism". The hunt for a personal style was perhaps a dramatisation of this breach with the parental household—a domestic anecdote shaping the morphological tier. Egoism is, or is not, transcendence.

Conventional young poets all give interviews stating how unconventional they are. As if I was in a room with 500 tousle-haired young poets, and shouted "Right! Everyone unconventional raise your hands!" and 500 hands shoot up. "No, I mean everyone who's different from all the others raise your hand!" 500 hands shoot up. Someone has got a wrong perspective here. I am so used to the gesture of revolt from the world of rock music, but I just can't think of a gesture of revolt in new-generation poetry.

Children have a structural need to appeal to adults for resources they want. There was a temptation for poets to appeal to the market by innocence and naivety, and writing about childhood was the least forgivable way of doing this. This was the direct continuation of the 1950s. This wholesomeness can usefully be evoked by the stylistic term Biedermeier, used for a period of Central European art which was childish because anything political was censored. The Biedermeier line saw the ascendancy of Betjeman. His verse autobiography, about family and education, was the unacknowledged model for much we would rather forget—Jackie Kay and Tony Harrison, for example. The match is between upwardly mobile individuals and downwardly mobile forms. The bare style in its entirety can be seen as a version of Biedermeier. So many people are willing to see poetry as an era of permitted infantility—a childhood state of language.

Poetry has been taken over by youth culture in the specific form of the student world. The '60s boom was closely linked, as Wolfgang

Görtschacher has carefully documented, to university towns and universities. Poetry has failed to expand its market share, but where it has expanded, this has involved residence in the world of students and academics. In order to understand the evolution of poetry, we would need to understand the evolution of the culture and ideology of students. At one level this is very conservative and some key things have remained constant since the '60s, but at another three years is a whole generation for studentdom.

It is possible that a grade of social experience is beautiful because we have never experienced it in sober reality. This is its idealistic quality, its suggestive and tantalising power. The suppressed area of the range of behavioural forms may be pre-selected as the realm of the aesthetic. Poetry thus offers a looking-glass image of reality. It proposes the exact converse of possessive individualism except that the poem seizes and possesses a style, the size and shape of a person, and refines that to a state of rare elaboration. What this points to is that the bareness of style, the degree zero of style, the pathological plainness and banality, of the era, are the continuation of the protest against possessive individualism and are structurally implied by the looking-glass role. Competence as an anti-business domain structurally implies incompetence at using language that rises above nattering at the supermarket. Blankness is proposed as the Before—before the damage arrives and is proclaimed as a social order. This is what folk song gave to the scene.

There is a line which projects aspirations for a more communal way of life not onto the future but onto a geographically neighbouring region, i.e. the "Celtic" realm around the Irish Sea. Regional differences in family structure may in fact correlate with a different and un-English line of poetry along the Atlantic and Irish Sea coast.

If possessive individualism manages to become aesthetic (to people in a society run on that rule), it is in the form of *dual narcissism*, where the consumer projects, narrowly, onto an artist who designs to receive that projection, and who presents a partial, projective, self-indulgent view of existence. Poetry was thus vulnerable to a takeover by single-issue politics, by the "politics of identity", the totalising of self-esteem. The singer songwriter genre was precisely the stylistic product which embodied this dual narcissism most glutinously and indulgently.

The atmosphere of poetry readings has in its foreground an intimacy which is part of a whole theory of depersonalisation. This is a visible phase of poetic life. This is where you can find the audience as well as the poets. This warmth is a protest against society being run on other principles, a critique so familiar that it is hardly audible any more. It fulfils a notion of authenticity. The abolition of distance is again compatible with linguistic bareness—imitating a voice is given priority over seeking out the ornate, the beautiful, and the intellectual. This is a continuity with the 1950s, which is when the modern idea of readings was developed.

For a brief moment in the mid-'70s we have a comprehensive list of all poetry publications, the great *Poet's Yearbook*. I went through this list for one year—without having read all the 800 or so books, I nonetheless recognise most of the names. What struck me was the level of unnecessary publication—the vacant heat. People "concerned with" poetry felt a need to publish poets without really believing in them. The facts of "being a poet" and the fact of "giving patronage to poetry" had an energy quite detached from things like being reviewed and reaching a market, which are normal parts of artistic endeavour. This blank benignity is surely central to the scene and its human warmth, even if its corollary is poetry of amazingly low technical standards. The difference in terms of reward between being a good poet and being a bad poet is minimal. The "significant others" who would form the primary audience, the *Textmilieu*, are simply absent—declining to invest in what will never "belong" to them. The ideal of an artists' community is largely a myth, poets generally write for themselves (the "nuclear poet", in fact).

The generational cycle built into the nuclear family patterns has implications for the transmission of styles and lines of experiment. The amazing willingness of the "editor tier" to print and publish bad poetry is a form of benignity which vitally contradicts rules of self-interest. The poetry scene is somehow outside capitalism. To be inside it we must be beside ourselves.

The idea of a field is that it links disparate cultural objects in a grid of mutually affecting energies. So, a style may represent assimilation to models and dissimilation, i.e. reaction against, other models. A new text captures and mutates existing texts, more exactly strands of signification present within older texts. Styles which you don't use may embody suppressed powers, forced into the nonfocal but latently there. But surely some objects really don't fit into a field. Given how much ignorance of the poetry scene is prevalent on the scene, it is plausible that "field effects" are weak and that even oppositions didn't have decisive results. So we might have to speak of multiple fashions—so there is no "style of the seventies" and there are ten "styles in the seventies". This corresponds to the educated minority growing in numbers to the point where knowledge cannot spread over the whole group—and huge tracts of it disappear over the horizon, as visible to any individual. To put this another way, the idea of a "period style" had depended on the cultural stratum being small enough to imitate each other and share one stylistic equipment.

With so much mutual incomprehension, balkanisation is a key word for the entire period. But if you find a slab of evidence which lets you look at a couple of hundred poets of roughly the same age, it is noticeable that most of them are not original. The balkanisation is theoretical and conformism is still a structural rule, part of socialisation. The idea that "the scene is endlessly diverse so my poetry is itself endlessly diverse" was corrupting.

A central place in British poetry was held by the bourgeois guardians, giving out legitimation and themselves legitimated by institutions. At the close of the 1950s, this group was especially confident, and especially hostile to the creative energies of poetry. Their power increased immeasurably with the growth of the universities but was doomed to overthrow because the expansion also increased the number of students and they were plugged into Youth Culture and hedonism—and this took over the new poetry. The "guardians", enfiefed in Oxford, the BBC, the quality press, and a few London publishers, were grimly plugging Disenchantment and empiricism all through the 1960s—but there was an era change, probably around 1979–85, which saw the "official" poetry world losing some of its inhibitions. Thus "the long 1950s" finally drew to an end. Because feminism did not want male moral authority, they withdrew approval from these "moral leaders", and thus accelerated or even caused the breakdown of this control system. Perhaps feminism did change the genre system.

Close reading. Pretty much everyone you talk to in the poetry world was impressed by Close Reading and that whole academic apparatus as they learnt to write clever essays. Pretty well everyone says that they had to forget all that in order to write poetry without seizing up and growing cold. Poetry may be created by the same people who study poetry in the classroom, but following a completely set of psychological imperatives.

In the 1950s, English poetry was still dominated by the Christian interest. This classically anti-capitalist energy and human vision mutated by shedding institutional power rather than vanishing from the scene. Thus, the Anglicans pioneered middle-class guilt and this remains a dominant factor on the scene. The Anglicans got into privatisation because of the decline of the parish as the most energetic unit of society and worship—and privatisation has been the theme of poetry ever since. The Protestant revolution which saw the Church emerge from the monasteries into the secular world is arguably being followed by a second one in which spiritual direction is taken away from the priests and descends on each of the parishioners. This implies a vast wave of innovation and diversification.

Intellectual Christians were, in the 1950s, involved with existentialism. This put a stress on the present moment and on bareness. The golden, half-Latin, language of Anglican theology and the alliance of the Church with the families who had the most wealth and education were both seen as the dominance of the Past, blocking out the reality of the Present. This bareness was defined as freedom. It is the single most important influence (among so many others) on the sparse language of the new poetry. This dissociation from the Past and from legacy structures mutated, in the atmosphere of the sixties, into a belief in spontaneity, improvisation, and hedonism.

In the wave around the Festival of Britain there was a great emphasis on what was cynically called "the box of beautiful things", which meant modest and charming English things like barge painting, Staffordshire pottery and folk songs. During the '50s, this evolved into the Folk Boom. The withdrawal from the archaic and too "rich" and governmental trappings of the Anglican Church, in a new craving for simplicity, found this as part of the available stock. It was natural to recur to the Middle Ages, as the cultural apex of the Christian civilisation, and this recovered a stratum of poetry and song which inevitably had a lot in common with folk music.

A third strand of Christian cultural development (there are so many) is the development into "personal" spirituality and away from legacy styles which can be seen variously in New Age spirituality and in Don Cupitt's "sea of faith" theology. The formal renewal of Christian poetry is striking, rarely more so than in the work of Pauline Stainer.

A strand which Tuma does not deal with is the one which John Press identified as energy (in his 1960 book on recent British poetry), which was represented for Press by Vernon Watkins, Edwin Muir, and Kathleen Raine. This *post-Symboliste* strand saw Yeats' *Oxford Book* as a reference point. Raine's intellectual project uncovered the whole history of the spiritual and "cosmic", of Western occultism. Poets who believe in Jung are surely a genre, both long-lived and vigorous. The Christian line, until recently the centre of English poetry, has migrated towards this personal and privatised manner.

Bibliography

References to my previous work as follows:

Centre-Periphery — *Centre and Periphery in Modern British Poetry* (Liverpool University Press, 2005)

FCon — *The Failure of Conservatism in Modern British Poetry* (Salt, 2003)

Heresy — *The Council of Heresy* (Shearsman, 2008)

Legends — *Legends of the Warring Clans. The Poetry Scene in the '90s* (published on the Internet at www.pinko.org)

Origins — *Origins of the Underground* (Salt, 2007)

Rules — *Fulfilling the Silent Rules* (as yet unpublished)

Introduction

Peter Barry, *Poetry Wars. British poetry of the 1970s and the Battle of Earls Court* (Cambridge: Salt Publishing, 2006)

Jauss, Hans Robert. 'Theory of Genres and Mediaeval Literature' (originally 1972) in *Towards an Aesthetic of Reception* (Brighton: Harvester Press, 1982)

Spectral investments and revisionist muzzle-flash

For the concept of liminal states, see Victor Turner, Dramas, fields, and metaphors; symbolic action in human society *(Ithaca, NY: Cornell University Press, 1974)*

Sydney Bolt, ed., *Poetry of the 1920s* (London: Longmans, Green and Co, 1967)

Adrian Clarke and Robert Sheppard, eds. *Floating Capital. New Poets from London* (Elmwood: Potes & Poets, 1991)

Crawford, Robert and Armitage, Simon, eds. *The Democratic Voice* (London: Viking, 1998)

Crozier, Andrew and Longville, Tim, eds. *A Various Art* (Manchester: Carcanet, 1987)

Enright, DJ, ed. *Oxford Book of Contemporary Verse, 1945–80* (Oxford: Oxford University Press, 1980)

Larkin, Philip, ed. *Oxford Book of Twentieth-Century Verse* (Oxford: Clarendon Press, 1973)

Sean O'Brien, ed. *The Firebox* (London: Picador, 1998)

Robert H. Ross, *The Georgian revolt 1910–22. Rise and Fall of a Poetic Ideal* (Carbondale: Illinois University Press, 1965)

Iain Sinclair, ed. *Conductors of Chaos* (London: Paladin, 1996)

Emmanuel Todd, *L'invention de la France* (with Hervé le Bras; Paris: Livre de Poche, 1981;

—— *L'enfance du monde. Structures familiales et développement.* (Paris: Seuil, 1984);

—— *L'invention de l'Europe* (Paris: Seuil, 1990)

Yeats, W.B., ed. *Oxford Book of Modern Verse 1892–1935* (Oxford: OUP, 1936).

Structure of the cultural field around 1960
see my previous remarks on 50s poetry in FCon, *pp.45–74.*

Allott, Kenneth, ed. *Contemporary Poetry* (1950; 2nd edition, about 50% larger, 1962) (London: Harmondsworth, 1950)

for Barker, George, see my comments in *Origins* pp.170–9

for Biedermeier, see Eda Sagarra, *A Social History of Germany 1648–1914* (London: Methuen, 1977)

Browne, E Martin, *Two in One* (Cambridge: Cambridge University Press, 1981)

Croft, Andy, ed., *A weapon in the struggle, the cultural history of the communist Party in Britain* (London: Pluto, 1998)

Fraser, Robert, *Chameleon Poet. The Life of George Barker* (London: Jonathan Cape, 2001)

Homberger, Eric, *The Art of the Real. Poetry in England and America since 1939.* (London: J M Dent, 1977)

Jones, Barbara, *Follies and Grottoes* (London: Constable & Co.,1953)

Lees-Milne, James, *Diaries 1942–54* (London: John Murray, 2006)

for Logue, Christopher, see my remarks in *Heresy* pp.92–7

Mellor, David, Saunders, Gill, Wright, Patrick, *Recording Britain, a Pictorial Domesday of Pre-war Britain* (Newton Abbot: David and Charles, 1990)

Nelson Parker, Anthony, *Pageants, their presentation and production* (London: Bodley Head, 1954)

Press, John, *Rule & Energy. Trends in British poetry since the Second World War* (London: Oxford University Press, 1963)

Seago, Alex, *Burning the box of beautiful things* (Oxford: Oxford University Press, 1995)

Thomson, George, *Marxism and Poetry* (London: Lawrence and Wishart, 1945)

Thurley, Geoffrey, *The Ironic Harvest. English poetry in the twentieth century.* (London: Edward Arnold, 1974)

Vidler, Alec, *Soundings. Essays concerning Christian understanding* (Cambridge: CUP, 1962)

Primary Texts:
Blackburn, Thomas, ed. *45–60. An anthology of English poetry 1945–60* (London: Putnam, 1960)

Fry, Christopher, *Venus Observed. A Play* (Oxford: Oxford University Press, 1950)

Fuller, Roy, *Brutus' Orchard* (London: Andre Deutsch, 1957)

—— *Collected Poems 1936–61* (London: Andre Deutsch, 1962)

Heywood, Terence, *Architectonic* (London: Fortune Press, 1953)
Key Poets, a pamphlet series (London: Fore Press, 1951)
Young, Andrew, *Out of the World and Back. Two Poems.* (London: Hart-
   Davis, 1958)

Christian Heads of Household
The religious style defined in The Council of Heresy *pp.67–91 (for Raine) and
   in Origins of the Underground pp.186–209 and 236–53.*
on watching high-status individuals: story in New Scientist *(19/1/08, pp.34–
   37), citing the 1960s work of Clifford Jolly and Michael Chance.*

de Waal, Frans, *Chimpanzee Politics* (Baltimore: Johns Hopkins University
   Press, 1989)
Dollimore, Jonathan and Sinfield, Alan, eds., *Political Shakespeare, essays in
   cultural materialism* (2nd edition, Manchester: Manchester University
   Press, 1994)
Mitchell, Stephen, trans., *Selected Poems of T. Carmi and Dan Pagis*
   (Harmondsworth: Penguin Books, 1976)
O'Brien, Conor Cruise *Writers and Politics* (Harmondsworth: Penguin, 1976)
Riley, Denise, see *Centre and Periphery*, pp.90–107
Weissbort, Daniel, ed. and trans., *The Poetry of Survival. Post-war poets of
   central and eastern Europe* (London, Anvil Press Poetry, 1991)

Domestic Anecdote
For a discussion of the Annales school, see Marc Ferro, ed., Social historians in
   Contemporary France *(New York: Harper and Row, 1972) and Jacques
   le Goff, Roger Chartier, Jacques Revel, eds.,* La nouvelle histoire *(Paris:
   C.E.P.L., 1978).*
For a discussion of privatisation, see Duncan on Logue in The Council of
   Heresy, *pp.92–6.*
For the theme of the white goods economy, see chapter on the 1950s, supra p.26.

Fuller, Roy, *The Middle of a War* (London: Hogarth Press, 1942); *Tiny Tears*
   (London: Andre Deutsch, 1973)
Roberts, Michèle, Kazantzis, Judith, and Wandor, Michelene, *Touch Papers*
   (London: Allison and Busby, 1982)
Jones, Brian, *Interior* (London: Ross, 1969)

Outsider Poetry
Anderson, J Redwood, *Approach* (London: Fortune Press, 1946), *The Fugue of
   Time* (London: Fortune Press, 1947?)

Bihalji-Merin, Oto, *Primitive Artists of Yugoslavia* (New York: McGraw-Hill, 1964)

Hayward, John, ed., *Poems 1951* (Harmondsworth: Penguin)

Szeemann, Harald, *Visionäre Schweiz* (Aarau: Verlag Sauerländer, 1991)

Formalism

Beecham, Audrey, *The Coast of Barbary* (London: Hamish Hamilton, 1957)

Holloway, John, *The Landfallers* (London: Routledge and Kegan Paul,1962)

Homberger, Eric, *Art of the Real* op. cit.

Logue, Christopher, *Songs* (London: Hutchinson, 1959)

Oral Poetry

Comments on Pop poetry in FCon, pp.96–100 and Origins, 291–6.

Booth, Martin, *Driving through the barricades: British poetry 1964 to 1984* (London: Routledge and Kegan Paul, 1985)

Patten, Brian, *Grinning Jack. Selected Poems.* (London: Flamingo, 1995)

Roche, Pete, ed. *Love Love Love. The New Love Poetry* (London: Corgi, 1967)

Smith, Ken Edward, *West Yorkshire Dialect poets* (Wilsden: Dialect, c.1982
—— see discussion of this line in *Centre-Periphery*, pp.126–30.

The singer-songwriter genre

Brend, Mark, *American Troubadours* (San Francisco: Backbeat Books, 2001)

Houghton, Mick, *Becoming Elektra* (London: Jawbone, 2010)

Mojo magazine (#204, November 2010, London) on Elektra Records, including interview with Jac Holzman

Virtuosity

Harper, Colin, *Dazzling Stranger: Bert Jansch and the British Folk and Blues Revival* (London: Bloomsbury, 2000)

Morgan, Edwin, *The Second Life: Selected Poems* (Edinburgh: Edinburgh University Press, 1968)

The Oxford Line

see my previous essay on Oxford poetry at www.pinko.org

Green, Martin *Children of the Sun* (New York: Basic Books, 1976)

Hamilton, Ian, ed., *The Oxford Companion to Twentieth Century Poetry in English* (Oxford: Oxford University Press, 1994)

Levey, Michael, *The case of Walter Pater* (London: Thames and Hudson, 1978)

Pater: *Imaginary Portraits*
Savage, D.S., *The Personal Principle. Studies in Modern Poetry* (London: Routledge, 1944)
Toynbee: see my comments in *Fulfilling the Silent Rules*, forthcoming.
Tuma *ut supra.*

Cerddi hir and Communalist Poetry
discussion of regional differences in Centre and Periphery, *pp.37–51.*
full text of Blackstone here: http://avalon.law.yale.edu/subject_menus/blackstone.asp#book2

Beveridge, Craig, and Turnbull, Ronnie, *Scotland After Enlightenment*, pp.104–10 (Edinburgh: Polygon, 1997)
Jones, Islwyn and Hughes, Gwilym Rees, eds., *Cerddi Hir* (Denbigh: Gwasg Gee, 1970)
van Bath, H Slicher, *Herschreven Historie* (Leiden: 1949). essay on 'Volksvrijheid en democratie' but also most of the other essays in the book.

Christian poets in a secular era
See my essays on Christian poetry in Origins of the Underground.

Abbs: Abbs has expressed his view of the arts in his own books and a series of anthologies, generally in favour of the Sublime and against any form of Modernity.
Booty, John, *The Church in History* (New York: Seabury Press, 1979)
Homberger, Eric, *The Art of the Real ut supra*
Humphreys: see a book by Thomas, M. Wynn, *Emyr Humphreys* (Caernarvon: Gwasg Pantycelyn, 1989) (in Welsh). This excludes his poetry. He has written many novels.
Levi, Peter: see interview from *Paris Review,* currently on the Net at http://www.parisreview.com/media/3379_LEVI.pdf .
—— *Collected Poems 1955–75* (London: Anvil Press, 1976)
Sinfield, Alan, 'Varieties of Religion', in *Society and Literature 1945–70*, ed. Sinfield, (London: Methuen, 1983)
Wilkinson, Alan, *Dissent or conform? war, peace and the English churches 1900–45* (London: SCM Press, 1986)
Young, Andrew, *Out of the World and Back. Two Poems.* (London: Rupert Hart-Davis, 1958)

My standpoint, my trajectory, my cherry-tree

Bense quoted from Domin, Hilde, ed., *Doppelinterpretationen* (Frankfurt am Main: Fischer, 1969)

Paterson, Don and Simic, Charles, eds. *New British Poetry* (Saint Paul: Graywolf Press, 2004)

Beautiful Illusions; Postmodernism and the Recovery of the m-stream

I wrote on the "sub-postmodernist" phenomenon a few years ago, see Legends of the Warring Clans *at www.pinko.org.*

I wrote on neo-conservatism in the 1980s and 1990s in FCon *pp.228–52 and 289–314.*

Barry, Peter, *Poetry Wars. ut supra*

Fuller, John, *Collected Poems* (London: Chatto and Windus, 1996)

Gregson, Ian, *Contemporary Poetry and Postmodernism. Dialogue and Estrangement* (London: Macmillan, 1996)

Joyce, Patrick quoted from *The Postmodern History Reader* (edited by Keith Jenkins, London: Routledge, 1997)

Lucas, John, *Starting to Explain* (Nottingham: Trent Books, 2003)

Schmidt, Michael, ed. *Some Contemporary Poets of Britain and Ireland* (Manchester: Carcanet Press, 1983)

Wainwright: see my essay on the poet in *FCon*, pp.204–6.

A new freedom?

MacBeth, George, *A Doomsday Book* (Lowestoft: Scorpion Press, 1965)

McKendrick, Jamie, *Sky Nails* (London: Faber, 2000)

Oswald, Alice, *Dart* (London: Faber, 2002)

Saxton, Robert, *Manganese* (Manchester: Carcanet, 2003)

Shapcott, Jo, *My Life Asleep* (London: Faber, 1998)

Stammers, John, *Panoramic Lounge-bar* (London: Picador, 2001)

Gold Audible in Death: Jeremy Reed

See my essay in FCon *pp.221–7.*

Reed, Jeremy, *Black Russian: Out-takes from the Airmen's Club* (Hove: Waterloo Press, 2011), introduction by Andrew Duncan.

—— *Red-haired Android* (London: Paladin, 1992)

—— *Heartbreak Hotel* (London: Orion, 2002)

Indigo and Arctic Fox: Pauline Stainer
Melangell was possibly 8th century but Brochwel was 6th century and there is
even a burial, dated to circa 560, with his name "brohmali".

Layard, John *The Lady of the Hare* (London: Faber and Faber, 1944)
Sinfield, Alan, 'Varieties of Religion', *ut supra*
Stainer, Pauline, *The Lady & the Hare. New and Selected Poems* (Newcastle upon
    Tyne: Bloodaxe Books, 2003)
Weaver, Mike, *The Photographic Art* (London: The Herbert Press, 1986) on Fox
    Talbot & Neoplatonism.

Muzzleflash Two
Gardiner, S.T., *The Poet's Yearbook 1978* (Cleethorpes: Poet's Yearbook Ltd,
    1978)

Index

Lightning Source UK Ltd.
Milton Keynes UK
UKOW032135070612

193977UK00001B/88/P